I0812796

IMAGES
of America

AVERY COUNTY

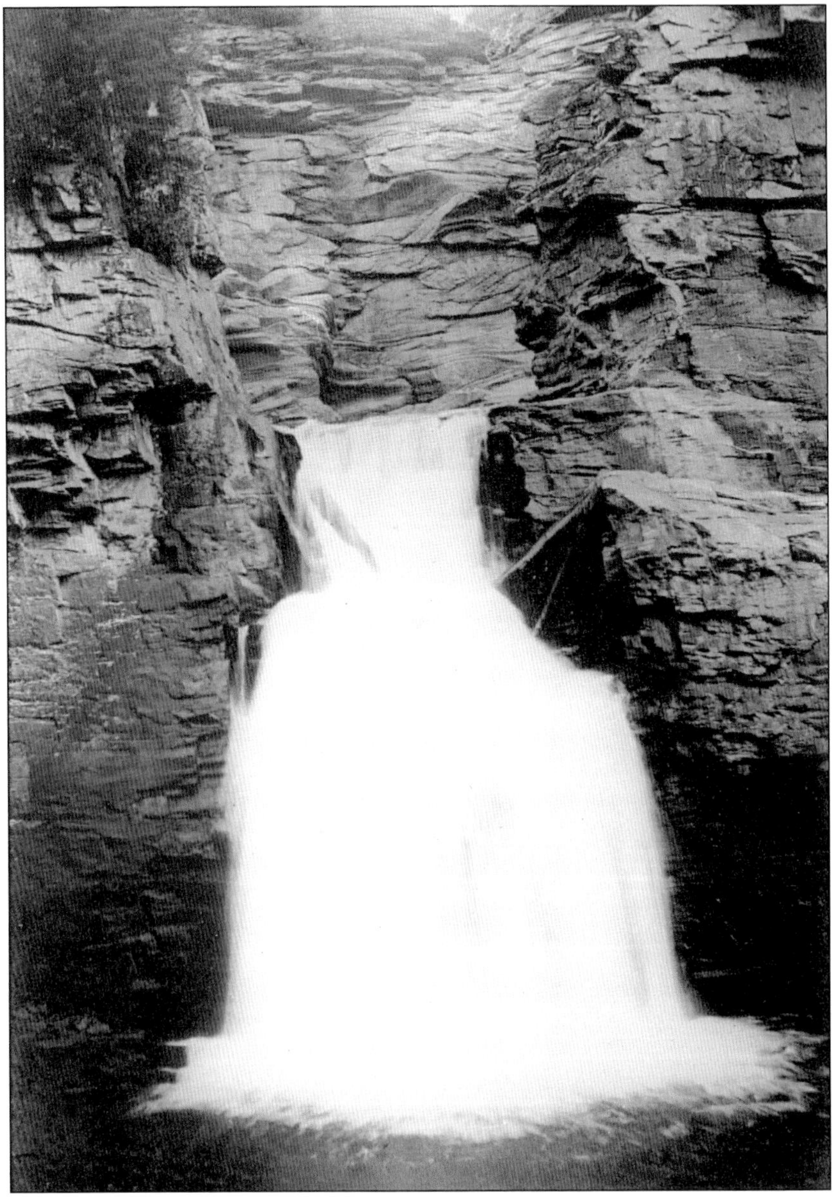

Linville Falls, called Eeseeoh or "river of many cliffs" by the Cherokee, has captivated visitors for many years. As the story goes, in 1766, William Linville, his son, John, and a 16-year-old named John Williams were camped out below the falls. They were attacked by the Cherokee while sleeping and the Linvilles were killed. Williams was shot through the thigh but was able to make his escape, carrying the tragic story to the outside world. The land for the Linville Falls Recreation area was donated to the National Park Service in 1952 by John D. Rockefeller Jr., with the stipulation that the land be preserved in its natural state. (Courtesy of the Avery County Historical Museum.)

On the Cover: This photograph, taken by local photographer W. R. Trivett, appears to depict Avery County residents engaged in the still-popular sport of bear hunting. Actually these men, Dudely Trivette, Leonard Story, and Willie Harmon, had been caught bear hunting out of season. (Courtesy of the W. R. Trivett Collection.)

IMAGES
of America

AVERY COUNTY

Michael C. Hardy

ARCADIA
PUBLISHING

ISBN 978-0-7385-4191-4

Published by Arcadia Publishing
Charleston, South Carolina

Printed in the United States of America

Library of Congress Catalog Card Number: 2005930511

For all general information contact Arcadia Publishing at:
Telephone 843-853-2070
Fax 843-853-0044
E-mail sales@arcadiapublishing.com
For customer service and orders:
Toll-Free 1-888-313-2665

Visit us on the Internet at www.arcadiapublishing.com

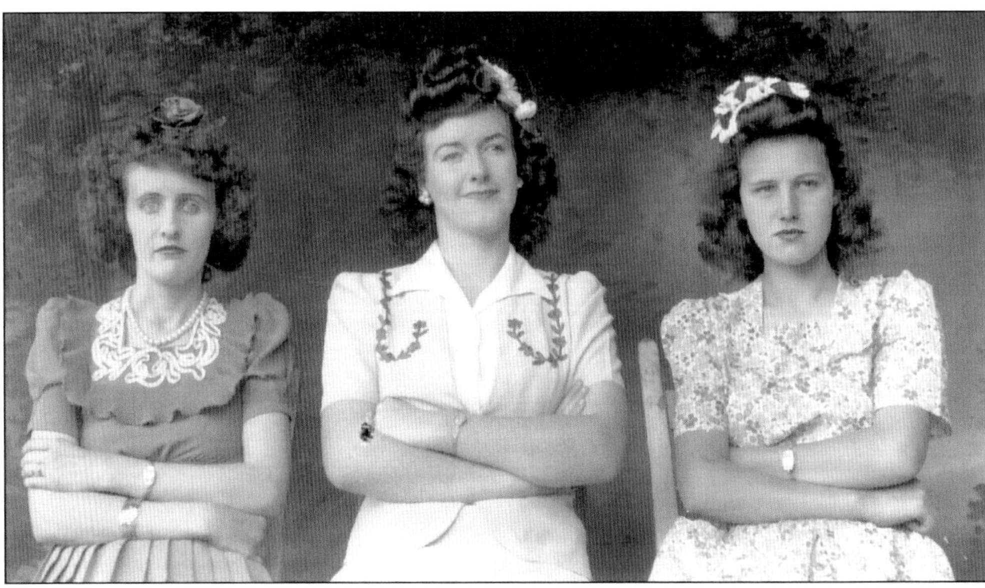

From left to right, Lowella Guy, Juanita Ward Guy, and Faye Guy Phillips pose in a c. 1943 photograph by local "picture man" W. R. Trivett. (Courtesy of the W. R. Trivett Collection.)

Contents

ACKNOWLEDGMENTS

No book, whether great or small, can be completed without the help of many people contributing on many levels. First and foremost, I would like to thank the members of the Avery County Historical Society and Museum for their help and support during the creation of this work. A large number of the photographs that make up this volume came from the museum's collection, the museum's resources were essential tools for information on people and communities, and the wonderful volunteers who make the museum successful were also vital in the completion of this project. The following institutions and people were also extremely helpful: Catherine Morton, Grandfather Mountain; Faye Williams, librarian at the James H. Carson Library, Lees-McRae College; Steve Massengill, North Carolina Division of Archives and History; and Zoe Rhine, Pack Memorial Library in Asheville. Thanks also to Ralph Lentz II, Johnny Graybeal, Neil and Sharon Stewart, Doyle Ollis, Ruffin Ayers, Roger and Irene Clark, Heidi Ellis, and Michelle Vance Scott for sharing photographs from their personal and family collections. This project would not have been possible without their generosity and interest. Many other individuals contributed information or helped identify people and places in these images so that their identities will not be lost to future generations. Lastly, I would like to thank my readers, Tense Franklin Banks and Elizabeth Baird Hardy.

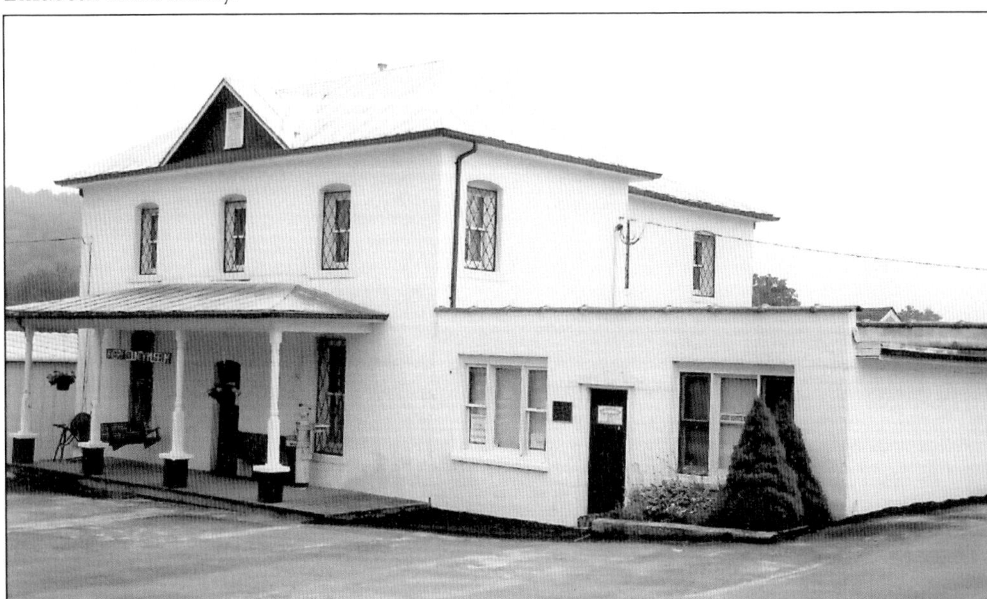

The Avery County Jail was designed by Wheeler and Runge of Charlotte and built by R. C. Campbell of Caldwell County in 1913. This structure not only housed prisoners but also the jailer and his family. The building currently serves as the home for the Avery County Historical Society and Museum. It was placed on the National Register for Historical Buildings in 1999. (Courtesy of Michael C. Hardy.)

INTRODUCTION

"Nature is adding new beauty to our country every day now," chronicled the *Avery Advocate* in April 1929. "Get the Kodak habit and preserve the many interesting scenes that come to you." Ever since Avery County was created in 1911, it has been lavished with photographers. Clifton Laws, who penned the above lines, ran a portrait studio in Elk Park in the late 1920s. He was preceded by the editor of the *Avery Advocate*, Frank A. Carr, and his wife, who were also photographers in the same area. Paul Buchanan, like his father, Fate Buchanan, photographed in Mitchell, Yancey, and Avery Counties. In the Linville Falls area of southern Avery County, James "Lenoir" Franklin photographed friends, neighbors, schools, and churches. On the opposite end of the county, Willie R. Trivett captured images of people in the Flat Springs and Beech Creek areas. Around the town of Crossnore, Dr. Eustace Sloop and his wife, Dr. Mary Sloop, founders of the Crossnore School, also purchased a camera. While they did not photograph for profit, they did record scenes of everyday life. All of these photographers were bi-vocational, taking pictures in addition to being farmers or business people.

The images created by these and by many, many more through the next nine decades have preserved unique glimpses of our common ancestors: farmers, laborers, teachers and pupils, ministers, blacksmiths, fathers, mothers, brothers, and sisters. Many of them were born, lived, and died within the confines of North Carolina's youngest county.

But their story only tells part of the history of Avery County. Roughly 200 years ago, the area's first white settlers, the Bright and Davenport families, started their settlement, while other visitors began to arrive, exploring the natural resources of our diverse ecological biosphere. Early explorers, like August Spangenberg, Andre Michaux, Elisha Mitchell, Asa Gray, and others, took their findings back to the intellectual centers of the new republic and beyond. Before long, the explorers and naturalists were replaced by excursionists and sightseers who came not for scientific exploration, but to enjoy the sheer beauty of the mountains that bear the names of Grandfather, Grandmother, Beech, Flat Top, Rattlesnake, and Hawshaw; they came to fish in the Toe, Watauga, and Linville Rivers and to appreciate the diverse plant and animal life.

It would be these two different groups of people, those who tilled the land and hunted the game and those who came to enjoy the scenic beauty, who would build the collective history of Avery County.

Avery County is named for Waightstill Avery (1741–1821), a Connecticut native and the first attorney general of North Carolina. Avery lived in Morganton but owned considerable land holdings in the county that today bears his name. The county seat is Newland, named after William C. Newland (1860–1938), mayor of Lenoir, a state representative, and a lieutenant governor. Prior to being named in honor of Newland, the community was known as Old Fields of Toe. Many of the communities within Avery County are named for the families that first settled the area: Pyatte, Whaley, Davis Mountain, Blevins Creek, Crossnore, Banner Elk, and Ingalls. Other communities or locales are named for events or activities: Powder Mill Creek, Ivy Heights, Cranberry, Devil's Race Path Branch, Buck Hill, and the Snake Den.

Some of these communities, such as Newland and Banner Elk, continue to thrive in the 21st century, and traces of their pasts can still be found under the façade of progress. Other communities, such as Crossnore, are fading, as businesses depart and venerable buildings disappear. Yet brief glimpses of history can occasionally be found emerging from the rubble. Some towns are completely gone, absorbed into development, dense underbrush, or young forests. Such is the fate of Childsville, which was built upon the original Bright and Davenport settlements, was a thriving community in the 1860s, and, under the name of Calhoun, served as the first county seat for Mitchell County.

Like these lost communities, many Avery County residents have also faded from view. For the most part, the photographs in this collection provide glimpses into the lives of people, as well as communities, that have long since vanished into the pages of history. Here are bustling towns that have since been become empty clearings by roadsides; beautiful homes and schools long ago consumed by fire and neglect; and smiling faces of men, women, and children who live on only in memories, in the descendants they left behind, and in these photographs.

People are still photographing Avery County today, recording our present before it becomes our past. Hugh Morton, owner of Grandfather Mountain, has made many images of the area, both on and around the mountain that dominates the northern portions of the county. And thanks to the Blue Ridge Parkway, many visitors come every year and leave with snapshots, fragments of Avery County, to add to their own history.

Clinton Laws, in another issue of the *Avery Advocate* in April 1929, admonished his readers to take better photographs, with still-relevant advice:

> We are getting some poor films made so by the failure to get a background for the objects taken. Faces will be flat with the sky or bright field covered with sunshine for a background. If you want good, clear faces get a dark background of trees, bushes, mountains, or anything but a clear sky behind the object you are trying to take. Always bring your pictures to us when you can and if there is anything wrong we can tell you about it.

One

Communities and Scenery

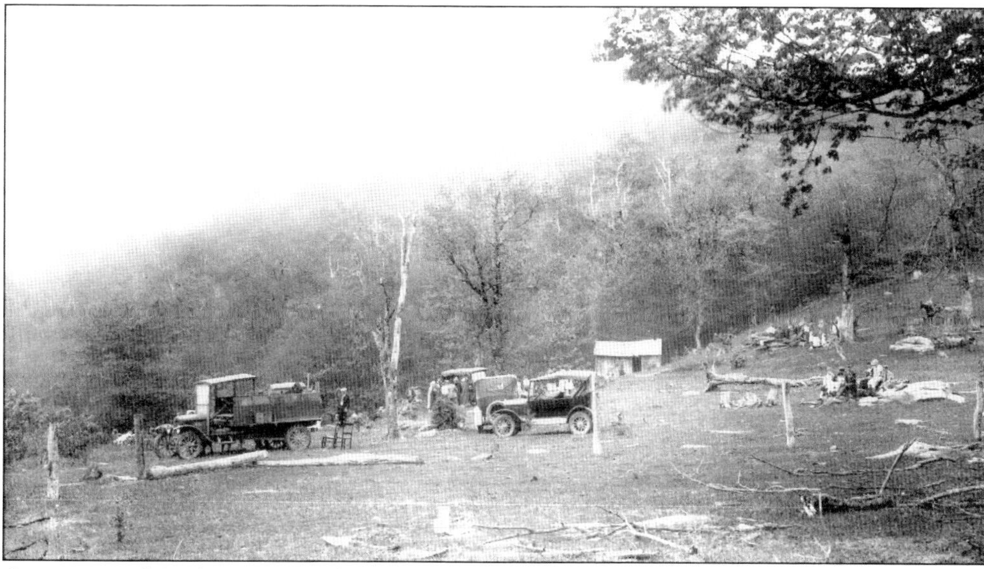

Once automobiles became popular, the mountains of Western North Carolina became common places for excursions and outings, as evidenced by these cars featured in a photograph taken on Beech Mountain, *c.* 1925. (Courtesy of the W. R. Trivett Collection.)

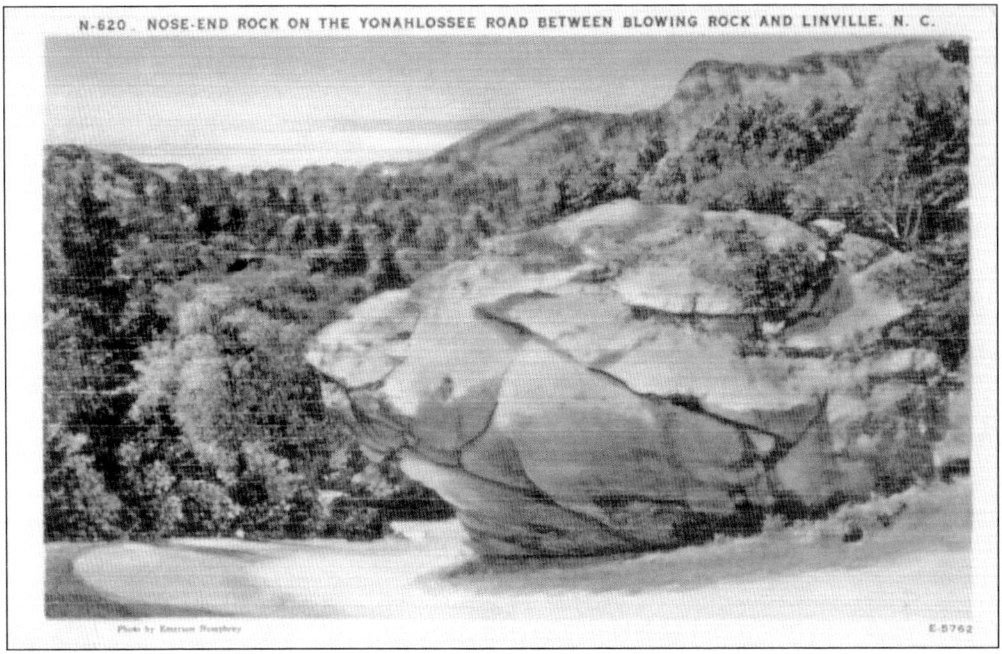

The Yonahlossee Road was constructed in 1891 by the directors and stockholders of the Linville Improvement Company. This new road provided a link between the already popular resort town of Blowing Rock and Linville. Yonahlossee means "passing bear" or "bear trail," so named because of the extensive amount of bear traps found by construction workers. Nose-end Rock was just one of the many scenic spots along the route. (Courtesy of Michael C. Hardy.)

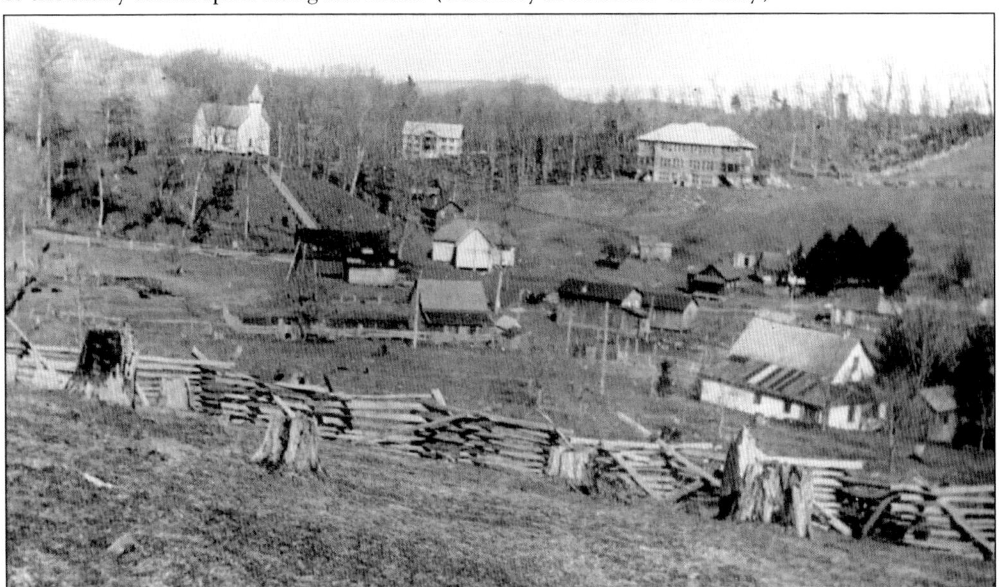

This early view of Crossnore shows the buildings of the Crossnore School and, on the left, the Baptist church, with the 100 steps that led from the bottom of the hill up to the church. Located in a valley between Davis, Hawshaw, and Snake Den Mountains, the town is named for George Crossnore, who lived in the area and operated a small store or trading post here in the 1790s. (Courtesy of the Clark family.)

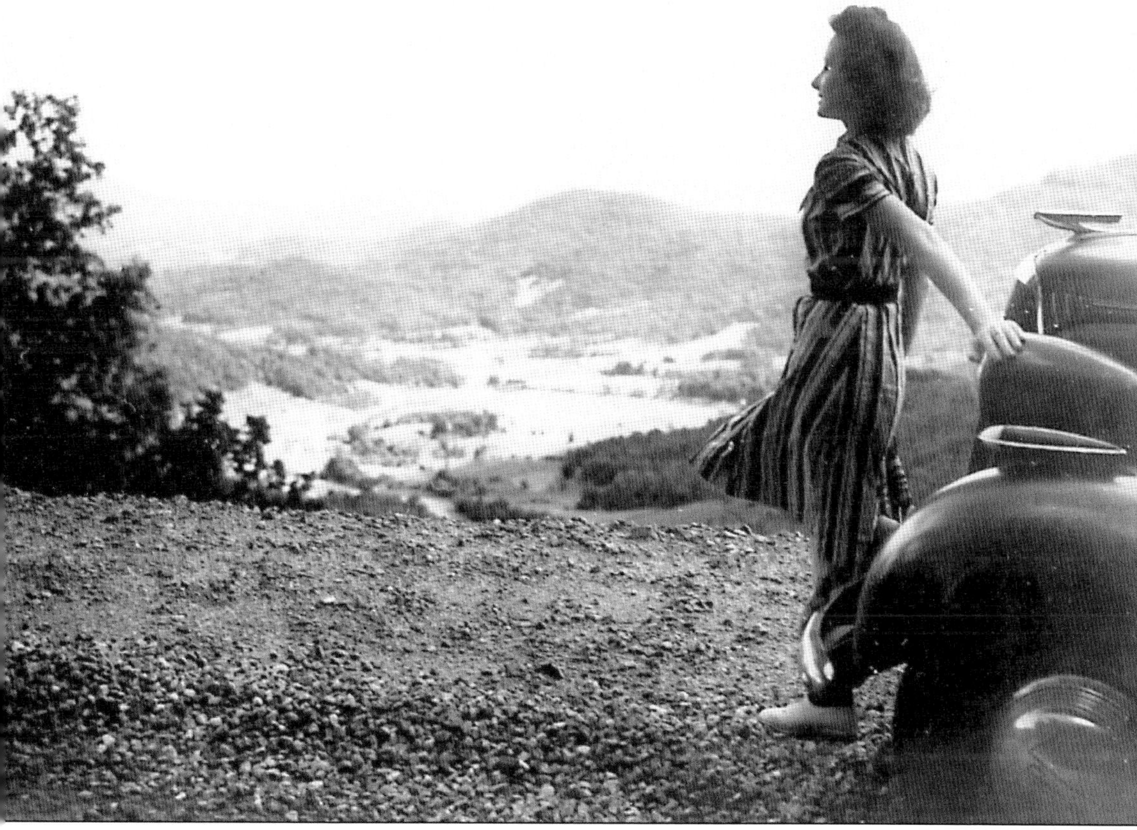

A young woman strikes a dramatic pose while looking down on the resort town of Linville. This photograph was undoubtedly taken from the Yonahlossee Road, now known as U.S. 221. (Courtesy of North Carolina Department of Archives and History.)

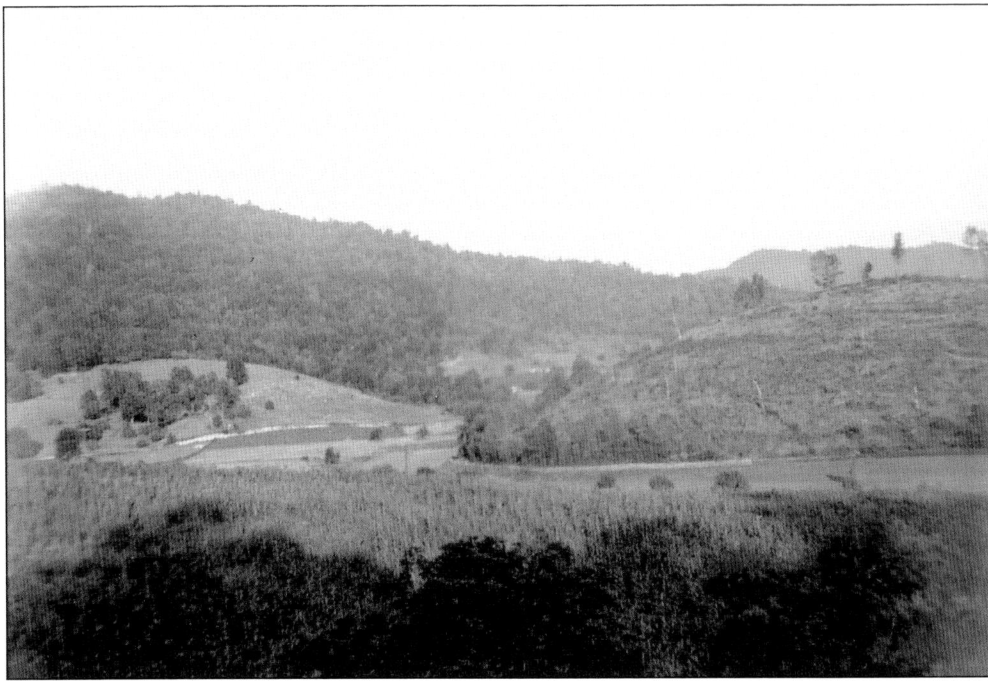

According to Horton Cooper's history of Avery County, Buck Hill, which is featured in this 1950s-era image, bears that name because an early hunter killed a large deer in the area. (Courtesy of the Phillips family.)

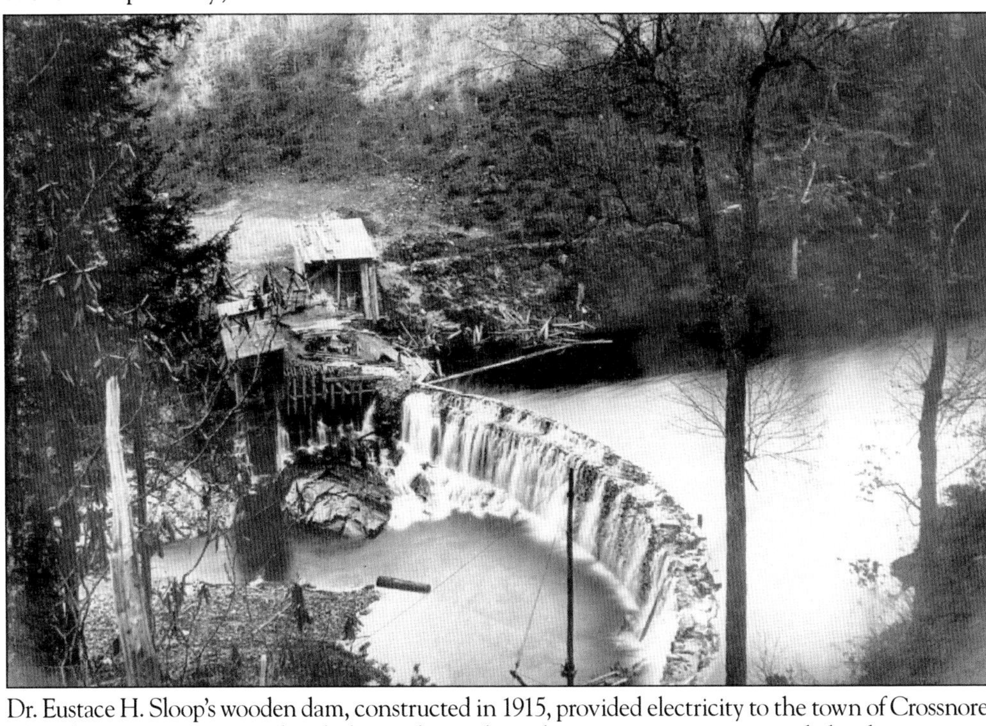

Dr. Eustace H. Sloop's wooden dam, constructed in 1915, provided electricity to the town of Crossnore. The Sloops were interested in helping their adopted community prosper, and the dam was just one of their many improvement projects. (Courtesy of the Avery County Historical Museum.)

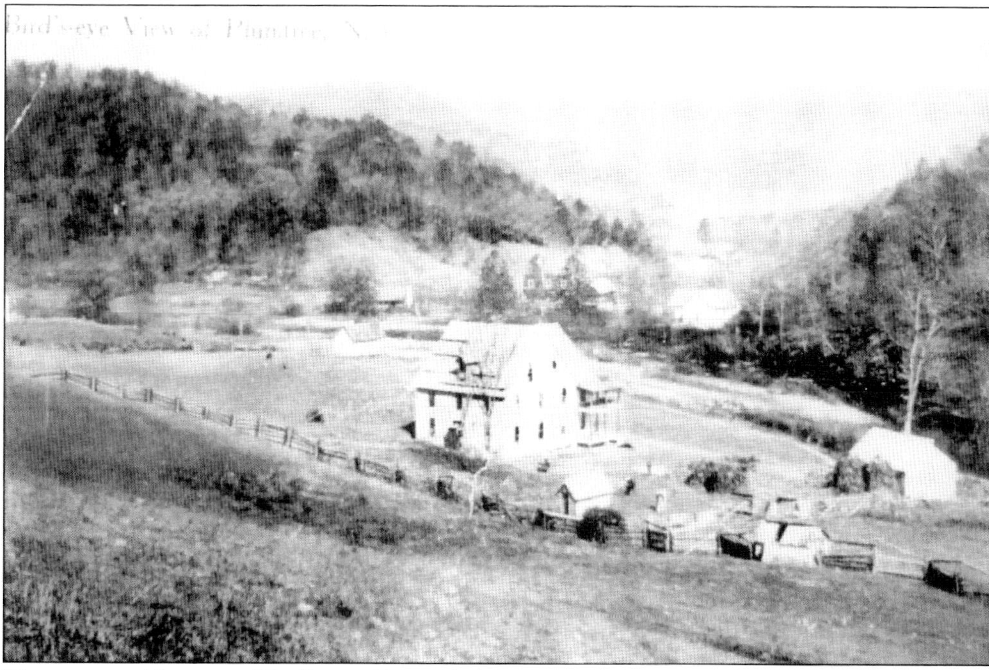

This postcard boasts a "Bird's-eye View of Plumtree." The community was originally known as Plumtree Orchards due to the orchards of plum trees cultivated by the Avery and Connelly families. (Courtesy of the Avery County Historical Museum.)

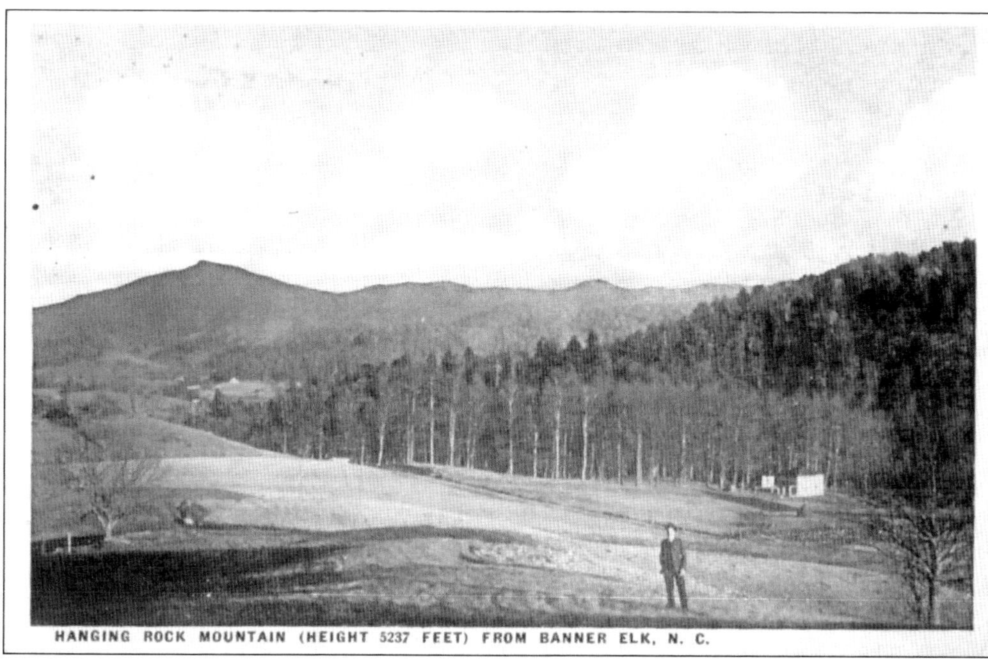

Hanging Rock Mountain, as seen from Banner Elk, is featured here on an early postcard. According to local legend, during the American Revolution, there was a camp on Hanging Rock in 1782 in which three members of the Triplett family died of measles. (Courtesy of Michael C. Hardy.)

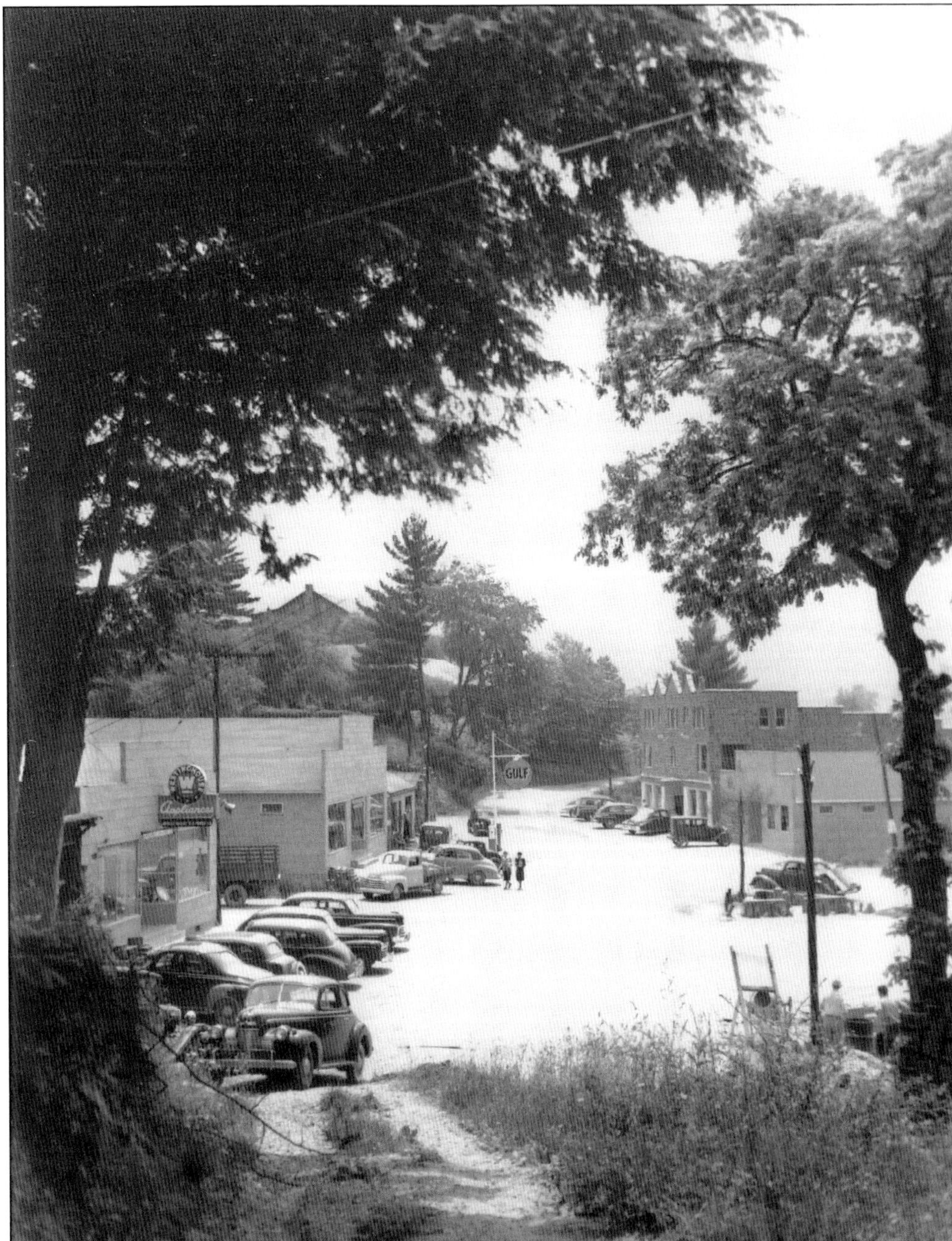

Crossnore in the early 1940s was a bustling community with several successful businesses. The town was incorporated in 1925 and by 1940 included a movie theater, a hospital, a swimming pool, two service stations, a Westinghouse appliance store, several cafés, a post office, and the Lewie Aldridge Music Company, then located in the old fish hatchery building, not to mention all of the buildings associated with the Crossnore School. (Courtesy of the North Carolina Division of Archives and History.)

Golfers at the Linville Golf Course in August 1939 enjoy their game as well as a splendid view of Grandfather Mountain in the distance. The first golf course in present-day Avery County was developed at Linville in 1895; just seven years later, the sport caught on in Yonkers, New York. (Courtesy of the North Carolina Department of Archives and History.)

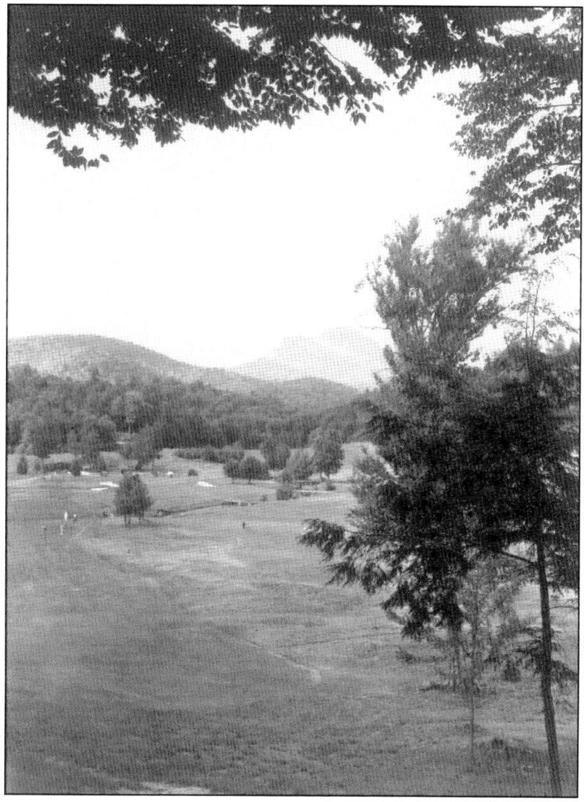

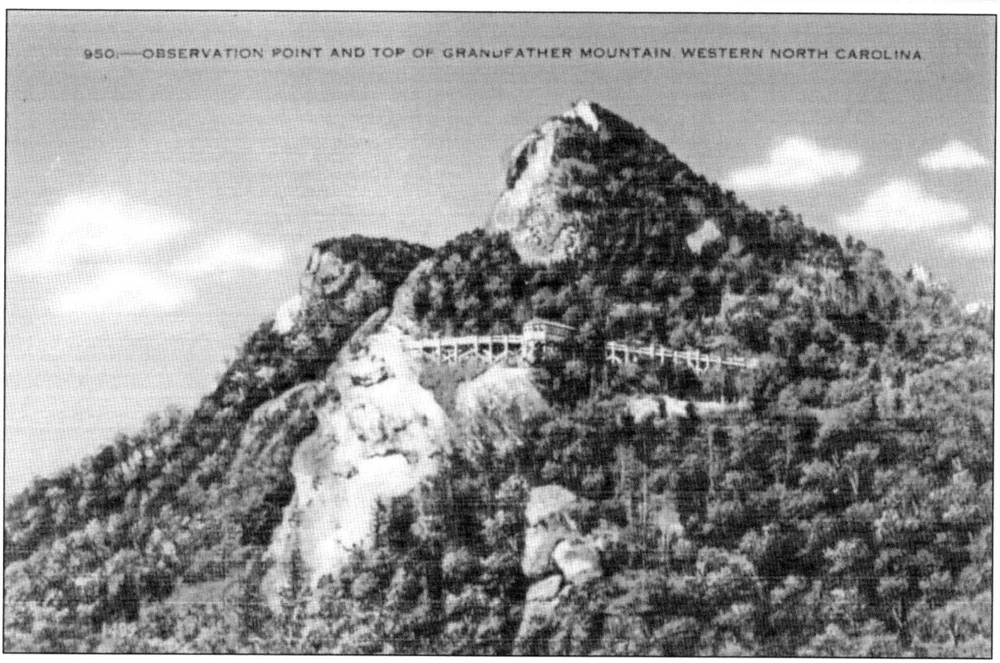

An early observation tower on Grandfather Mountain allowed intrepid visitors to enjoy spectacular views. Grandfather Mountain has been a popular spot for tourists since the 19th century. (Courtesy of Michael C. Hardy.)

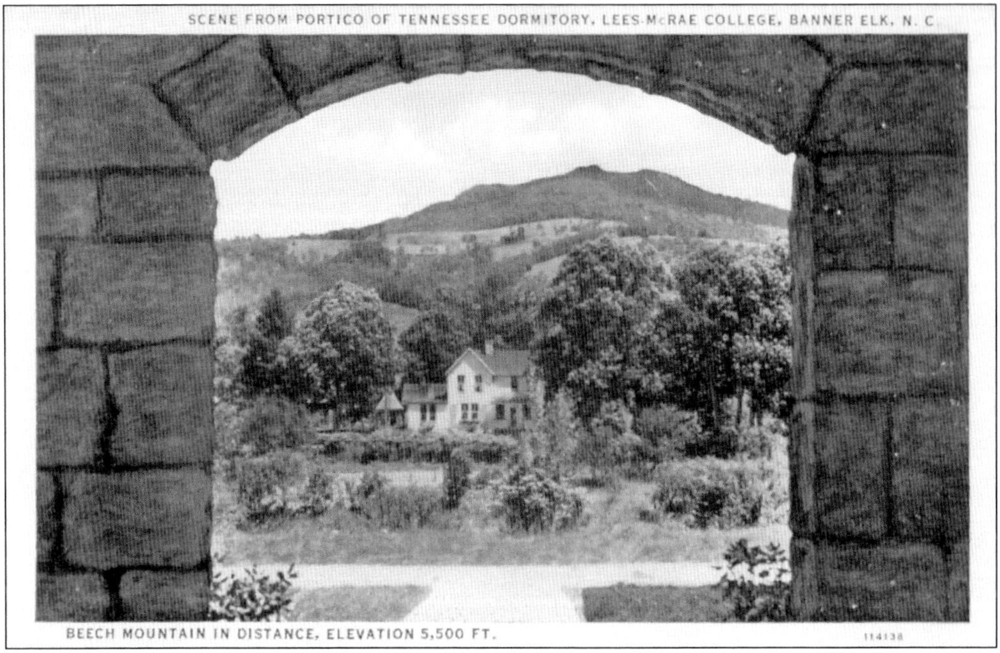

A view seen from the Tennessee Dormitory of Lees-McRae College reveals Beech Mountain in the distance. (Courtesy of Michael C. Hardy.)

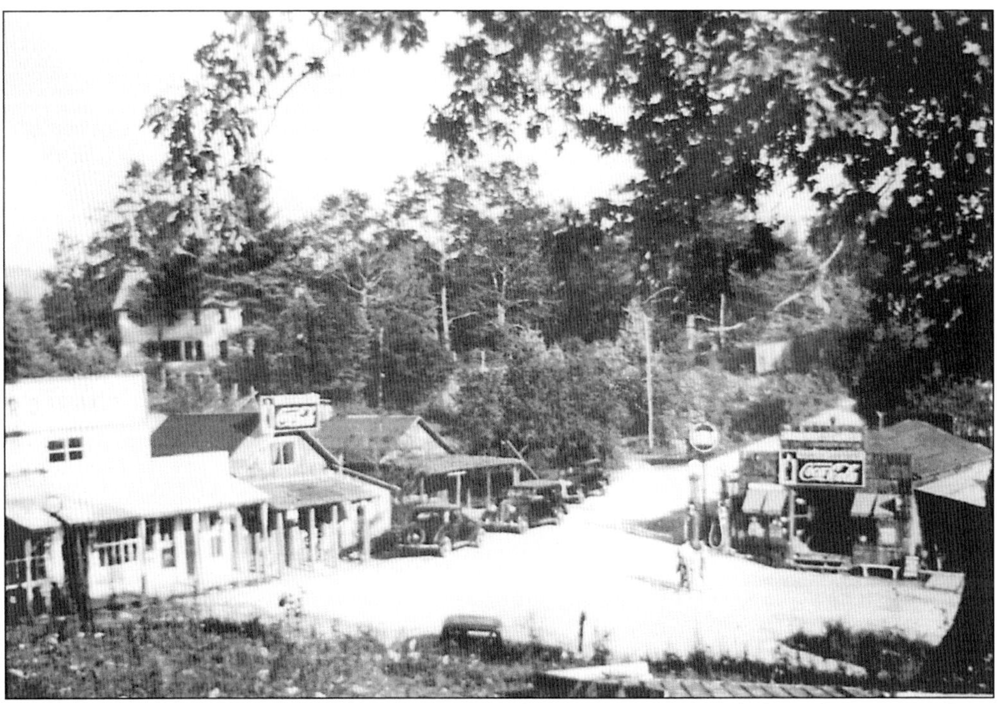

The town of Linville Falls in the 1930s was a bustling community, including the stores and gas station seen here. (Courtesy of Tense Banks.)

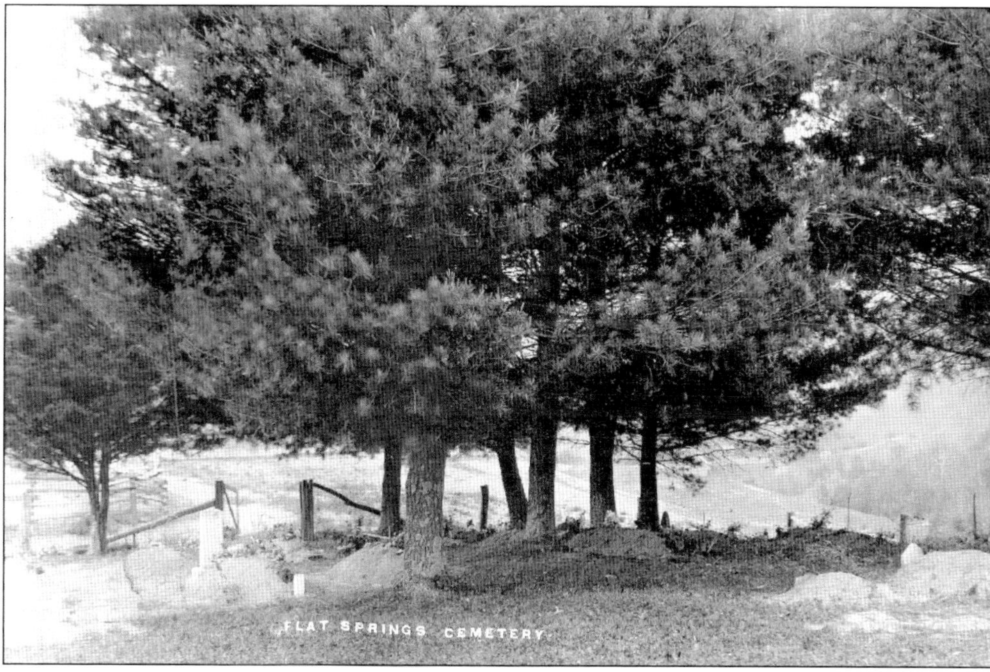

Flat Springs Cemetery is located beside the Flat Springs Church. This cemetery holds the remains of members of the Greene, Guy, Harmon, Henson, McGuire, Norris, and Trivett families. (Courtesy of the W. R. Trivett Collection.)

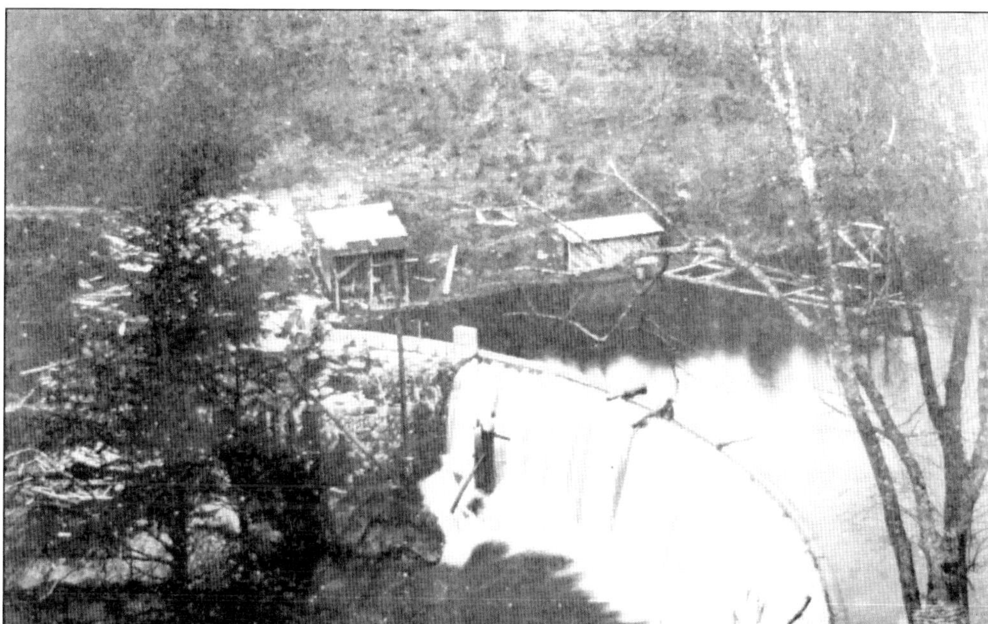

Dr. E. H. Sloop's second dam, built between 1924 and 1926, remained stable even during the devastating flood of 1940 that washed away lives, homes, and businesses. (Courtesy of the Avery County Historical Museum.)

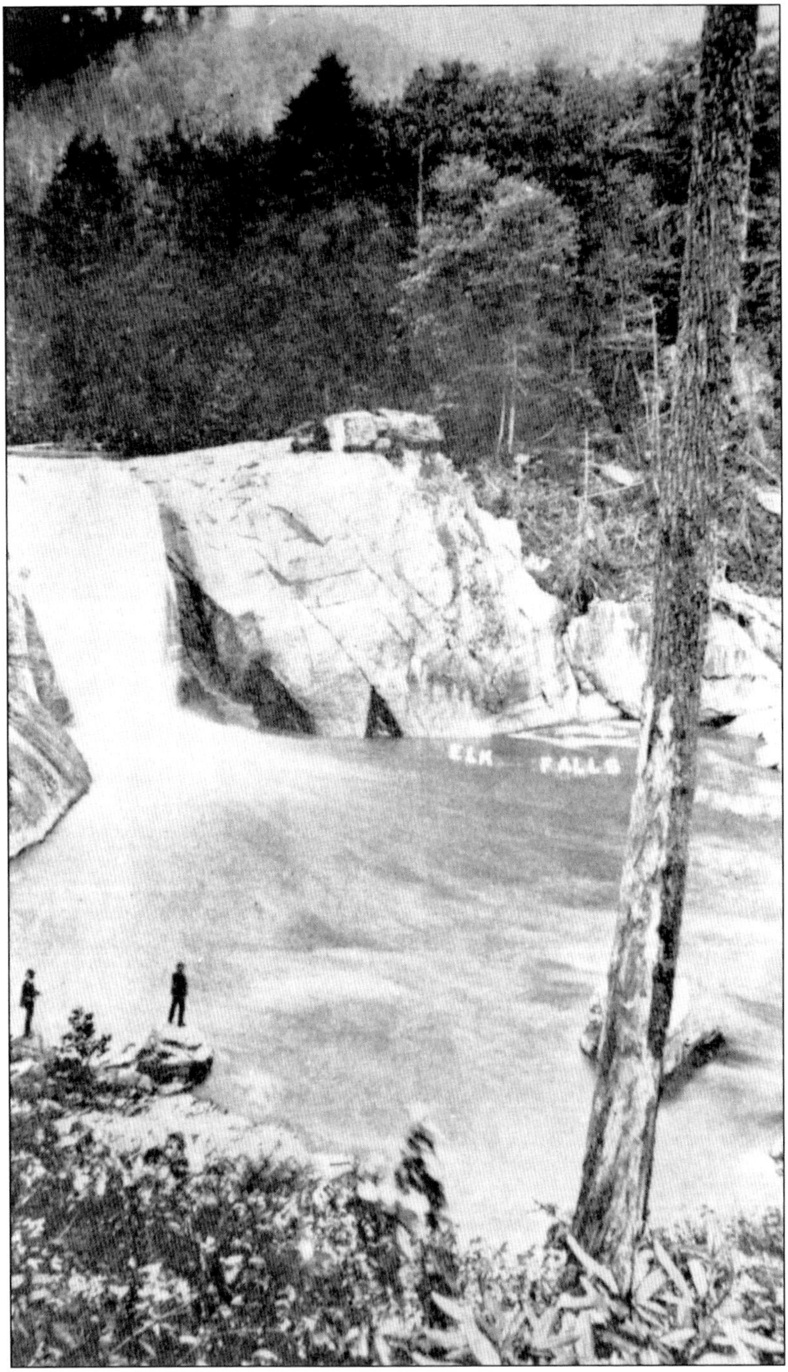

Popular local attraction Elk River Falls is shown here on an early postcard. The Elk River and the town of Elk Park were named for the massive elk that once ranged over the mountains and the Hump Mountain, which resembled a park. Under the pressures of hunting and human settlement, the elk in Western North Carolina were all gone by the early 1800s. Elk River Falls plunges 50 feet into one of the deepest pools in North Carolina and is today still a very popular swimming hole among locals and students from Lees-McRae College. (Courtesy of the Baird family.)

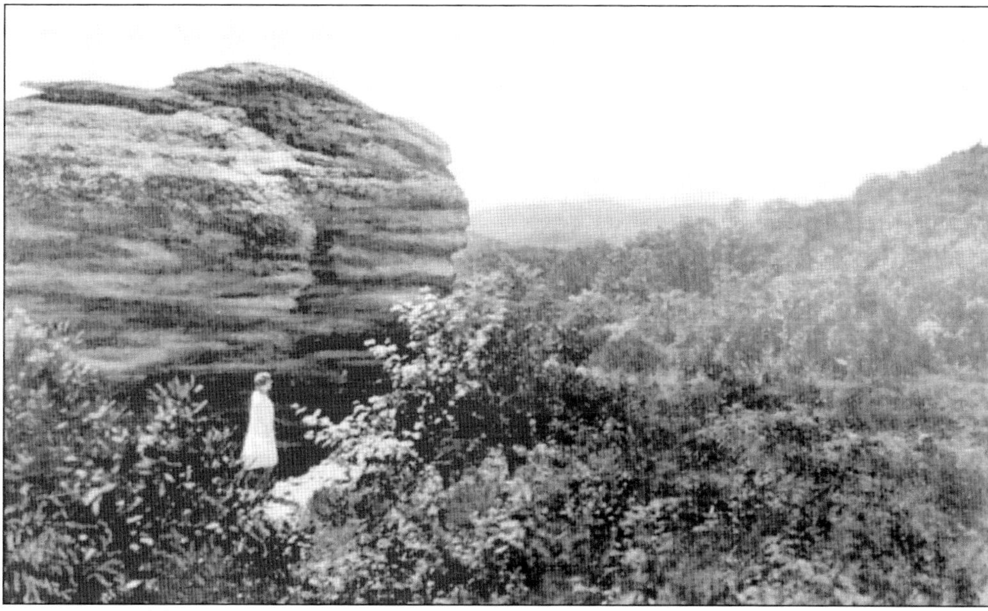

This postcard features an unidentified early visitor to Grandfather Mountain. (Courtesy of Pack Memorial Library.)

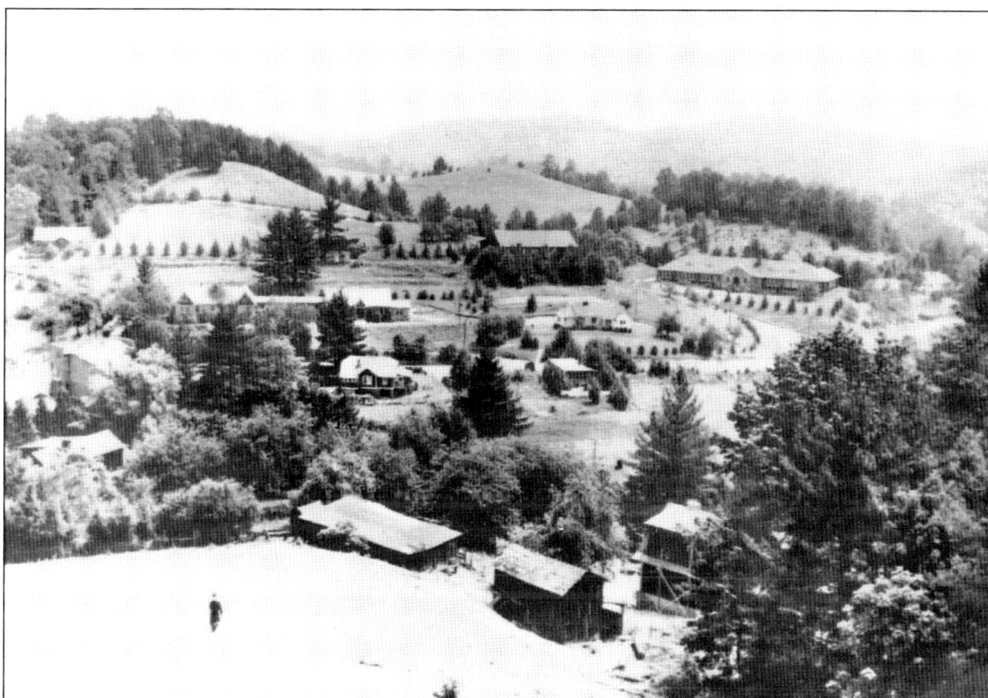

In this early view of Crossnore, Garrett Memorial Hospital is on the left, and the high school is the large building on the right. After being concealed inside a more recent hospital structure for decades, the original hospital is once again visible and scheduled for restoration. (Courtesy of the Clark family.)

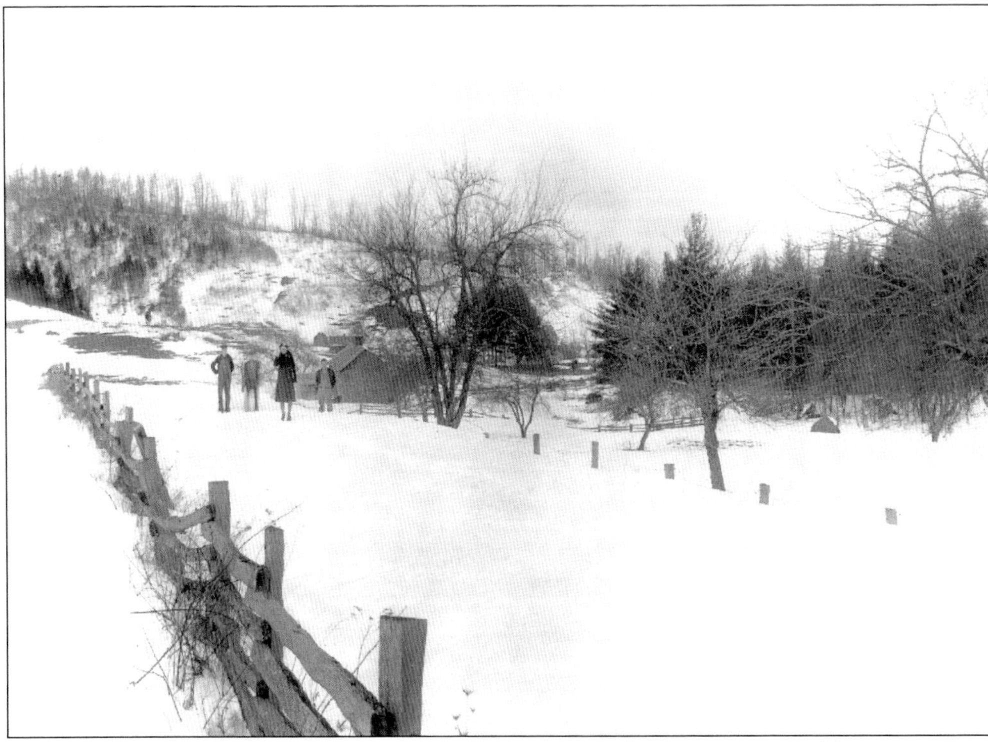

From left to right, Haskell Trivett, Willie Trivett, and Mertie Trivett enjoy a typical late-season snow in the Flat Springs community on March 12, 1942. (Courtesy of the W. R. Trivett Collection.)

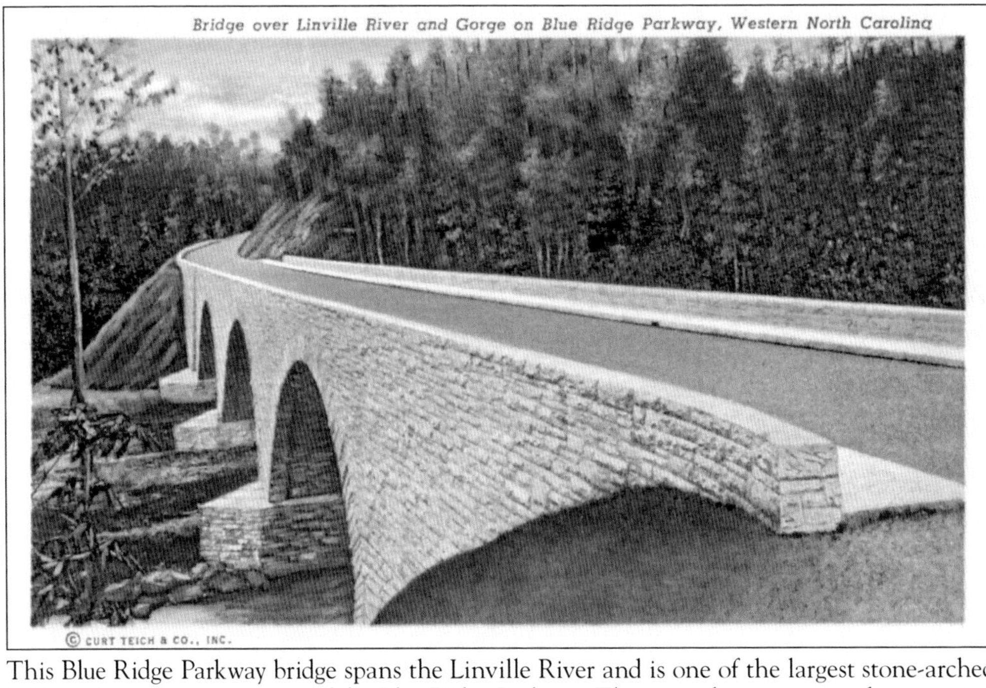

This Blue Ridge Parkway bridge spans the Linville River and is one of the largest stone-arched bridges along the entire route of the Blue Ridge Parkway. There are three spans, each measuring 80 feet. (Courtesy of Michael C. Hardy.)

Many of Crossnore's early buildings, like this one, were of log construction. This photograph was taken by Monimia F. MacRae. (Courtesy of Pack Memorial Library.)

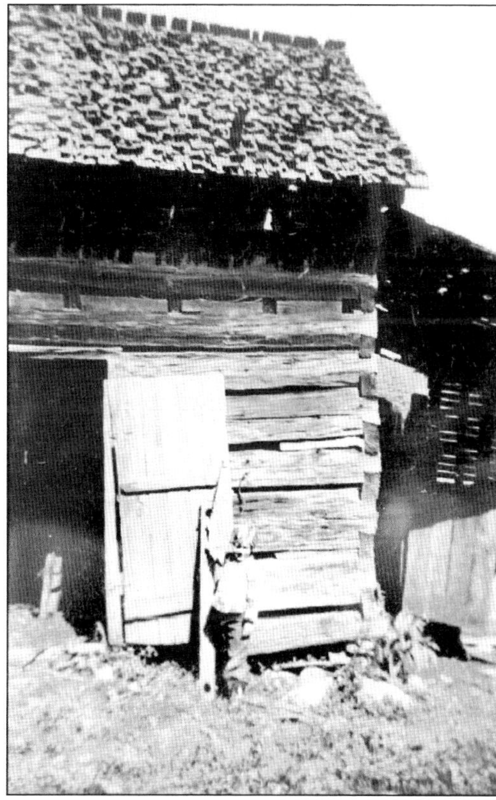

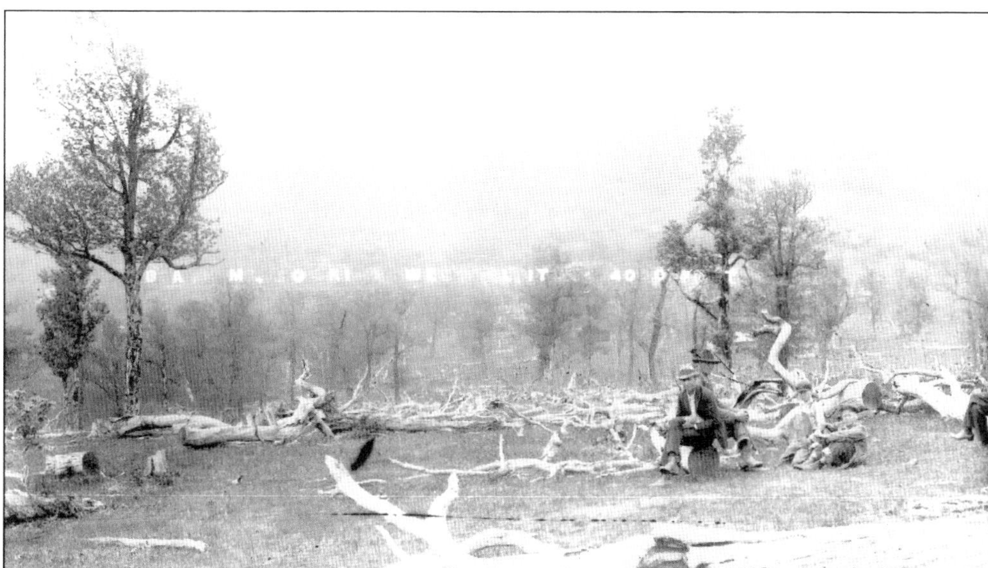

A group of early visitors pose among deadwood on Beech Mountain. (Courtesy of the W. R. Trivett Collection.)

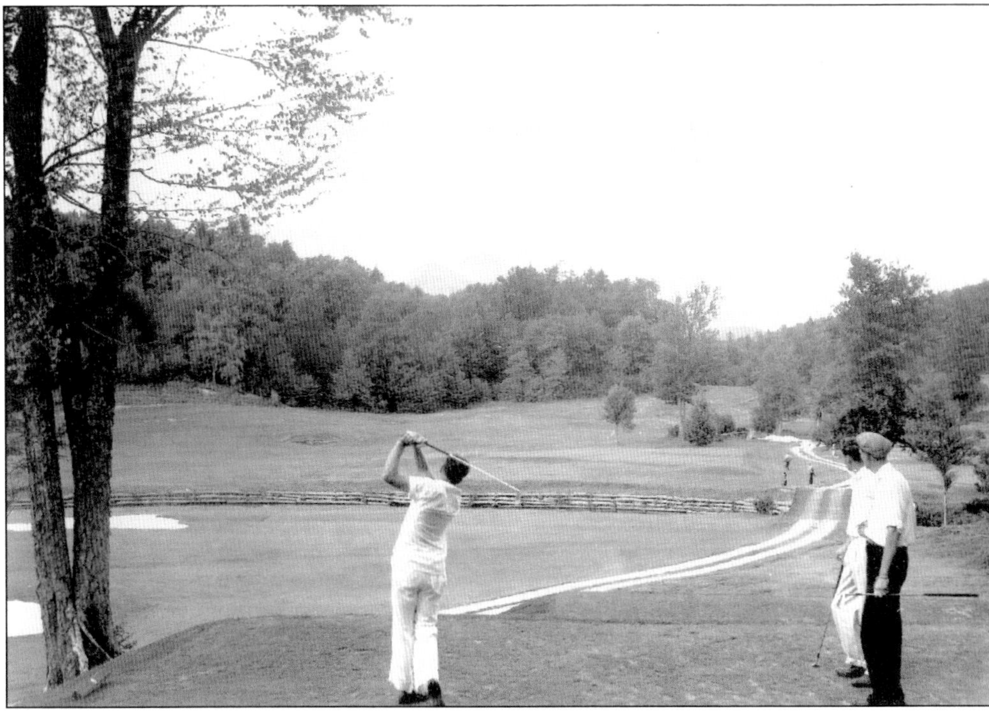

A golfer tees off on the Linville Golf Course in August 1939. (Courtesy of the North Carolina Division of Archives and History.)

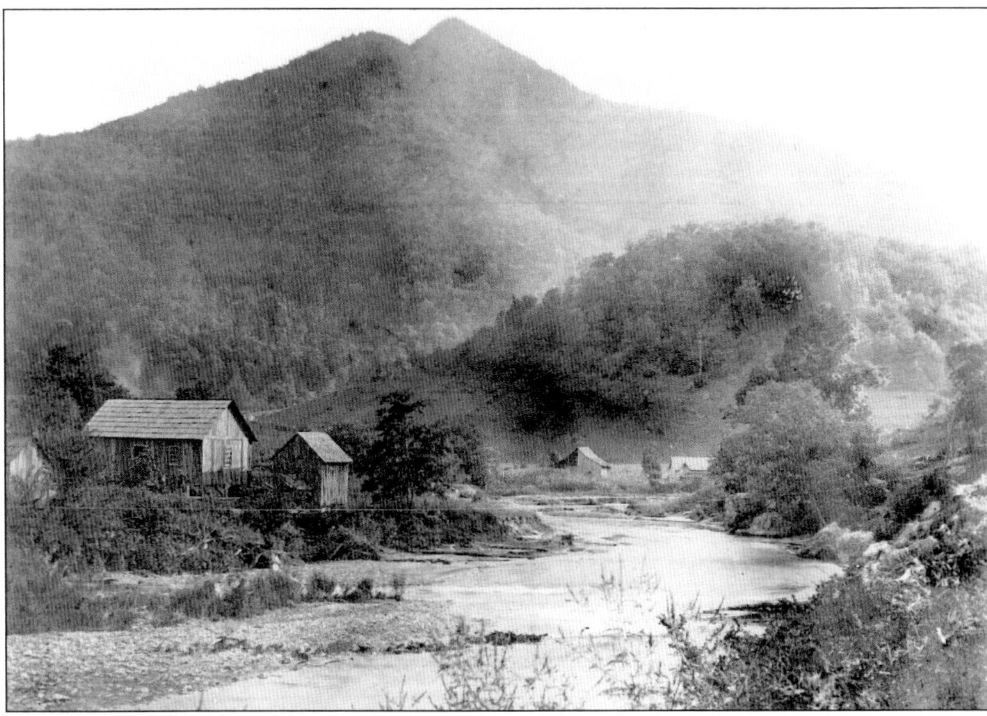

This farm at the foot of Grandfather Mountain, in a c. 1908 photograph, is typical of many of the farms in the area. (Courtesy of the North Carolina Department of Archives and History.)

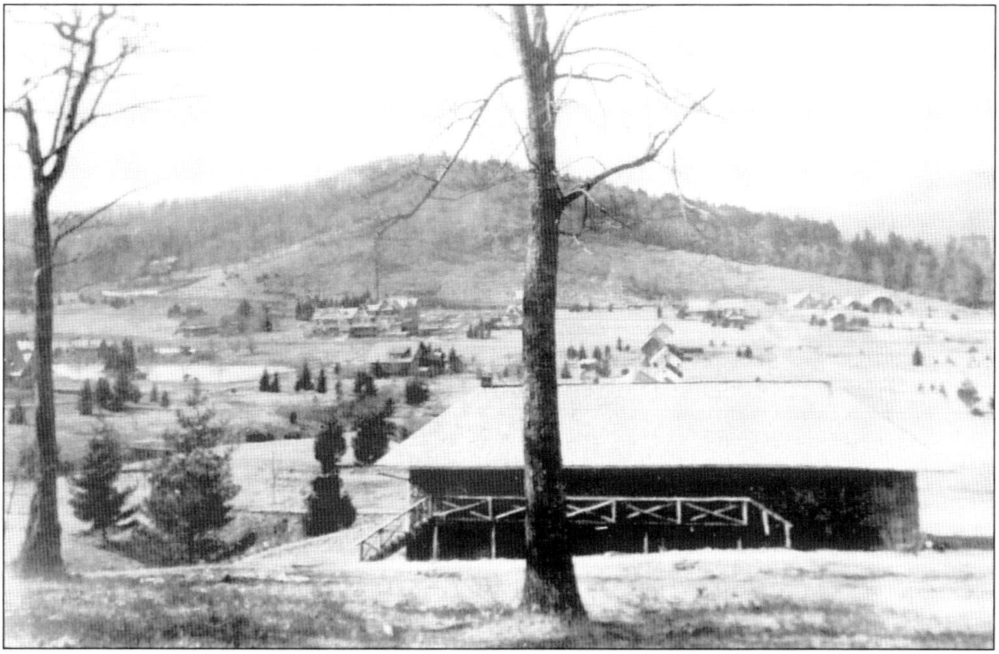

This image captures an early view of the town of Linville. The town was originally called Clay in 1883, then changed to Porcelain in 1885, and finally to Linville in 1888. It was built under the direction of the Linville Improvement Company. The Eseeola Inn can be seen in the left center of the photograph. (Courtesy of Tense Banks.)

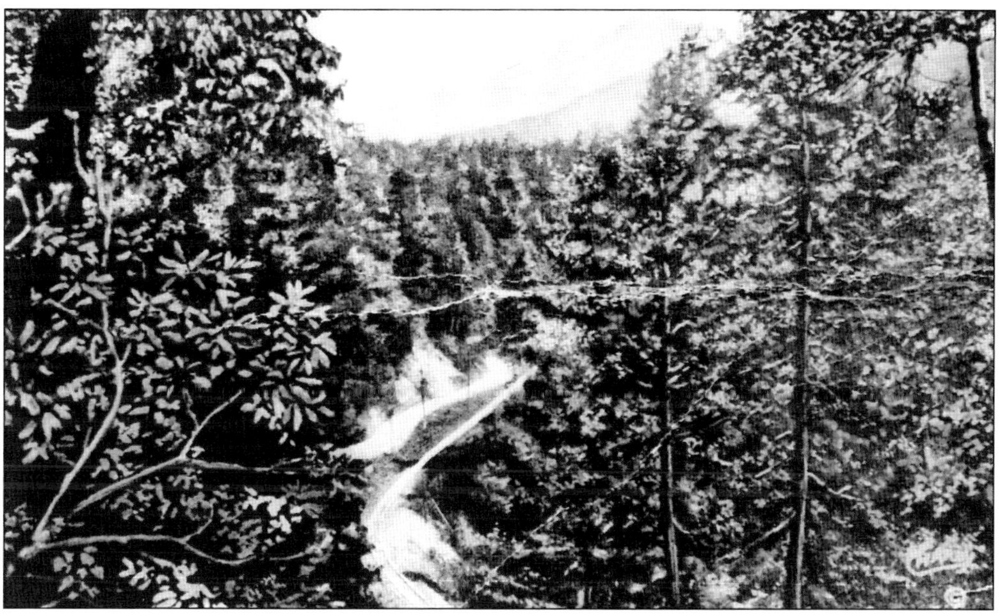

A road paralleling the Linville River Railway near Grandfather Mountain provides a good example of the diverse methods of travel in the mountains. After leaving Linville, the railroad headed north into Linville Gap. At 4,100 feet above sea level, Linville Gap was the highest point east of the Mississippi River serviced by railroad. (Courtesy of the Baird family.)

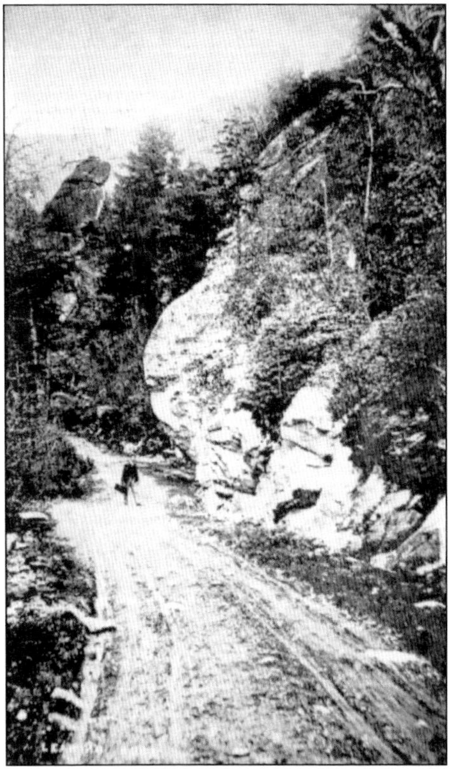

In this image taken on the old Yonahlossee Road, the Leaning Rock, a popular photographic stop for excursionists, can be seen in the background. (Courtesy of the Baird family.)

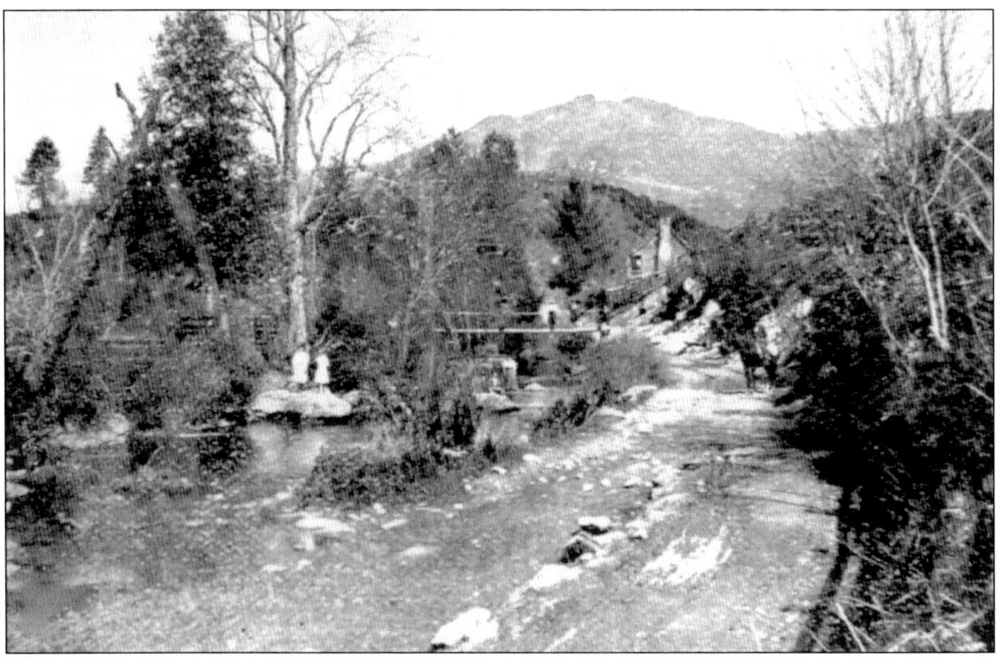

Beech Mountain can here be seen from Banner's Ford in the Banner Elk area. The community of Banner Elk, called Banner's Elk prior to 1911, was named after the Banner family; two brothers, Martin L. Banner and Lewis B. Banner, settled in the area in the mid-1800s. (Courtesy of the Baird family.)

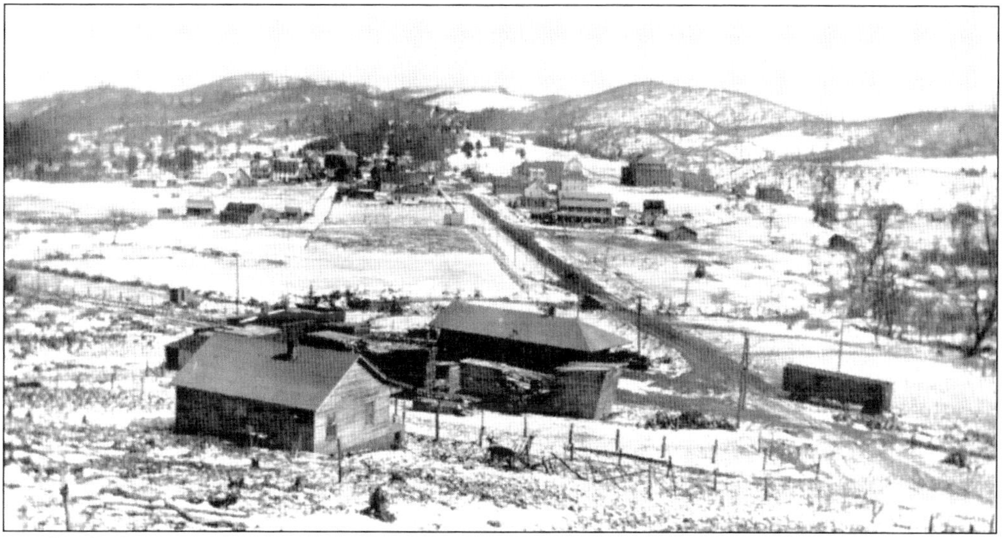

Newland is here seen on a snowy day with the railroad depot in the foreground and the courthouse and jail in the background. Prior to being renamed in honor of William C. Newland, the area was called Old Fields of Toe and was used as a militia muster field when the area was still a part of Burke County. (Courtesy of Michael C. Hardy.)

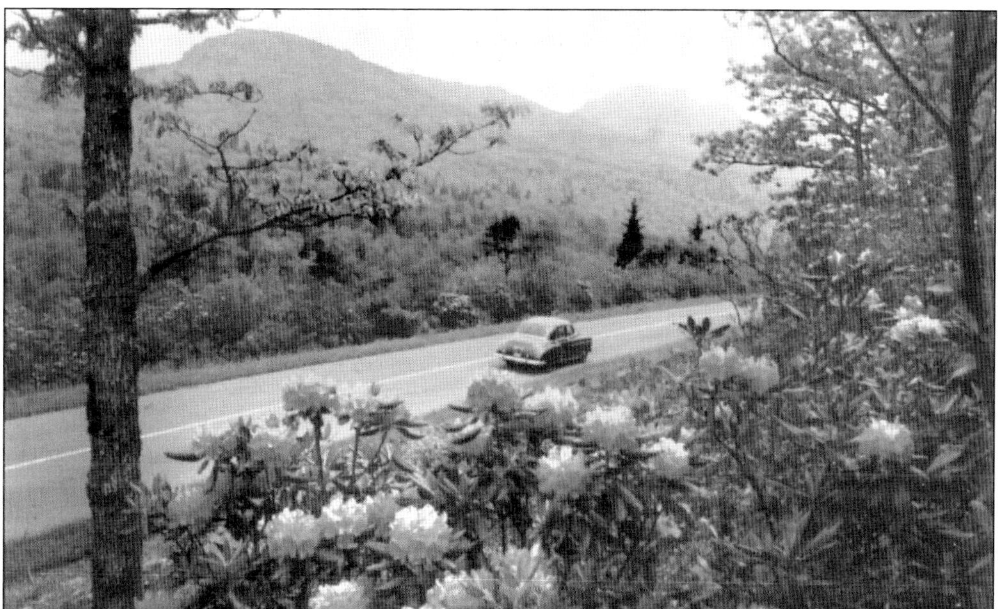

The Blue Ridge Parkway, with Grandfather Mountain in the distance, continues to draw locals and visitors for its beautiful year-round scenery, such as the rhododendron blooms seen in the foreground here. (Courtesy of Michael C. Hardy.)

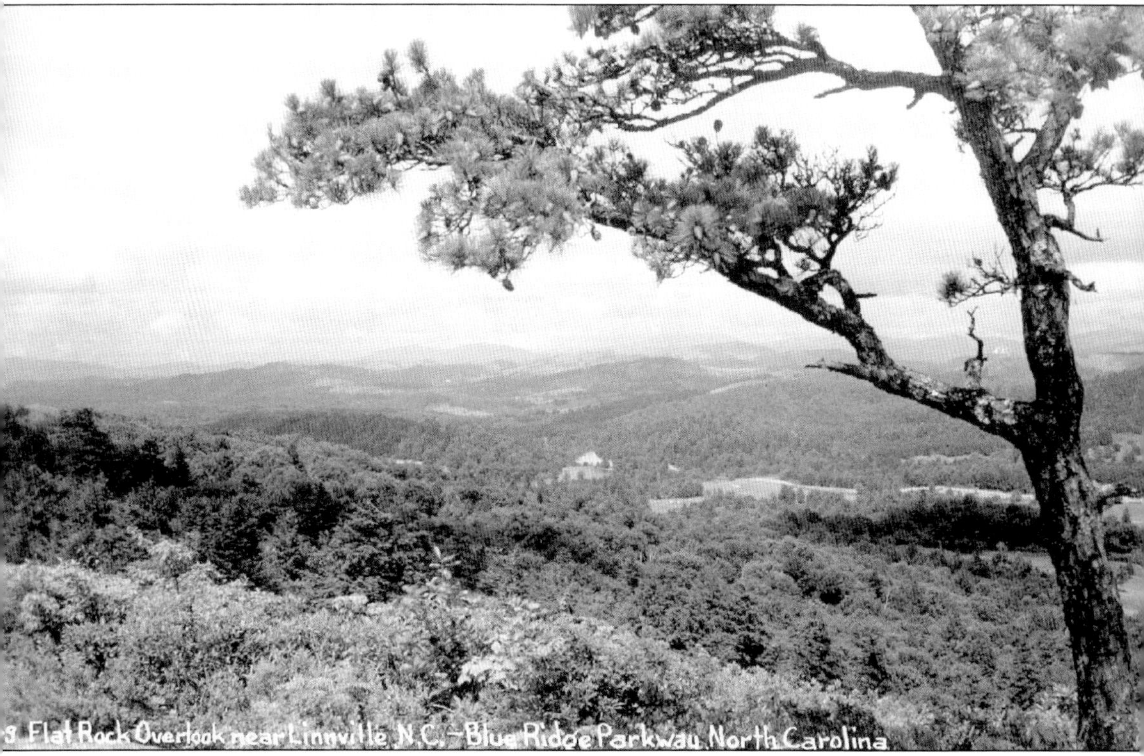

This photograph was taken from the popular Flat Rock Overlook off the Blue Ridge Parkway. The quartzite outcropping looks across Linville Valley and Grandfather Mountain toward Roan Mountain, Tennessee. The 469-mile Blue Ridge Parkway, begun in 1933, stretches from the Shenandoah National Park in Virginia to the Great Smoky Mountains in North Carolina. Almost 20 miles of the parkway lie within the boundaries of Avery County, from the Linn Cove Viaduct in the north to Linville Falls in the south. (Courtesy of Michael C. Hardy.)

Two

CHURCHES AND SCHOOLS

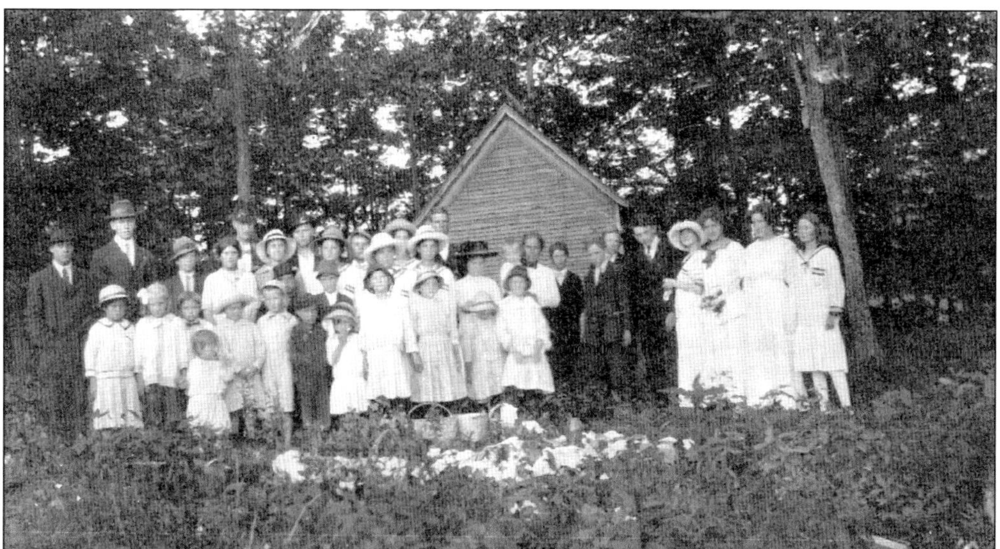

Members are dressed up for a festive occasion at the Pine Grove United Methodist Church. Churches often served the communities where they were located as places of worship, schools, and community centers. (Courtesy of the Phillips family.)

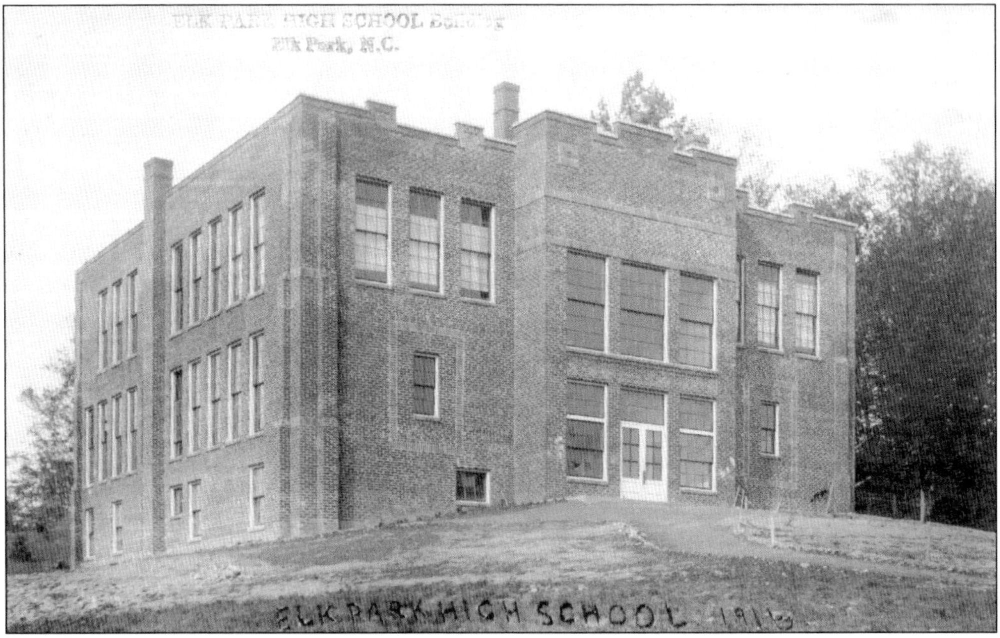

When this photo-postcard of the brick Elk Park High School was taken in 1916, Avery County was just five years old. (Courtesy of Naomi Houston.)

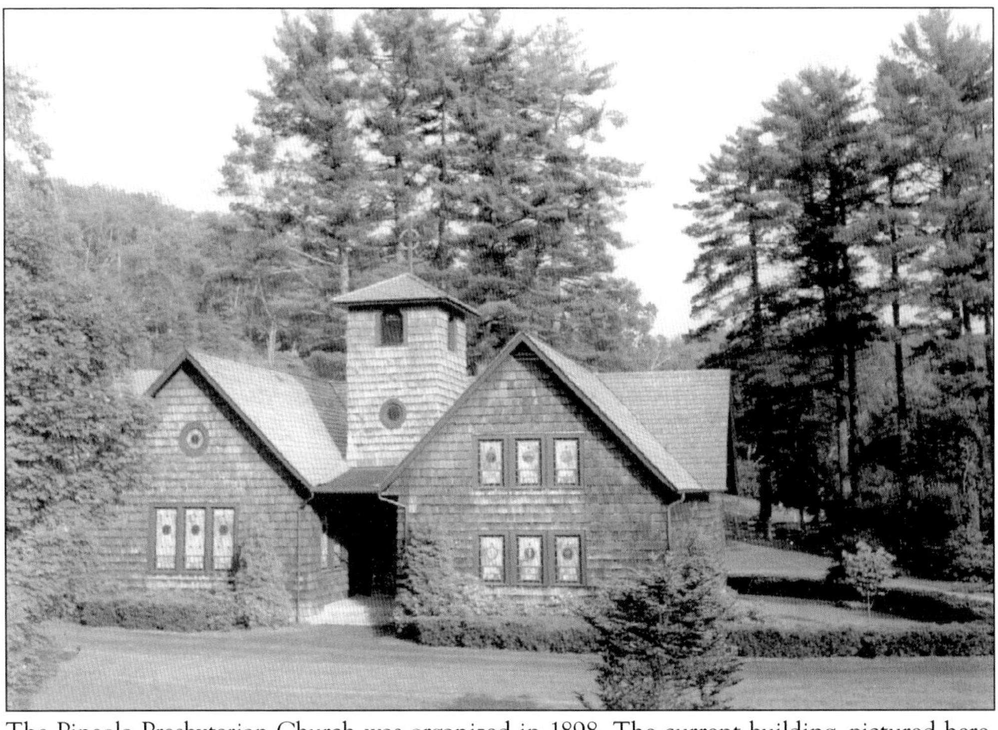

The Pineola Presbyterian Church was organized in 1898. The current building, pictured here, was built in 1927, replacing a one-room structure. It was originally covered in chestnut bark that was later replaced by cedar shingles. (Courtesy of the Stewart family.)

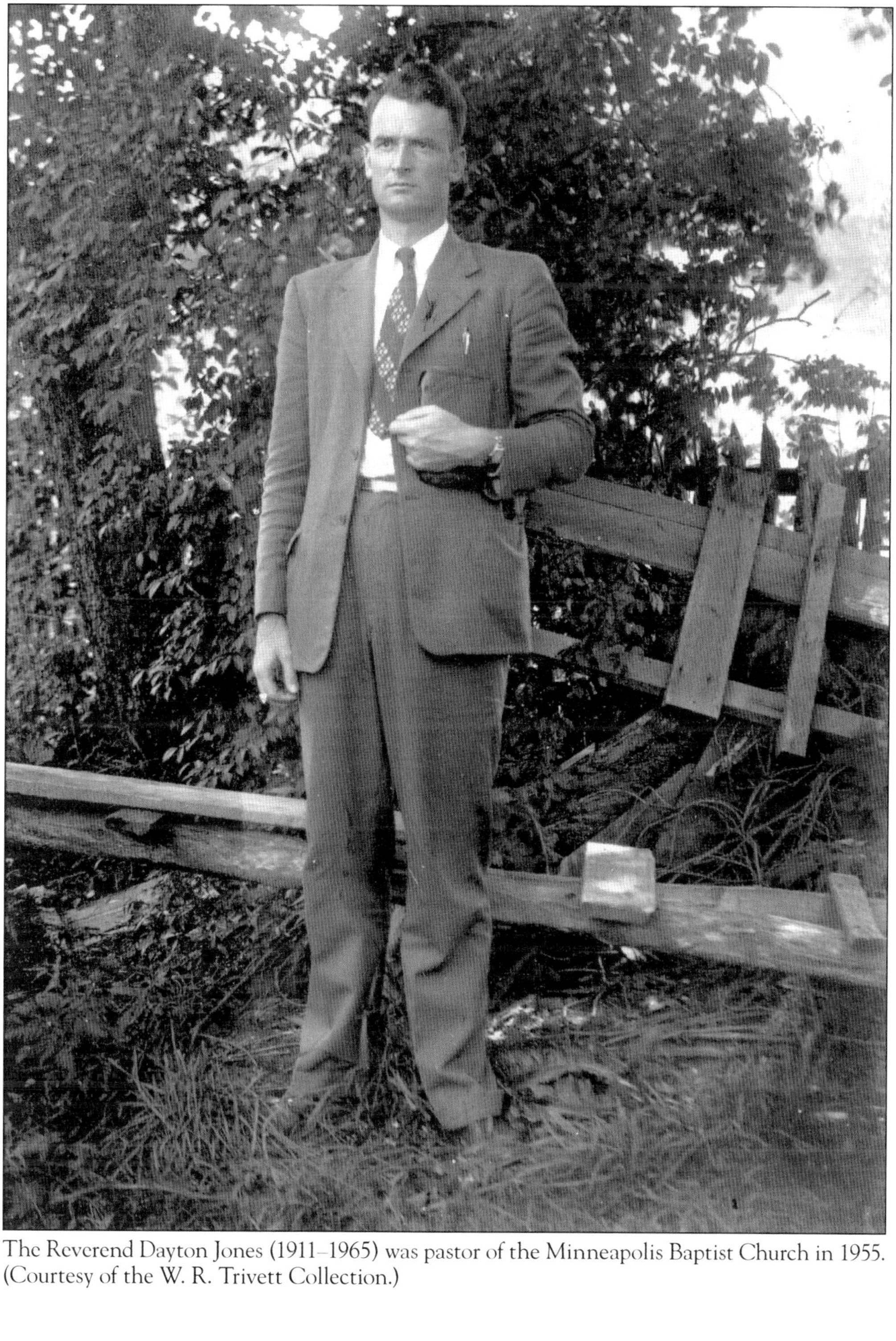

The Reverend Dayton Jones (1911–1965) was pastor of the Minneapolis Baptist Church in 1955. (Courtesy of the W. R. Trivett Collection.)

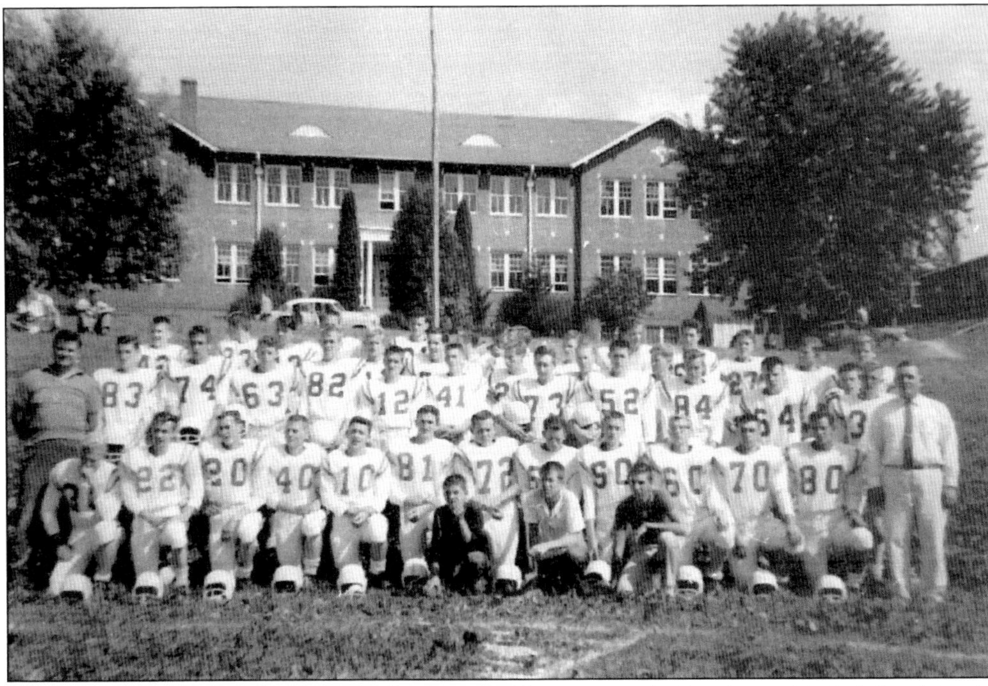

The Cranberry High School football team of 1959 poses with Cranberry High School in the background. (Courtesy of David C. Vance Sr.)

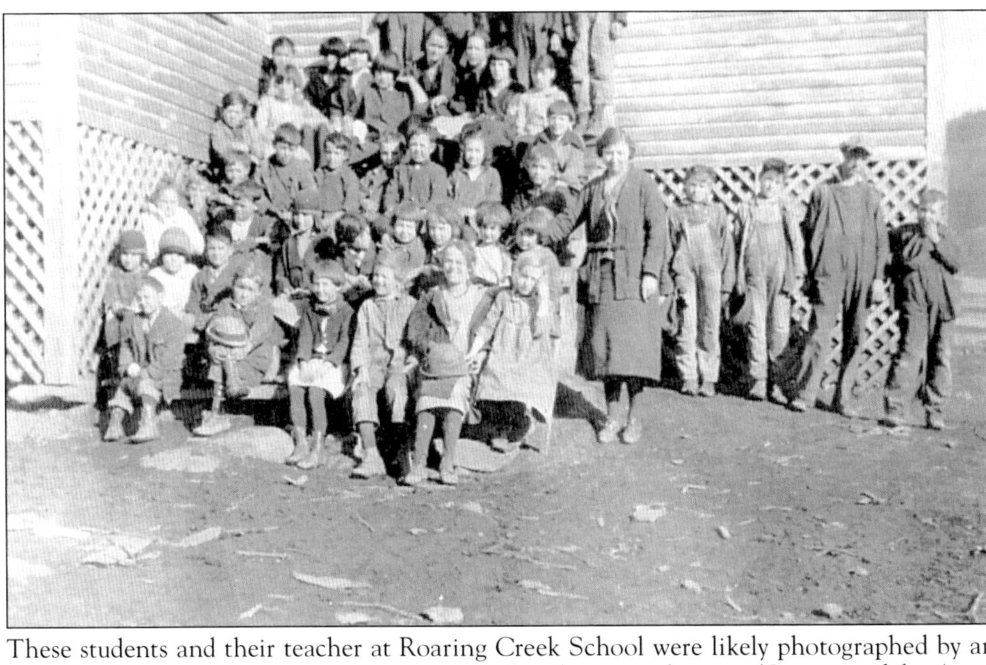

These students and their teacher at Roaring Creek School were likely photographed by an amateur since the top row of students was cut off in the original image. (Courtesy of the Avery County Historical Museum.)

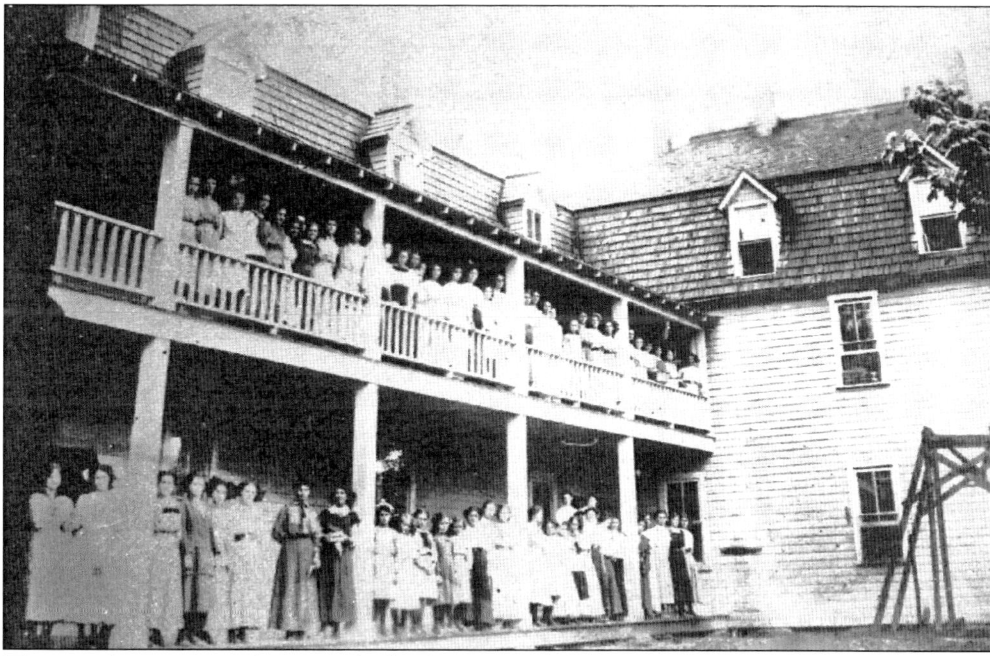

These students are standing outside the dormitories of Lees-McRae College, c. 1911. The school opened in 1900 as the Elizabeth McRae Institute, and for some time, only female students lived in the dorms; men were admitted as day students but did not live on campus. (Courtesy of Lees-McRae College.)

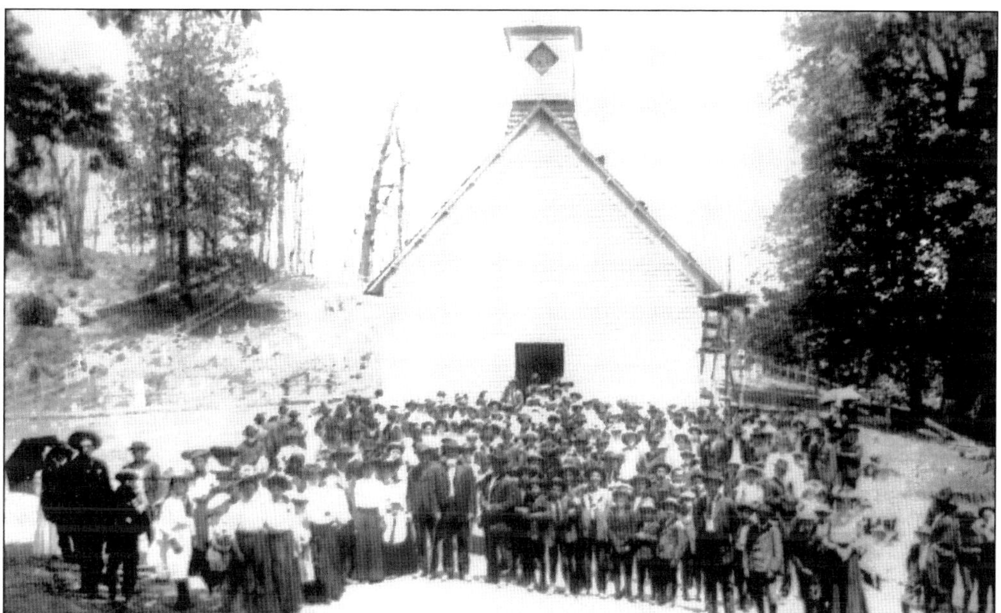

Family and friends are here seen attending a postponed funeral at the Pisgah United Methodist Church. Funerals could be delayed for a variety of reasons, including weather or the absence of a minister. While the deceased individual was buried soon after death, the formal service would sometimes not be held until months later. Several funerals might even be conducted on one day. (Courtesy of Tense Banks.)

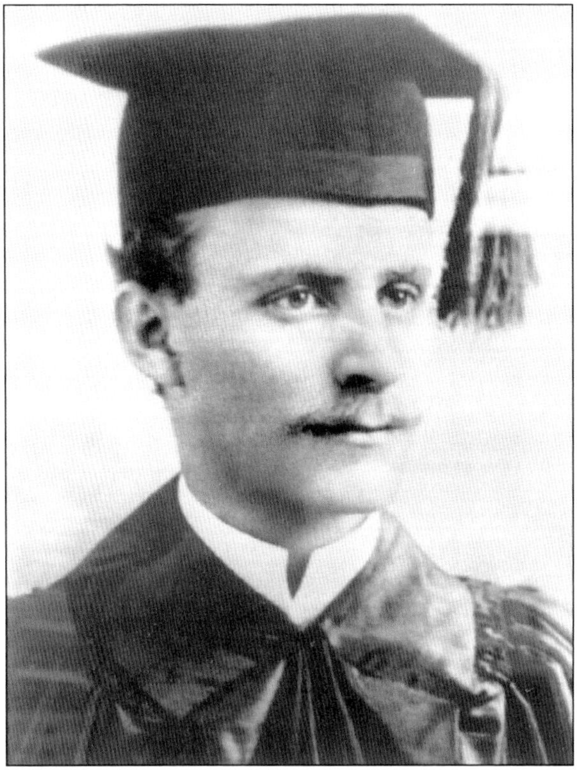

The Reverend Edgar Tufts (1870–1923) founded Lees-McRae College in Banner Elk. After growing up in Maitland, Florida, Tufts came to Banner's Elk in 1901. He also established Grace Hospital and the Grandfather Orphanage, which became the Grandfather Home for Children. (Courtesy of Lees-McRae College.)

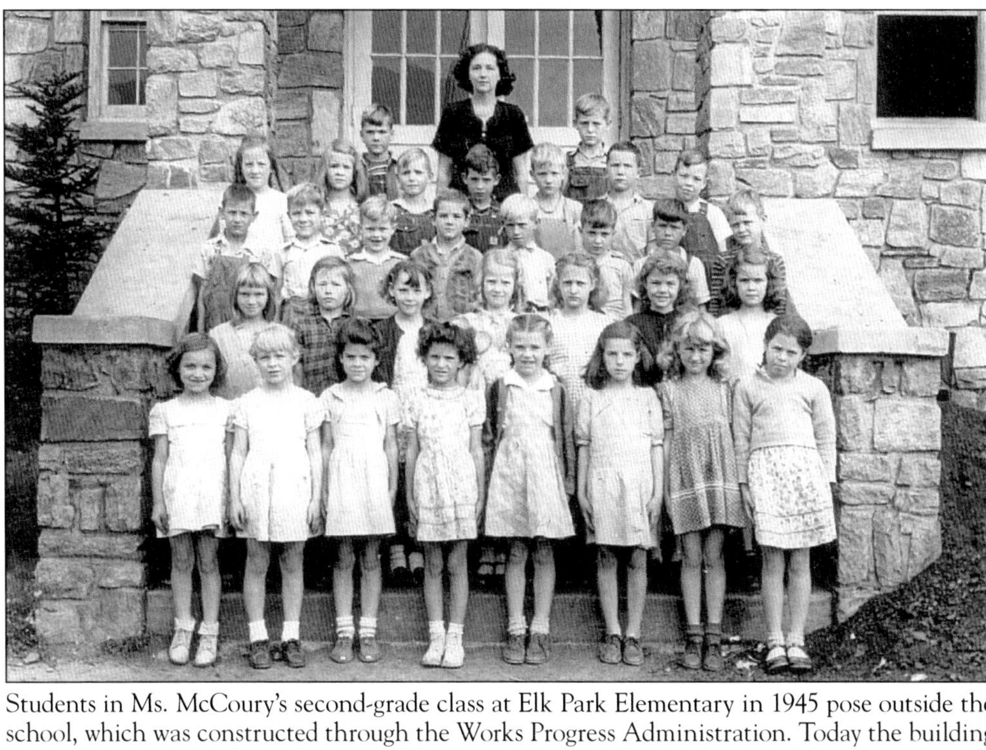

Students in Ms. McCoury's second-grade class at Elk Park Elementary in 1945 pose outside the school, which was constructed through the Works Progress Administration. Today the building is an apartment complex. (Courtesy of the Avery County Historical Museum.)

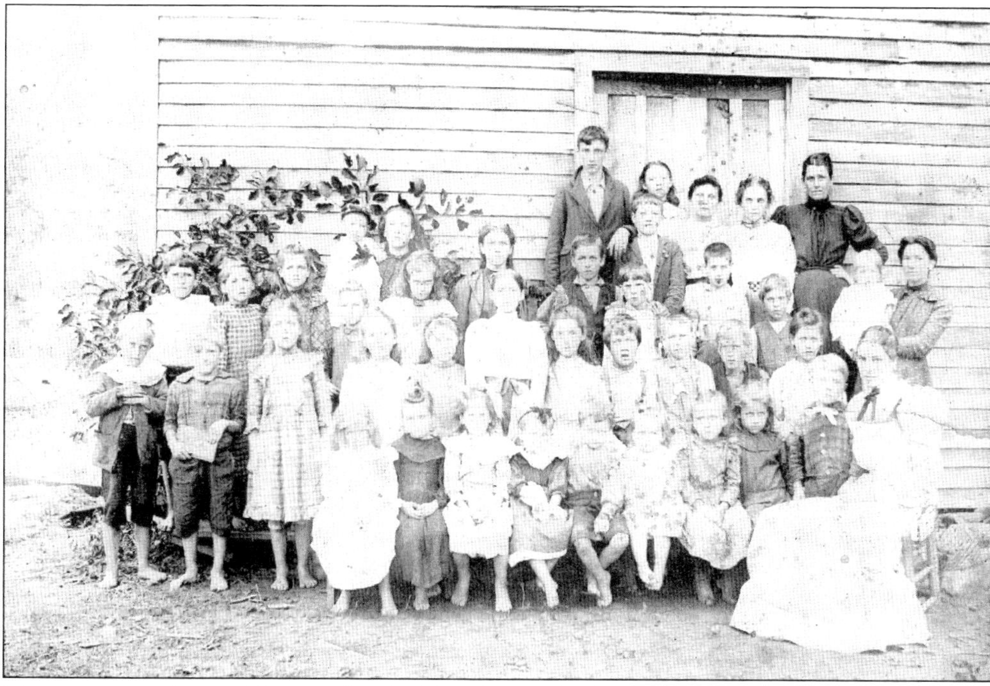

This picture, taken at Henson Creek School, *c.* 1900, bears the photographer's stamp on its back: "A. L. Buchanan, Clarrissa, NC," indicating that the image was struck by a professional photographer. (Courtesy of the Avery County Historical Museum.)

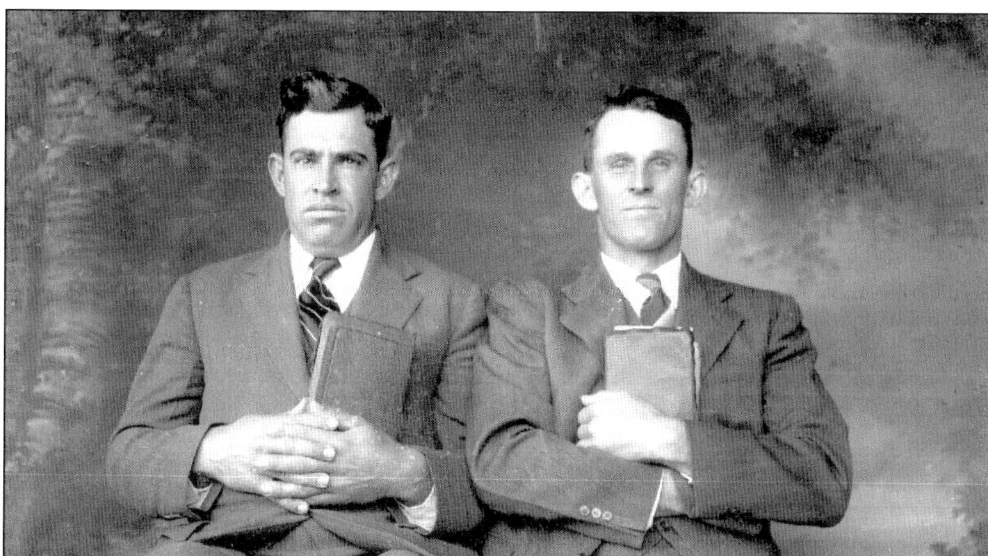

Rev. Victor Trivett (left) and another (unidentified) Avery County preacher pose with their Bibles prominently displayed. (Courtesy of the W. R. Trivett Collection.)

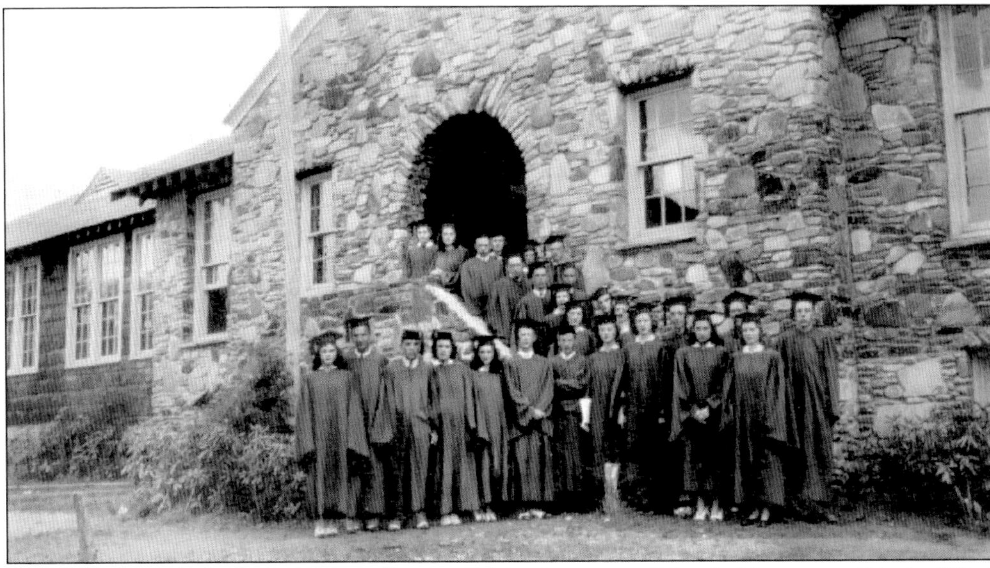

The class of 1942 stands proudly on the steps of the Crossnore School. (Courtesy of Doyle Ollis.)

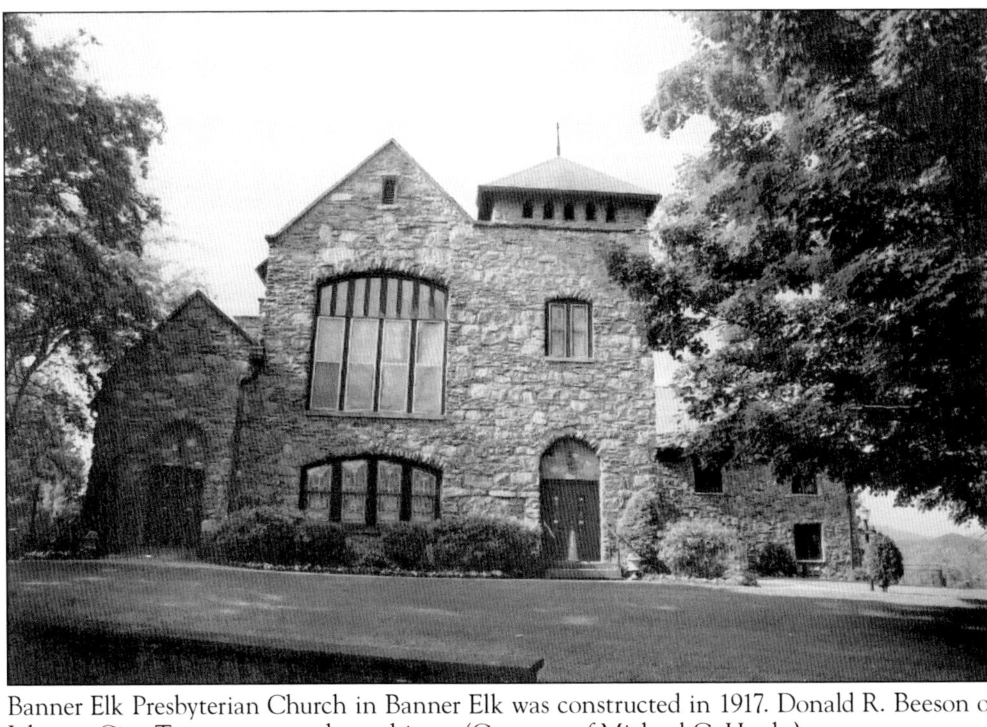

Banner Elk Presbyterian Church in Banner Elk was constructed in 1917. Donald R. Beeson of Johnson City, Tennessee, was the architect. (Courtesy of Michael C. Hardy.)

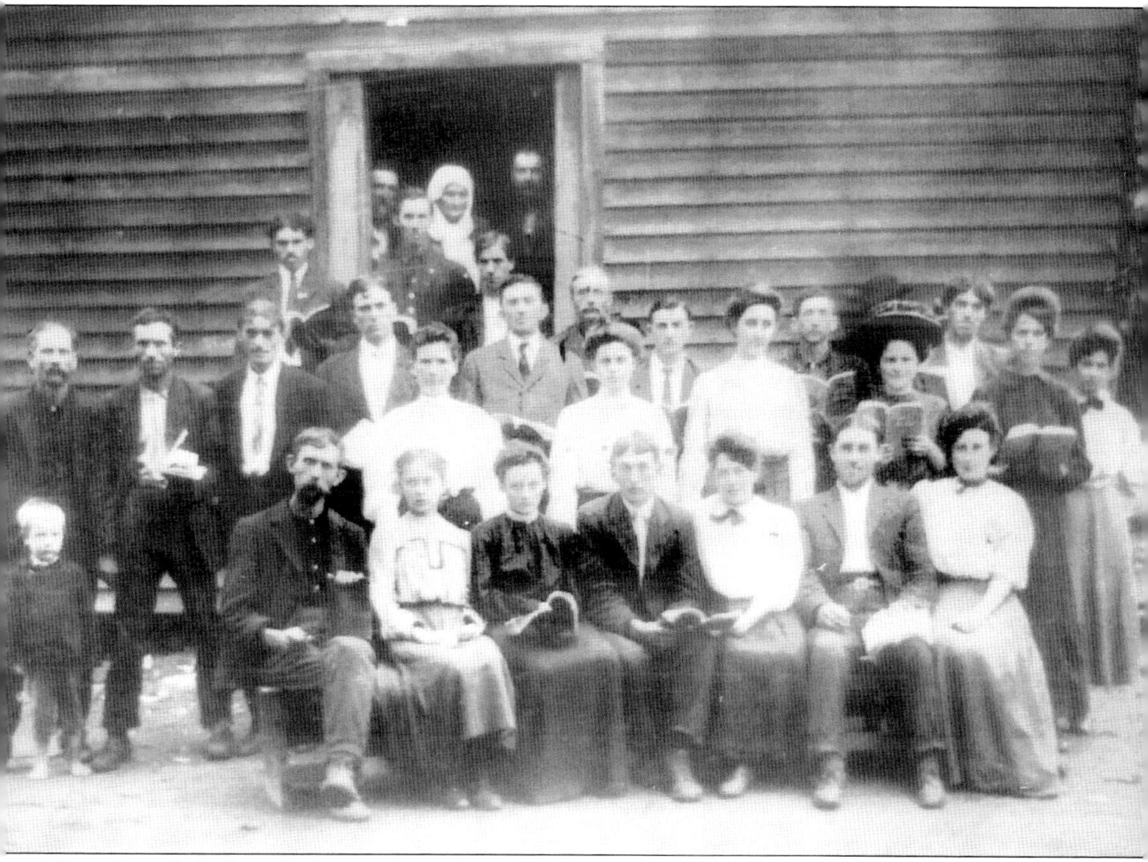

These Linville Falls and Three Mile residents are taking part in a shape-note singing school. This style of musical notation, in which the notes are indicated by a shape, as well as by their position on the musical staff, allowed many people, otherwise untrained in music, to enjoy singing in the distinct harmonic style that was produced. Singing schools, often using the Sacred Harp hymnal, were held at churches and communities throughout rural America to teach shape-note singing. This school was led by Lenoir Franklin and included members of the Wise, Carpenter, Franklin, and Dellinger families. (Courtesy of Tense Banks.)

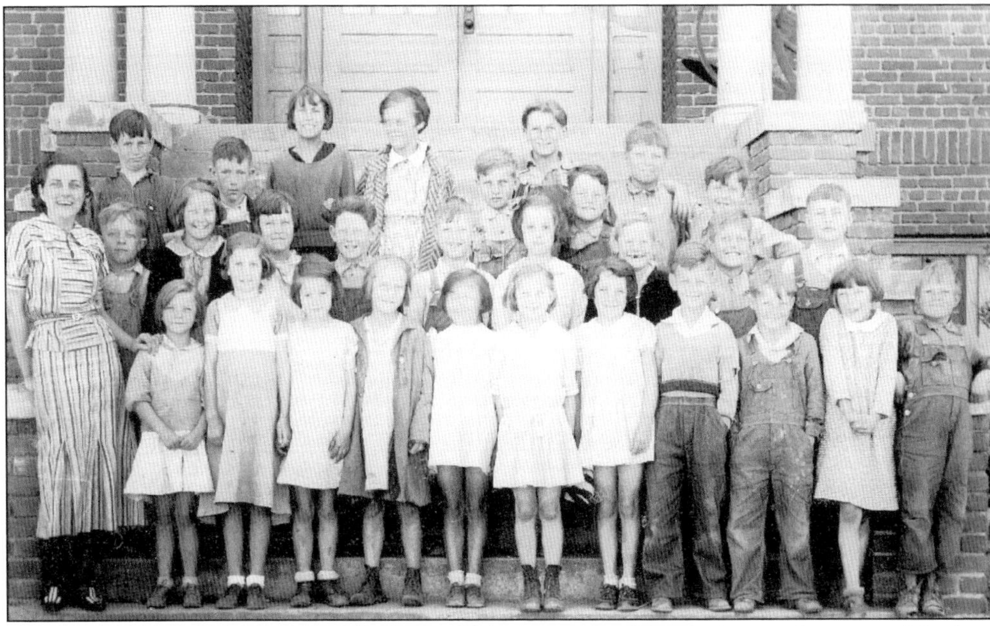

Sybil Ayers Thompson stands with her cheerful-looking second-grade class on the steps at Newland Elementary School. (Courtesy of the Avery County Historical Museum.)

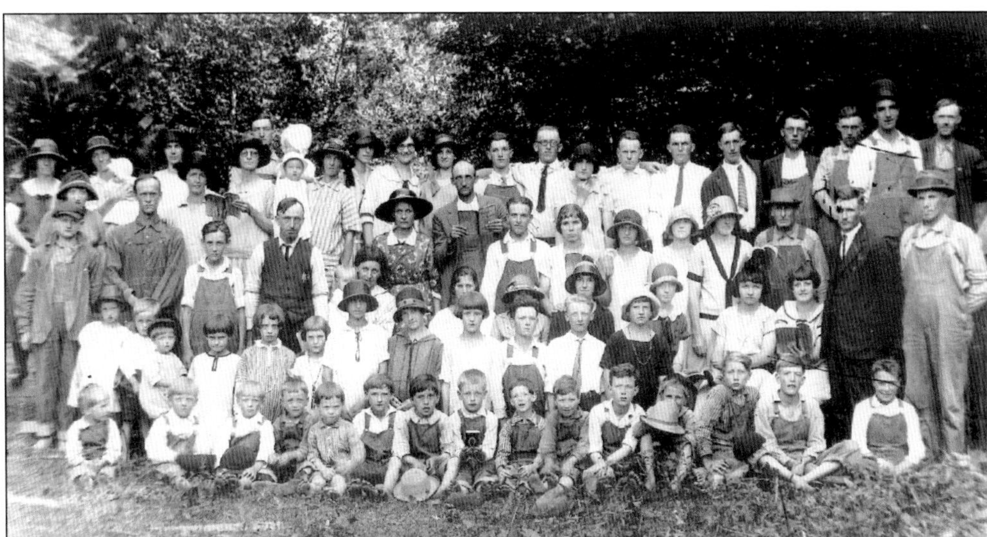

The congregation of the Flat Springs Baptist Church of Christ, c. 1928, included their hymnals, as well as church members of all ages, in their photograph. The church was formed in 1902 by 17 believers, 9 women and 8 men. (Courtesy of the W. R. Trivett Collection.)

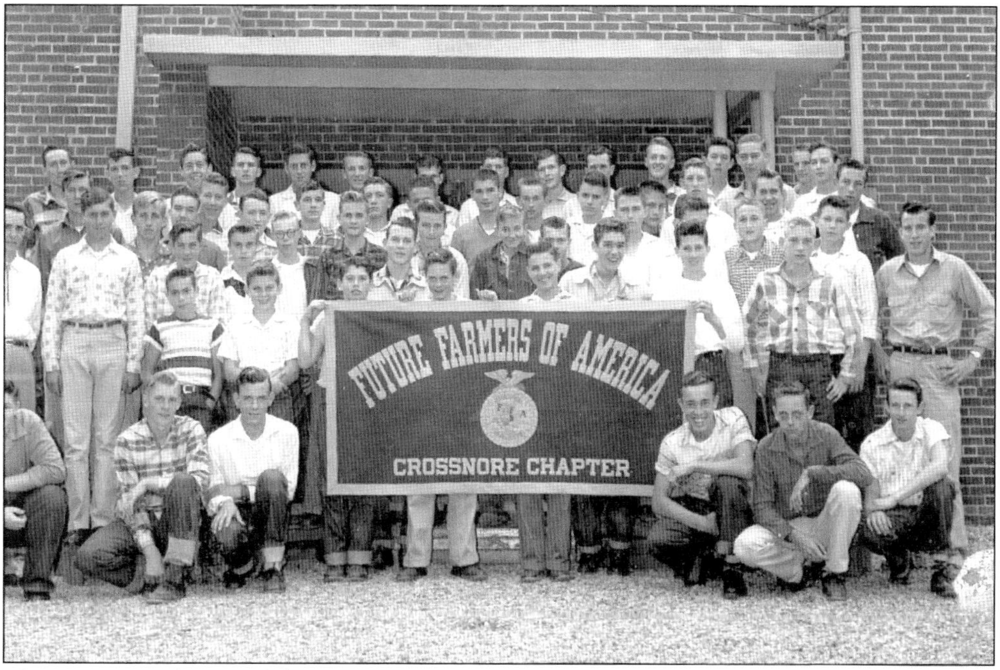

The Crossnore chapter of the Future Farmers of America, c. 1955, displays its banner. (Courtesy of the Phillips family.)

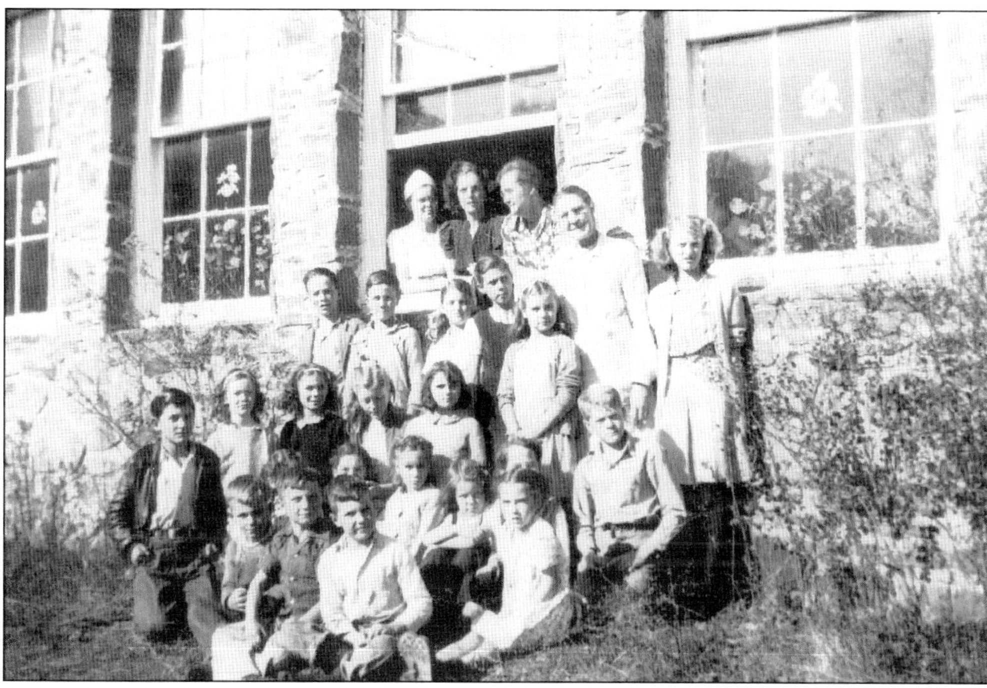
A fourth-grade class at Riverside Elementary School stands between flowers growing inside the classroom on the windowsills. This was a longtime practice of this teacher, Arizona Houston Hughes, lovingly known to many students as "Miz Shoes." (Courtesy of the Avery County Historical Museum.)

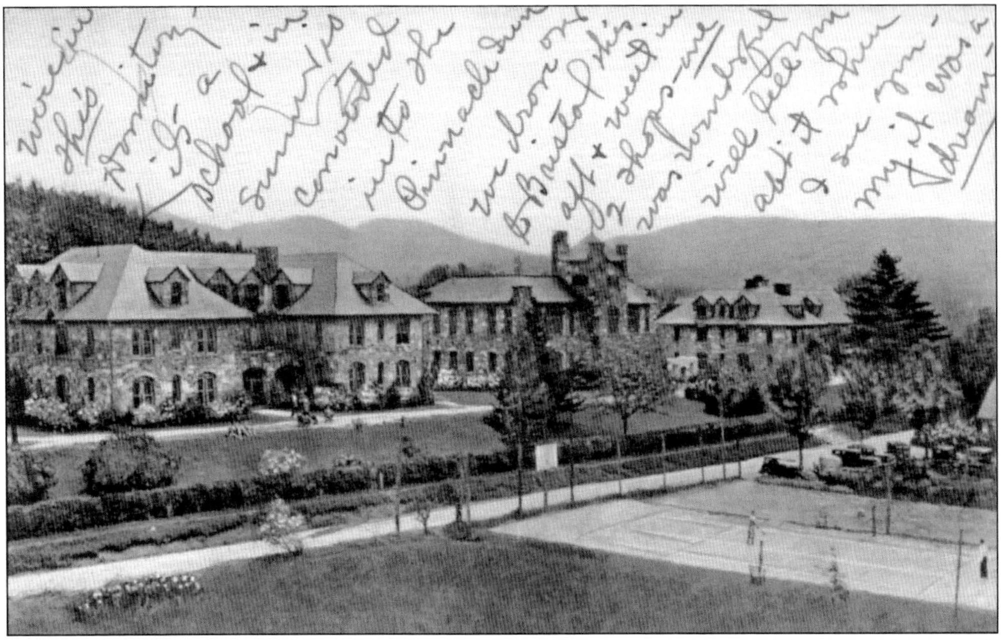

This image of school buildings at Lees-McRae College is accompanied by an early visitor's enthusiastic remarks about the area. (Courtesy of Michael C. Hardy.)

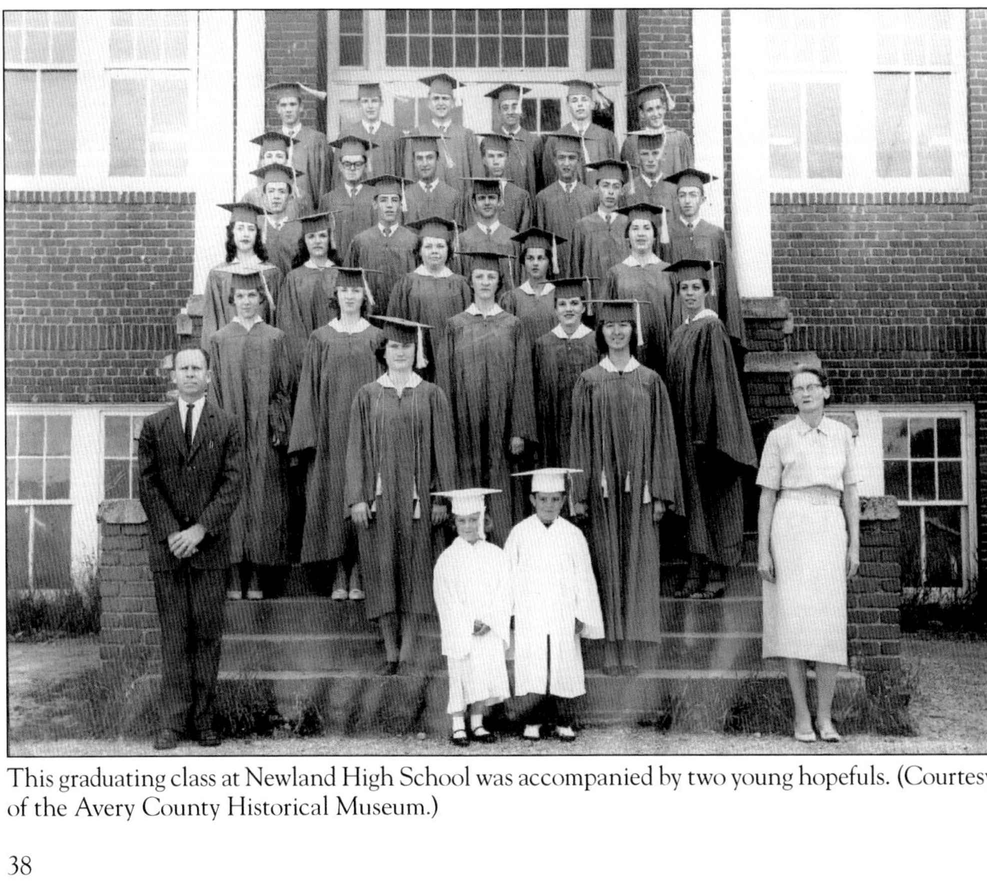

This graduating class at Newland High School was accompanied by two young hopefuls. (Courtesy of the Avery County Historical Museum.)

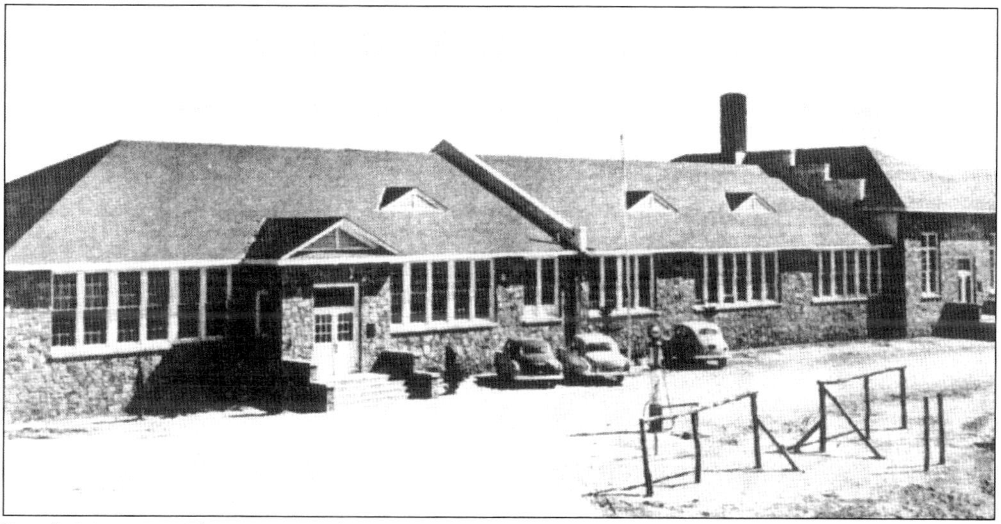

Beech Mountain Elementary School, c. 1953, is pictured here. Note the cars, the gas pump, and the hitching post in the yard—testimony to the variety of transportation methods still being used. The building was constructed by the Works Progress Administration as one of its many projects to provide work and create useful structures. (Courtesy of Ralph E. Lentz II.)

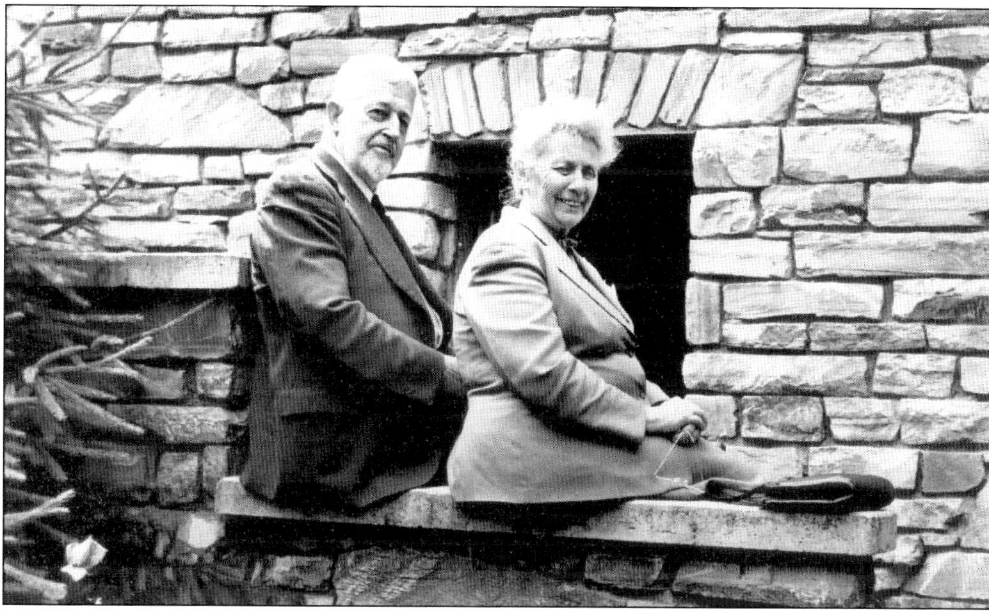

Doctors Eustace H. and Mary M. Sloop were founders of the Crossnore School. Eustace was born in 1878 in Mooresville, North Carolina. He first came to present-day Avery County in 1906 where he began his medical practice. In 1911, he and his wife, Mary, moved to Crossnore, and in 1928, he helped build Garrett Hospital. He died in 1961. Mary Turpin Martin was born in 1873 in Davidson, North Carolina, and received her medical degree in 1906. Turned down for mission service for being "too old" (she was in her early 30s), she married Eustace Sloop in 1908. She was chosen the first North Carolina Mother of the Year and became the American Mother of the Year since she had been a mother to so many children through the school. She also received doctorates in education and humanities and wrote her autobiography, *Miracle in the Mountains.* (Courtesy of the Avery County Historical Museum.)

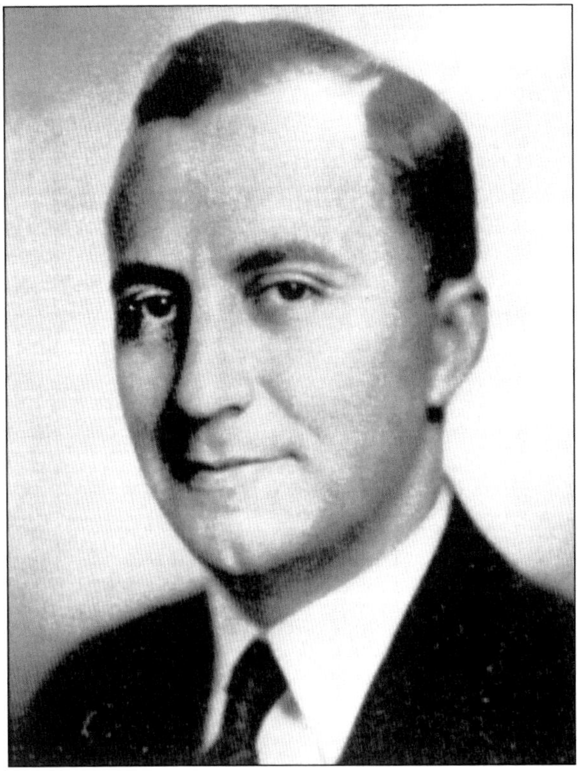

Edgar Hall Tufts Jr. was president of Lees-McRae College from 1923 through 1942. Tufts was only 23 years old and fresh from college when his father died, and he became head of the Lees-McRae Institute, Grace Hospital, and the Grandfather Orphanage. (Courtesy of Lees-McRae College)

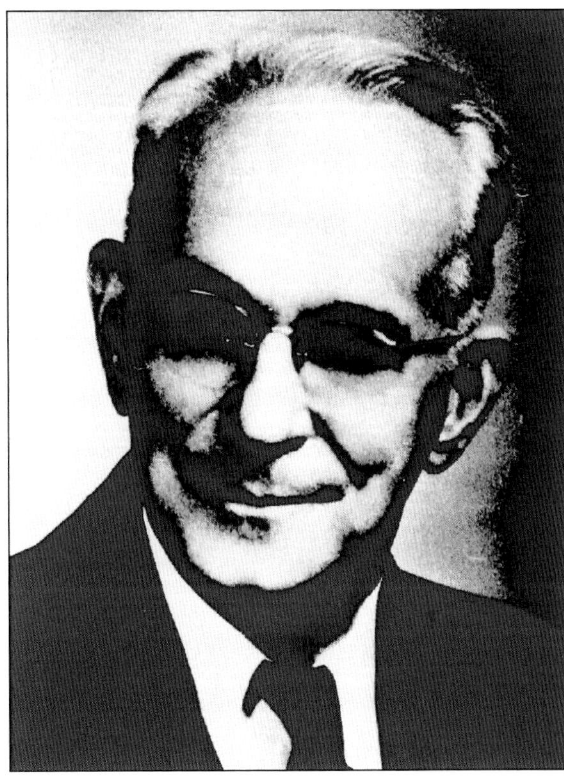

Dr. William Cummings Tate (1886–1960) was president of Lees-McRae College from 1947 to 1950. A native of Tennessee, he came to present-day Avery County in 1908 to work as company physician for the Ritter Lumber Company of Pineola. His friend Edgar Tufts convinced Tate to use his medical skills to minister to the people of Banner's Elk. He served patients throughout the area, sometimes with the help of his wife. He served as the director of Grace Hospital from 1910 to 1951. In 1922, he organized the bank of Banner Elk and served on its board for nearly 40 years. He also served as mayor of Banner Elk. (Courtesy of Lees-McRae College.)

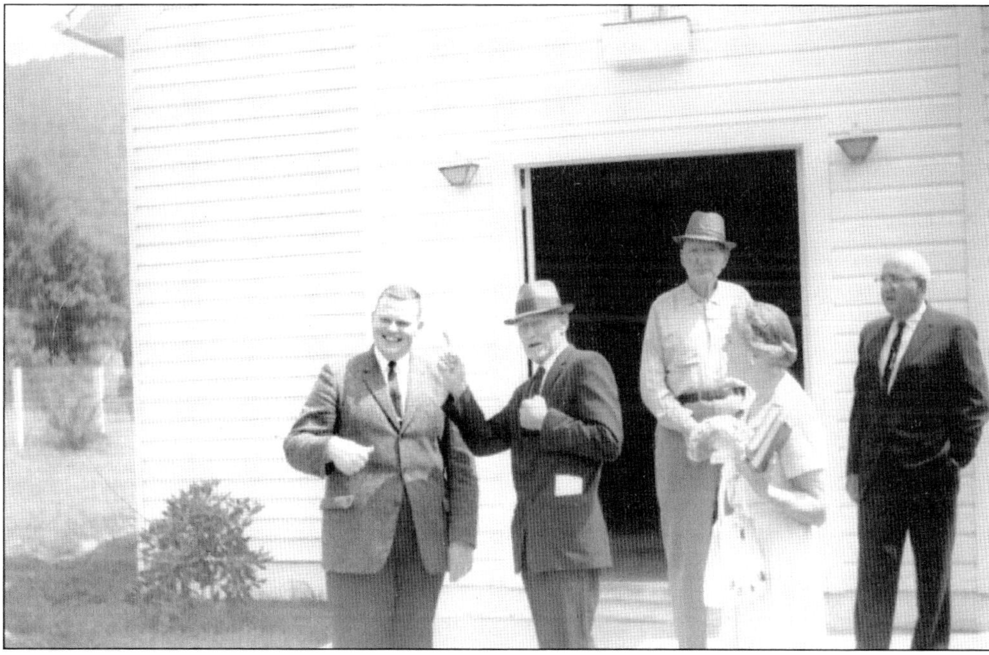

From left to right, John Duvall, Mr. Erickson, Mr. Turks, Mrs. J. L. Blanchard, and an unidentified man are seen here leaving a service at Pine Grove United Methodist Church. (Courtesy of the Phillips family.)

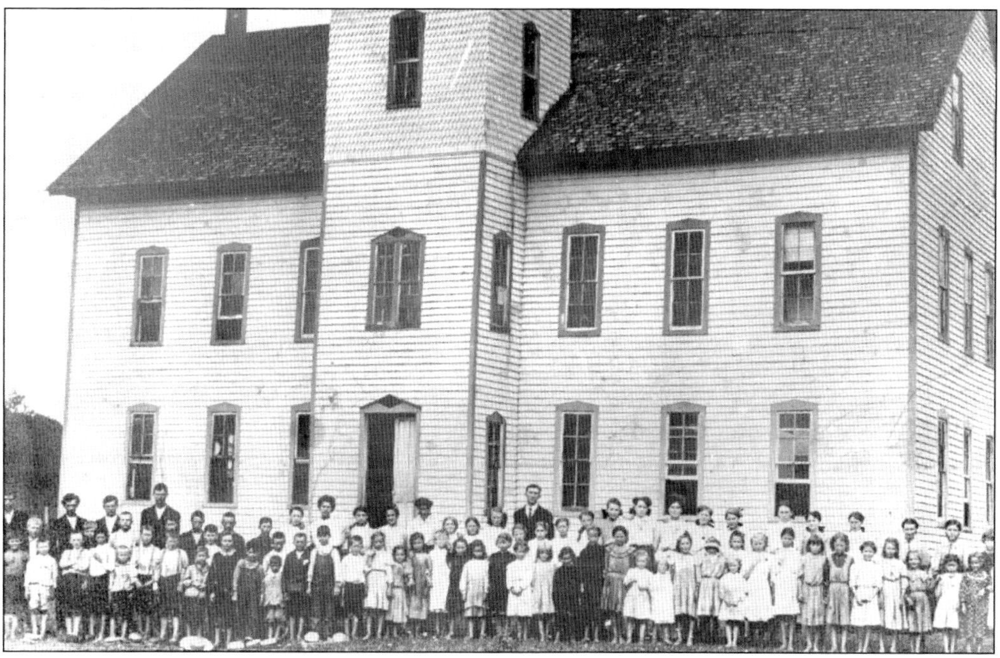

The Aaron Seminary was established in 1890 by the Blue Ridge Conference of the Methodist Church. It existed in the Aaron community, now known as Montezuma. The two-and-a-half-story building housed classrooms for local children and for Methodist church services. The building was torn down and the lumber used to construct a Methodist church. (Courtesy of the Avery County Historical Museum.)

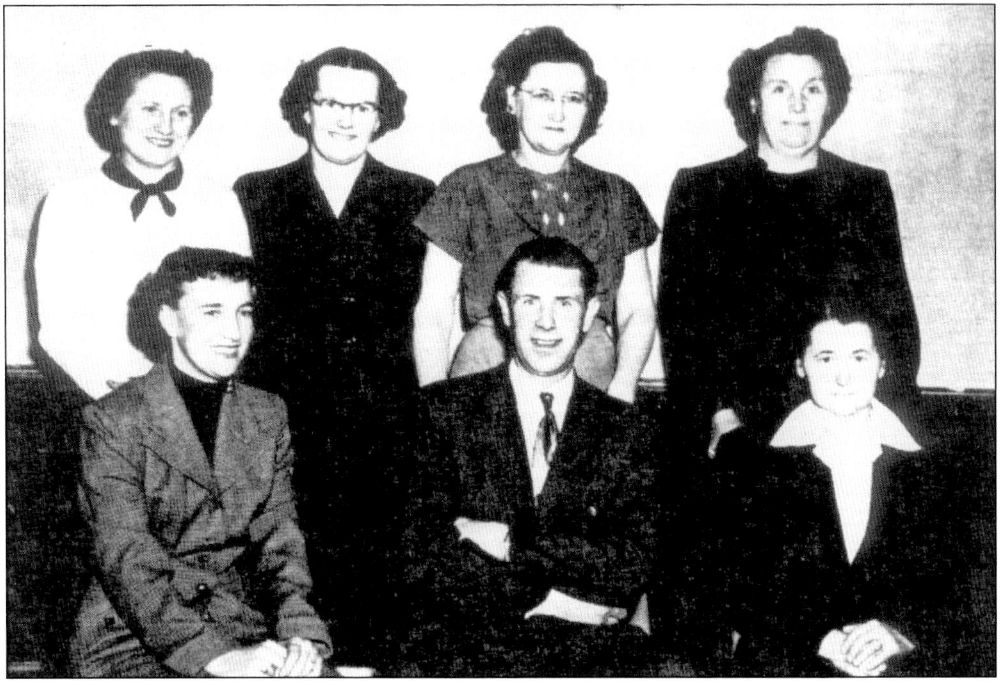

In 1953, there were eight teachers at Beech Mountain Elementary School: Ruby G. Young, Cloyce Harmon, Nell J. Buchanan, Ella Faye Phillips, Clara V. Phillips, Beulah Dugger, and Virginia Johnson. Six of those teachers are featured here with Principal N. E. Johnson (center, first row). (Courtesy of Ralph E. Lentz II.)

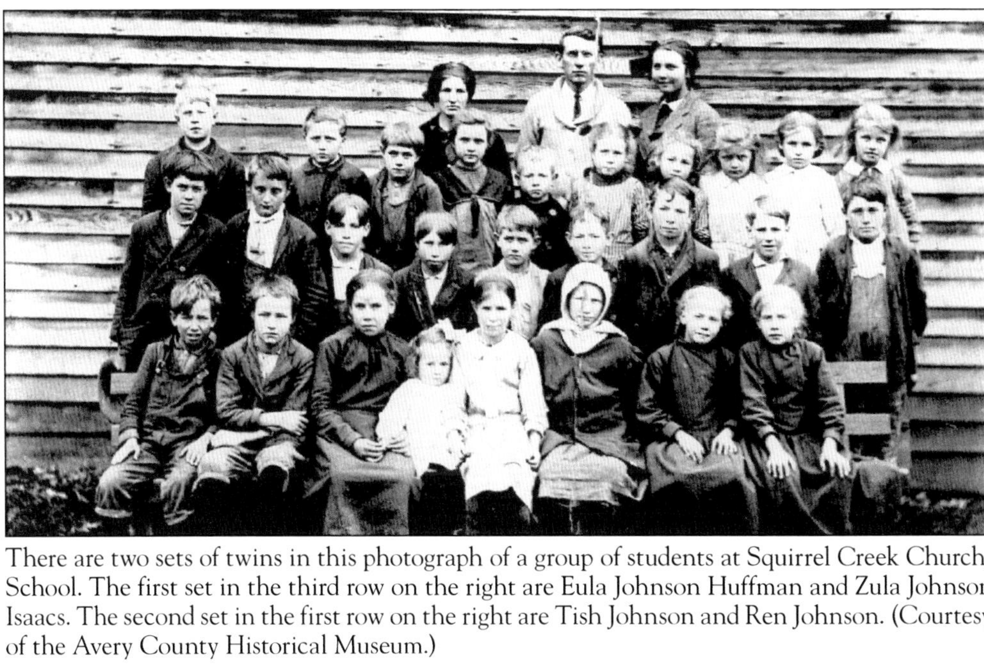

There are two sets of twins in this photograph of a group of students at Squirrel Creek Church/School. The first set in the third row on the right are Eula Johnson Huffman and Zula Johnson Isaacs. The second set in the first row on the right are Tish Johnson and Ren Johnson. (Courtesy of the Avery County Historical Museum.)

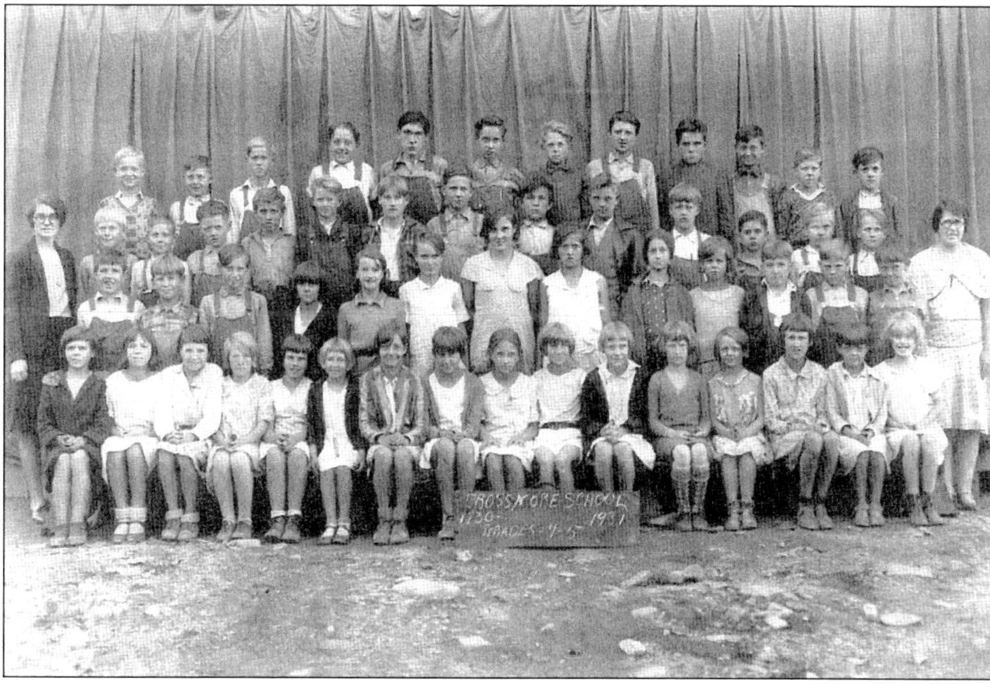

These students are members of the fourth-grade class at Crossnore Elementary, 1930–1931. (Courtesy of the Avery County Historical Museum.)

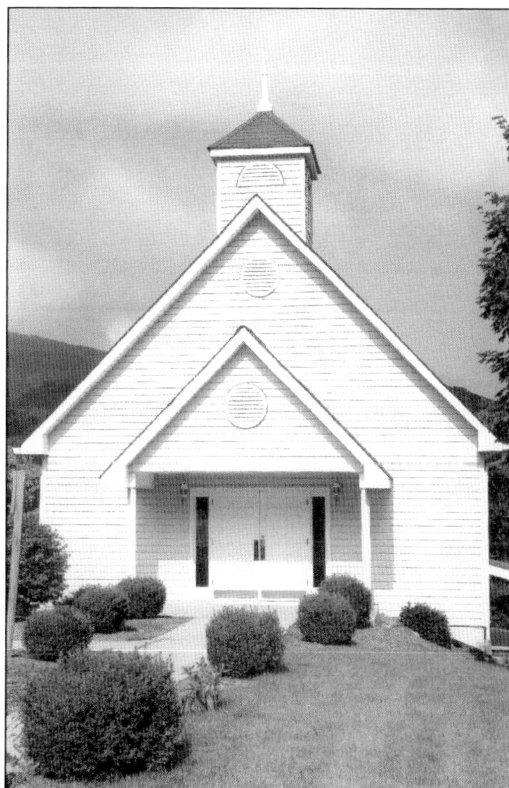

The Church of Christ in Norwood Hollow continues to see active service. (Courtesy of Michael C. Hardy.)

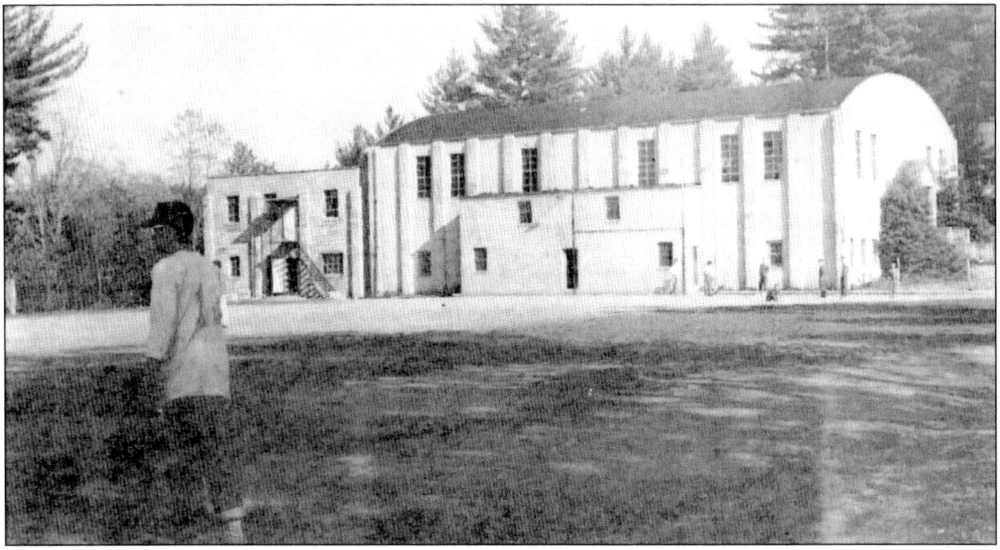
The David Allen Memorial Gymnasium and Recreation Hall has stood for many years on the grounds of the Crossnore School. (Courtesy of the Avery County Historical Museum.)

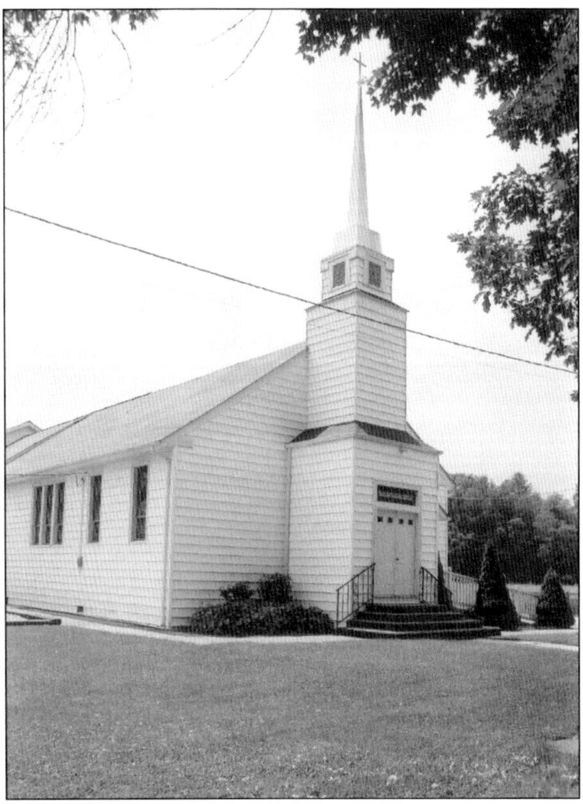
Dedication services for the Altamont United Methodist Church were held on September 13, 1925. The charming building is still in use today. (Courtesy of Michael C. Hardy.)

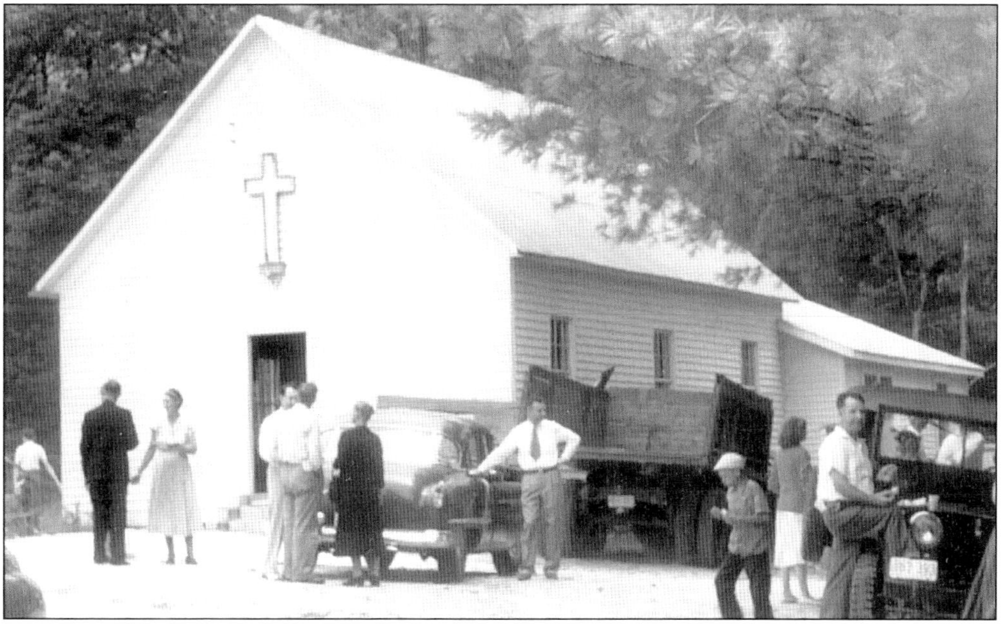

Members are seen here visiting outside Pine Grove United Methodist Church, *c.* 1953. (Courtesy of Linda Taylor.)

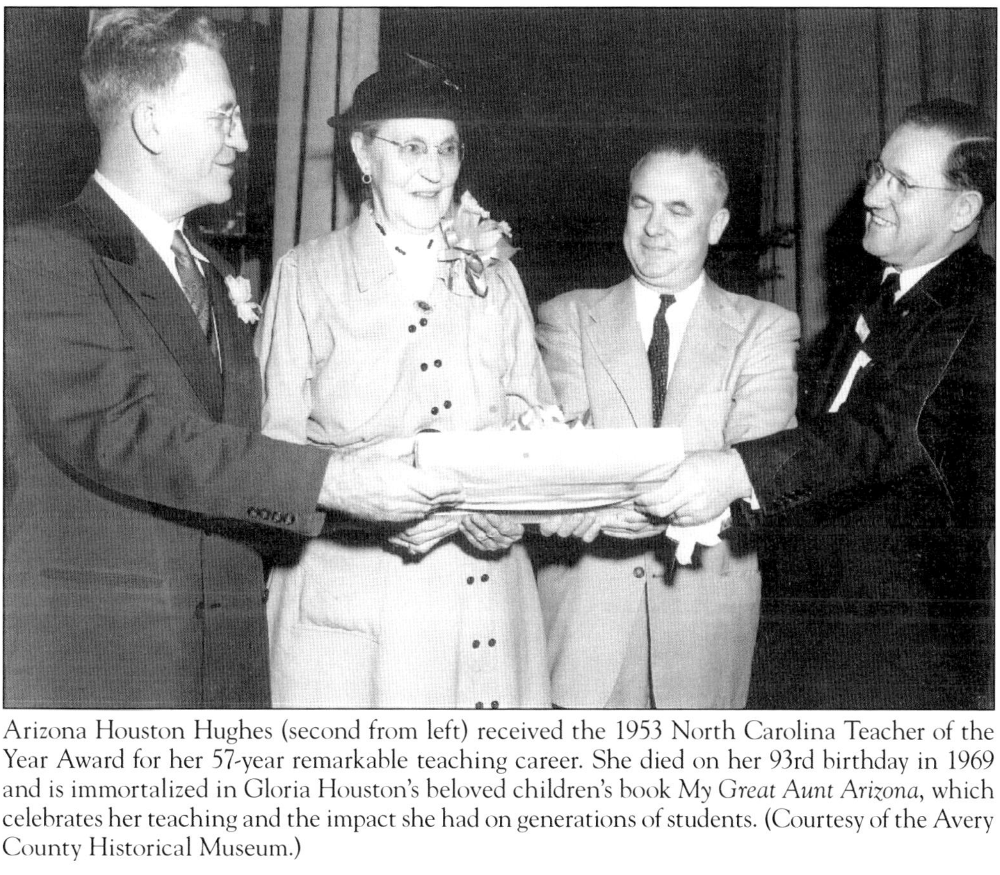

Arizona Houston Hughes (second from left) received the 1953 North Carolina Teacher of the Year Award for her 57-year remarkable teaching career. She died on her 93rd birthday in 1969 and is immortalized in Gloria Houston's beloved children's book *My Great Aunt Arizona*, which celebrates her teaching and the impact she had on generations of students. (Courtesy of the Avery County Historical Museum.)

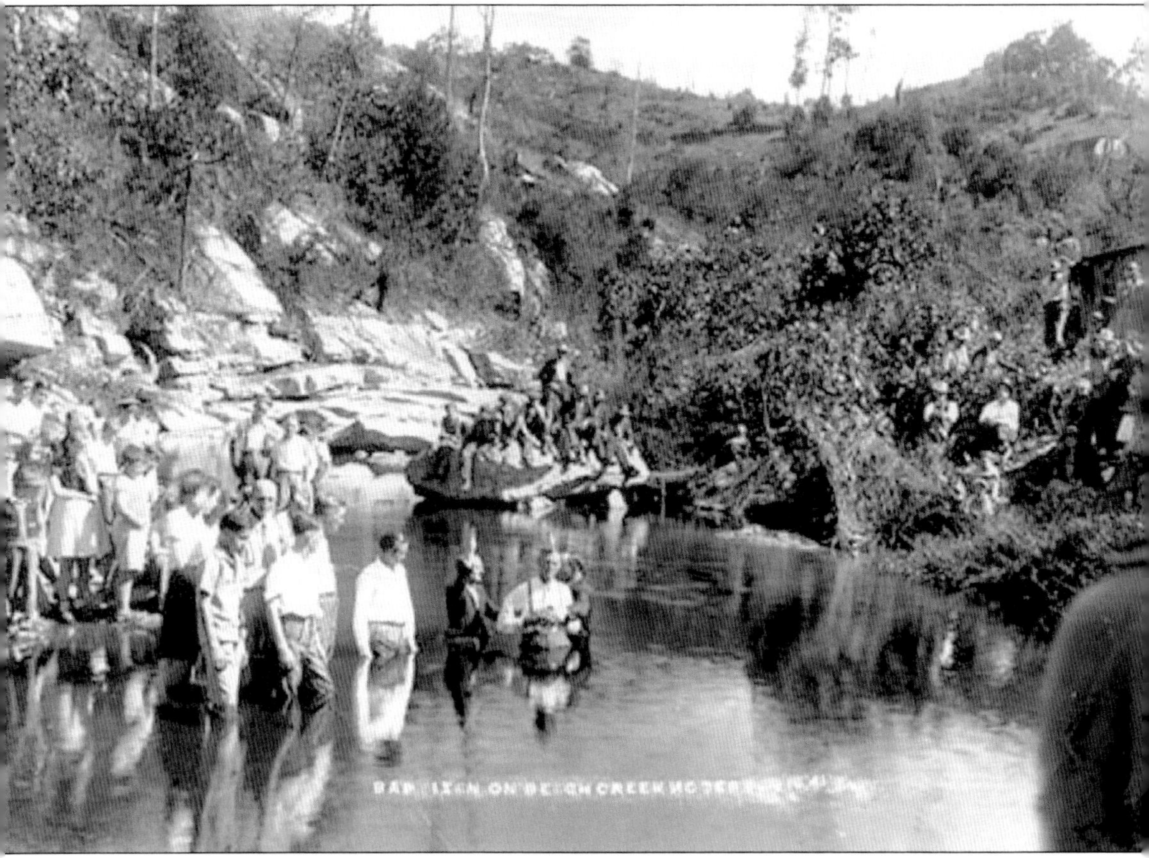

Monroe Ward was baptized by Dwight Edmisten in Beech Creek, September 28, 1941. (Courtesy of the W. R. Trivett Collection.)

Three

Friends and Neighbors

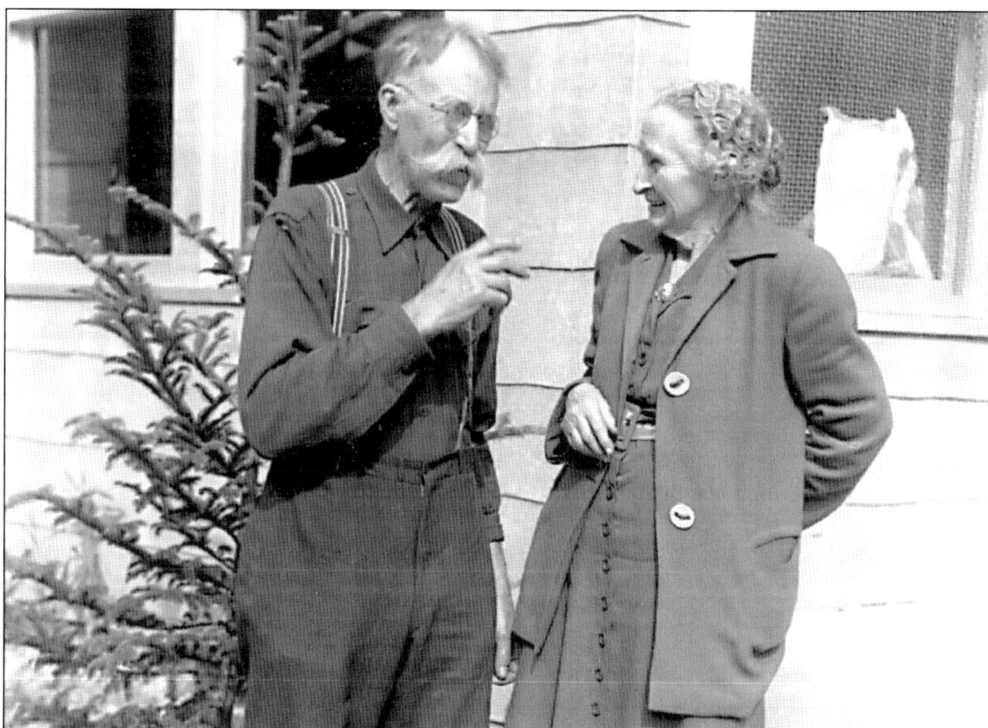

"Uncle Gilmer" and "Aunt Pop" were local characters and operators of the Community Store in Crossnore. This photograph was taken in July 1948. (Courtesy of the North Carolina Division of Archives and History.)

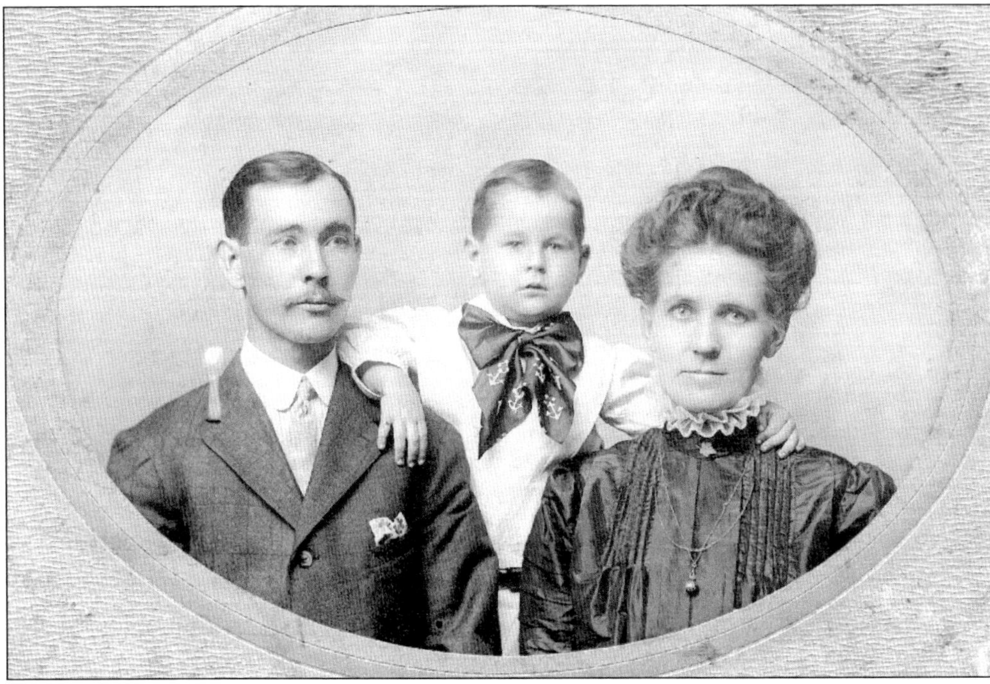

Robert and Sallie McGrath are photographed here with their son, Harold, who was later a postmaster of Linville. (Courtesy of the Avery County Historical Museum.)

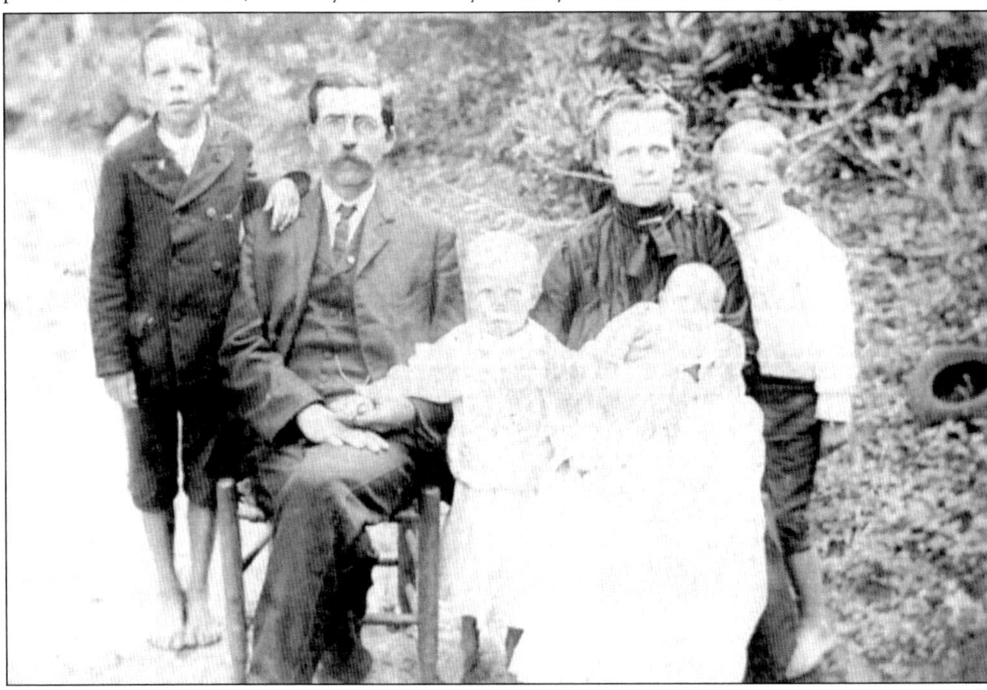

Augusta and John Riddle had five children: Otis, Clyde, Earnest, Carl, and John, four of whom are seen here. The younger boys are wearing gowns, typical of all children until the early 20th century. Until they were toilet trained, both boys and girls wore gowns, also making it easier to prepare a layette, regardless of gender. (Courtesy of Doyle Ollis.)

Edward and Josie Wiseman were the parents of Scotty Wiseman and part of the famed musical Wiseman family. (Courtesy of the Avery County Historical Museum.)

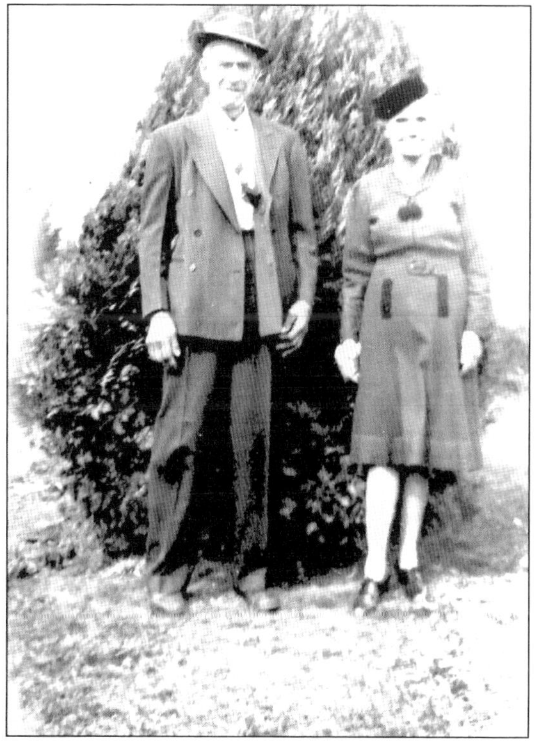

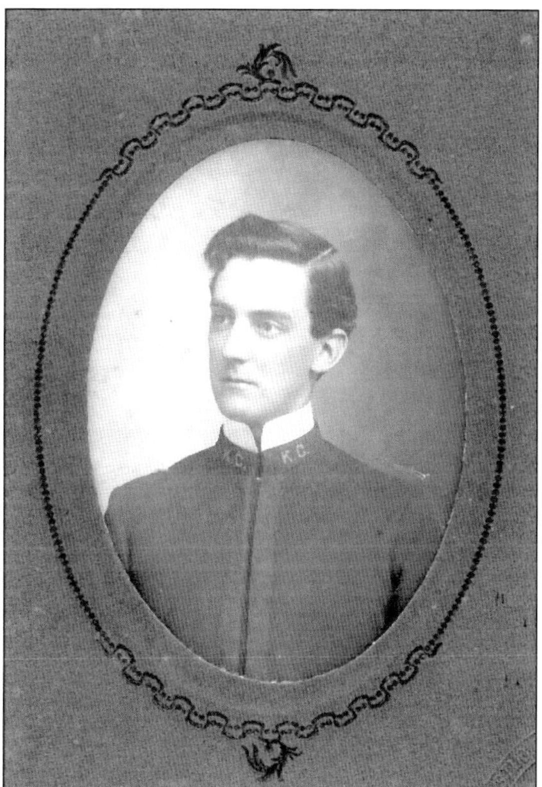

Plumtree's Dr. W. B. Burleson (1882–1958), here seen as a student, was secretary of the Avery County Medical Association and served as both master and worshipful master of the Plumtree Masonic Lodge. (Courtesy of the Avery County Historical Museum.)

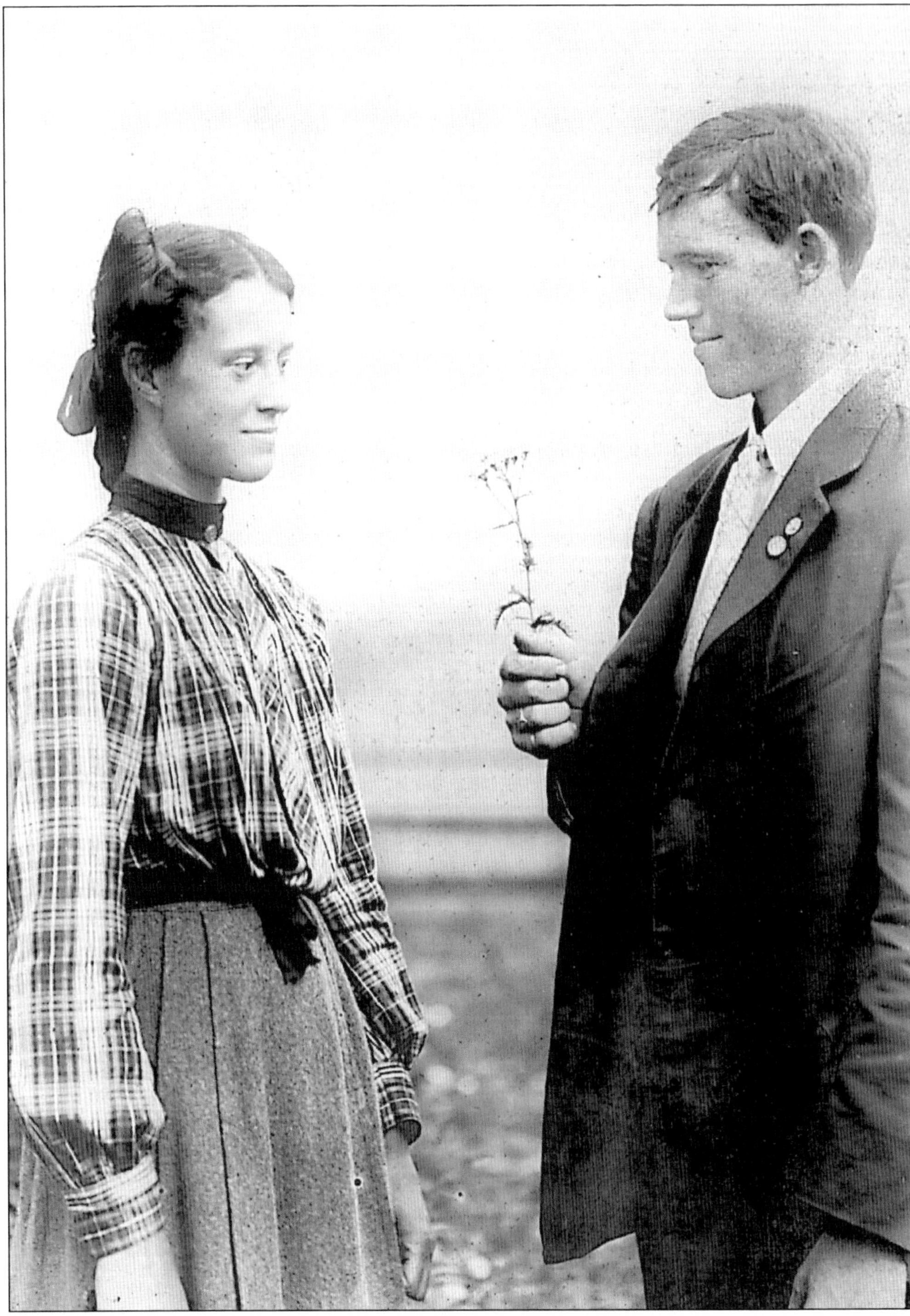

This photograph of Mertie Weaver and Willie R. Trivett was probably taken to commemorate their engagement *c.* 1911. Trivett was a portrait photographer or "picture man" in the Beech Creek and Flat Springs area of Avery County. (Courtesy of the W. R. Trivett Collection.)

Watauga County native Doc Watson is here seen playing at Lees-McRae College in the late 1960s. (Courtesy of Lees-McRae College.)

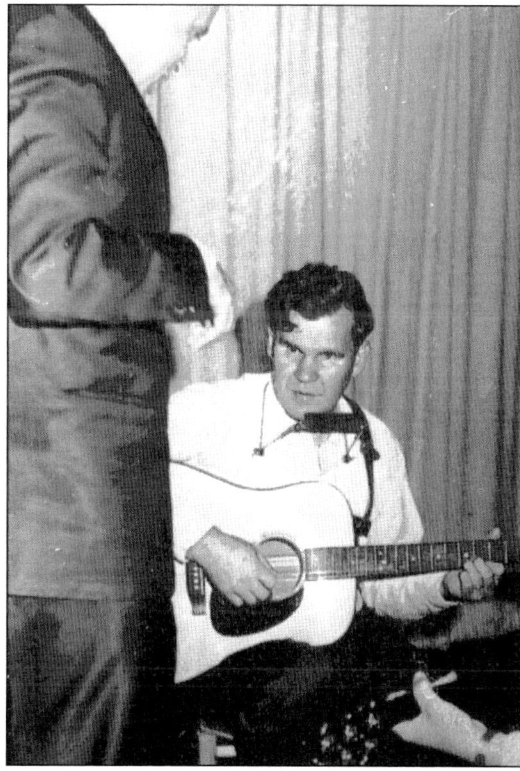

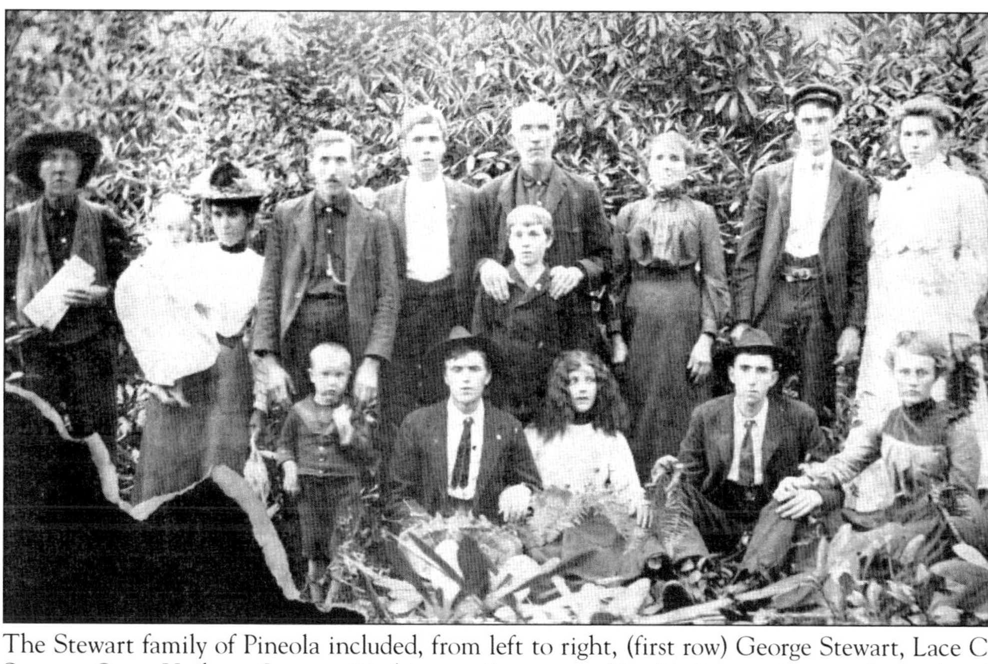

The Stewart family of Pineola included, from left to right, (first row) George Stewart, Lace C. Stewart, Grace Hoilman Stewart, Washington Stewart, and Lockie Fortner Stewart; (second row) Charles D. Stewart, Eugena Stewart, Maggie Green Stewart, William Nelson Stewart, Charlie Stewart, Fred Stewart, James M. Stewart, Jane Faye Stewart, unidentified, and Rittie Stewart Clark. (Courtesy of the Stewart family.)

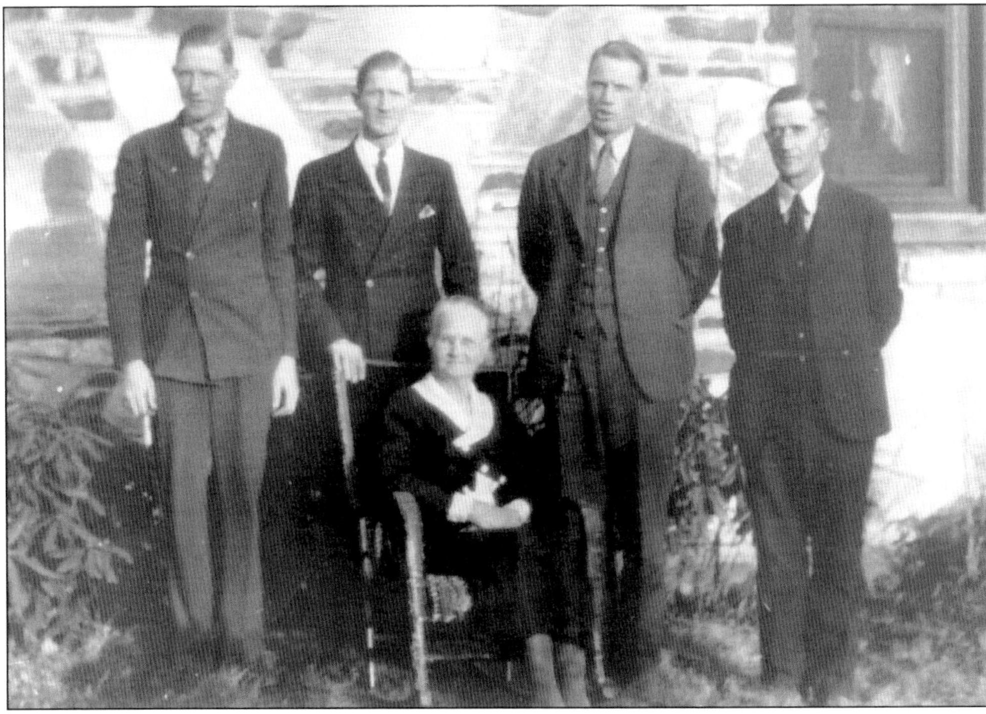

Standing here with their mother, Nancy Henderson Vance, are, from left to right, Toss Vance, Todd Vance Jr., Paul Vance, and Jim Vance. (Courtesy of Heidi Ellis.)

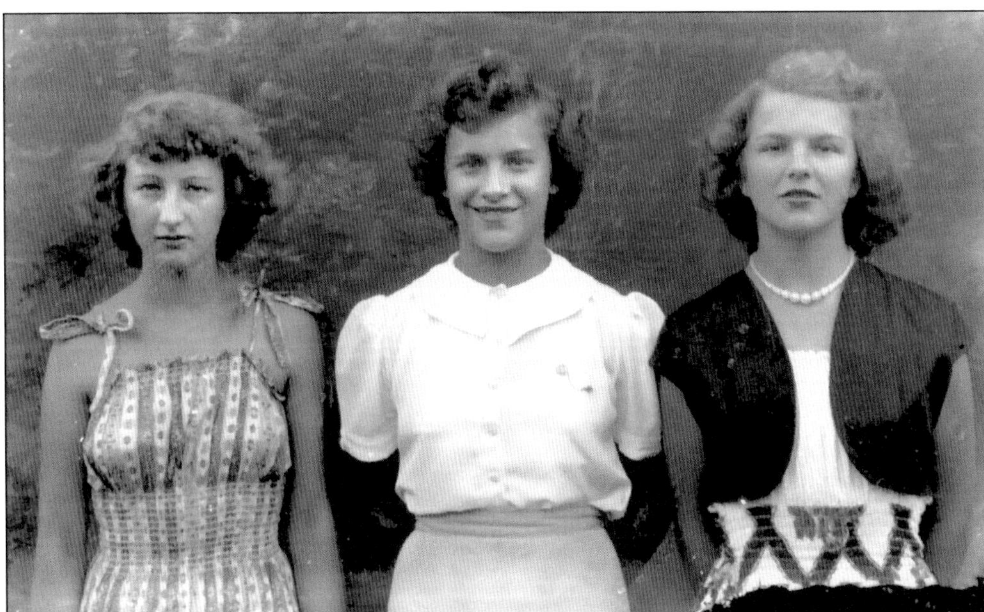

Louise Harmon (left), Betty Harmon (center), and Helen Harmon pose for one of W. R. Trivett's many portraits taken in Avery County. (Courtesy of the W. R. Trivett Collection.)

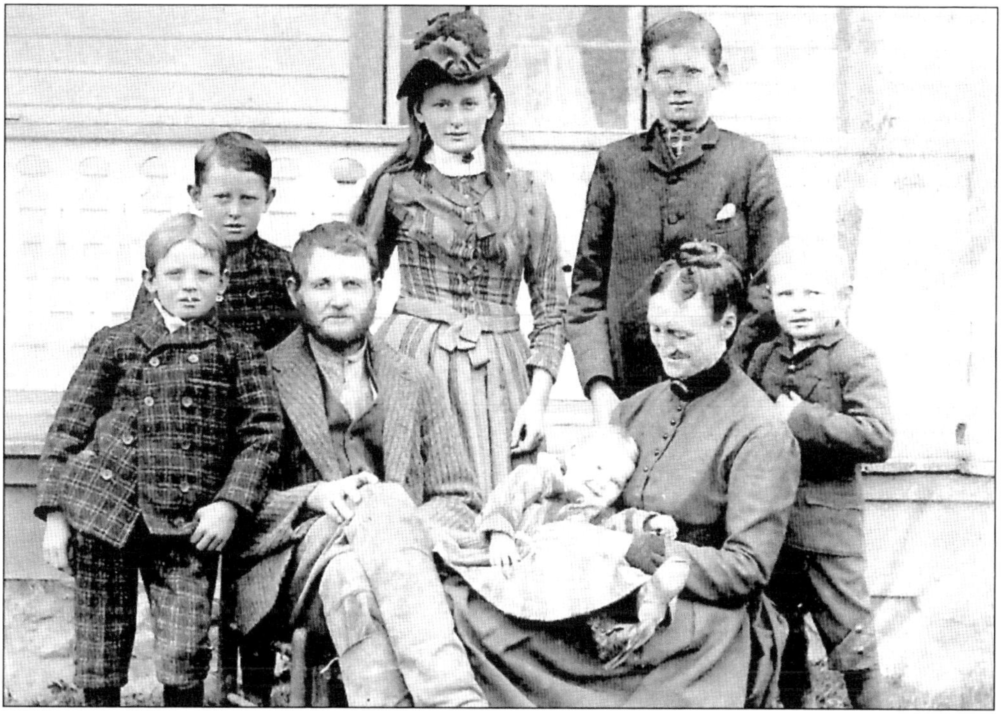

This photograph was taken by F. W. Tyler of Ledger, Mitchell County, North Carolina. Since early photographic techniques required people to sit completely still for several seconds while the picture was taken, it is unusual to see such an old photograph with such natural expressions on a mother and child. Children often blur in these photographs because they could not stay still. Shown here from left to right are (first row) Mack Phillips, John G. Phillips, Kate Phillips (infant), Minerva ("Tuppy") Phillips, and Ed Phillips; (second row) Lynn Phillips, Hettie Lee Phillips, and Jim Phillips. (Courtesy of the Phillips family.)

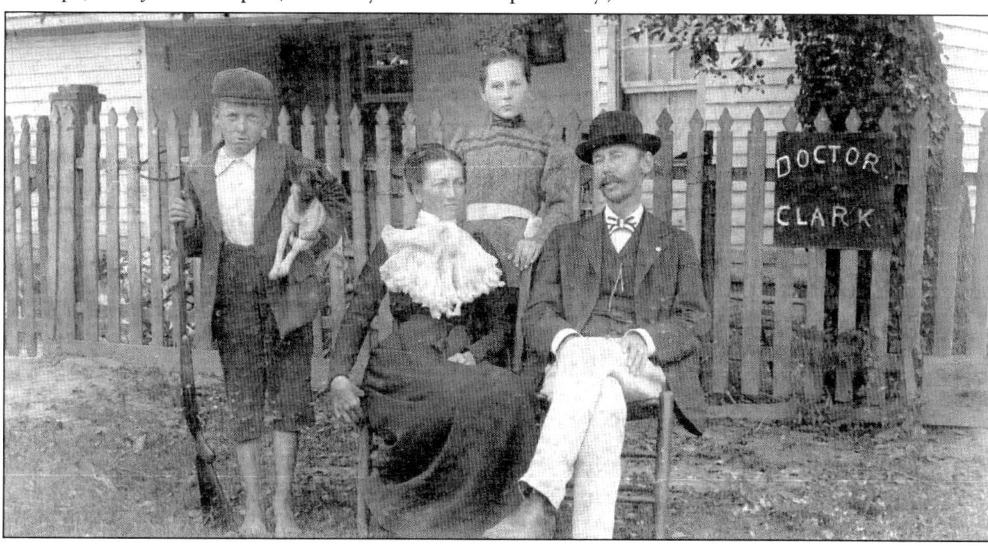

Dr. Lyman C. Clark owned the Appalachian Inn in Minneapolis, and he operated his medical practice out of the back part of the building. He is seen here with his wife and family. (Courtesy of the Avery County Historical Museum.)

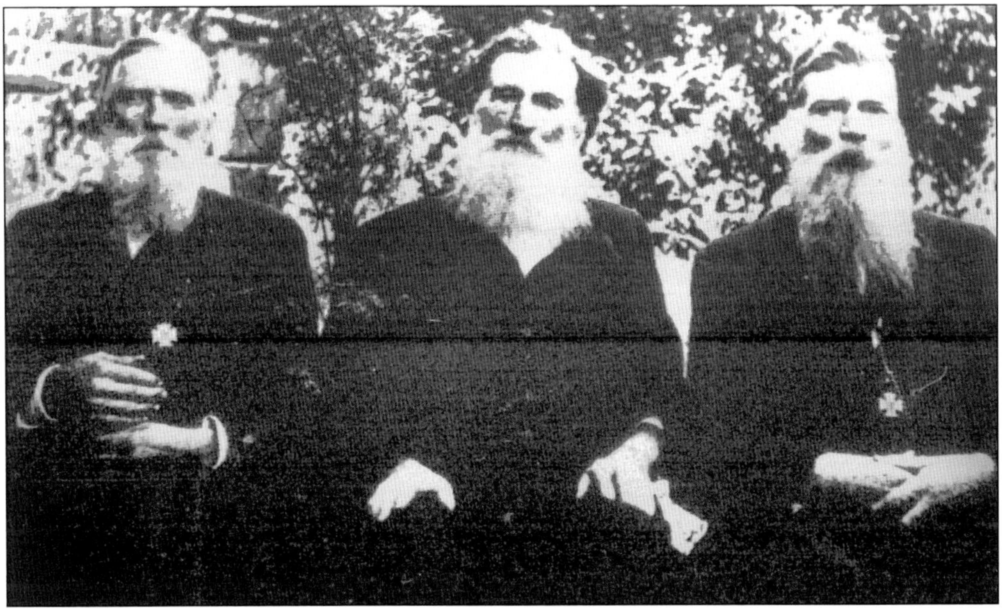

Tom Wise (left), John Wise (center), and Newton Wise were three brothers who all served in the Confederate army and who all attended the 50th anniversary of the Battle of Gettysburg in 1913. They were the only set of three brothers at the reunion in Pennsylvania. (Courtesy of Tense Banks.)

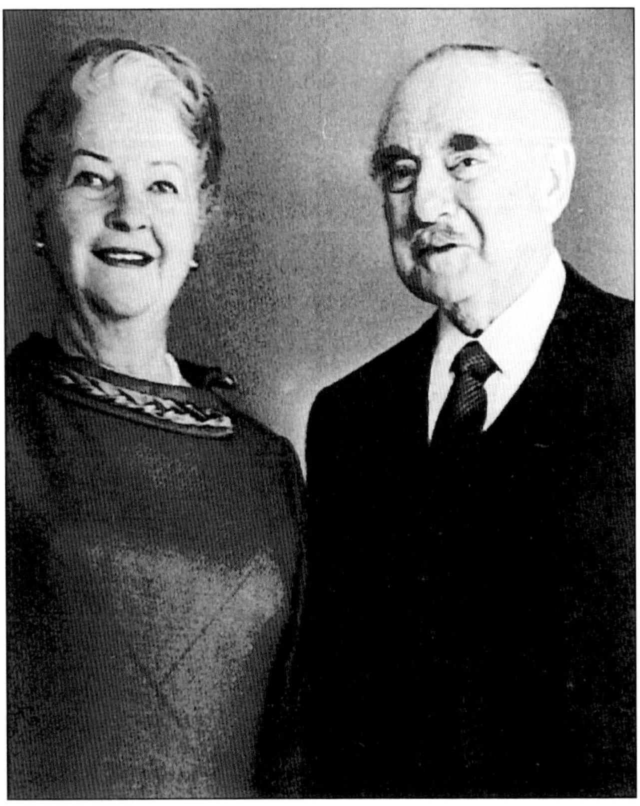

The stadium at the Avery County High School is named for Mr. and Mrs. N. J. MacDonald. (Courtesy of the Avery County Museum.)

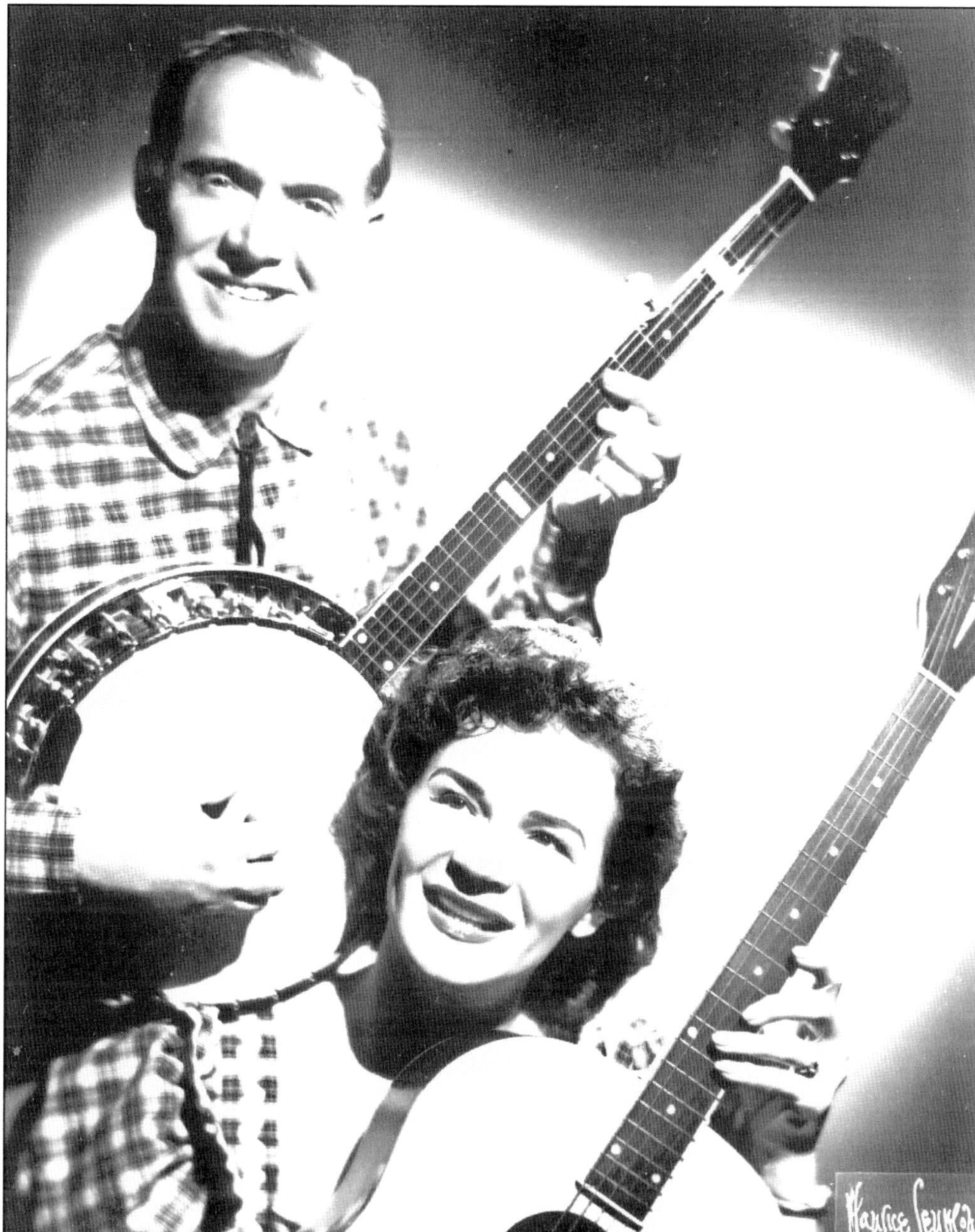

Scotty and Lula Belle (Myrtle Eleanor Cooper) Wiseman were featured on the WLS (a Chicago radio station) Barn Dance for over 25 years and appeared in seven films. Among the most influential performers in the early days of country music, they retired to the Ingalls community, and Lula Belle represented the area in the North Carolina General Assembly from 1975 to 1978. (Courtesy of the Avery County Historical Museum.)

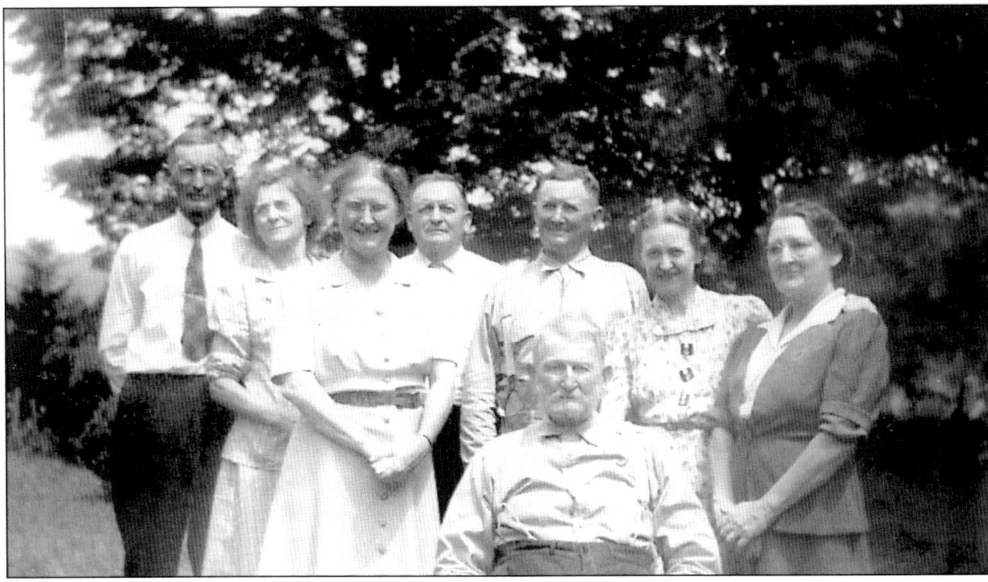

John G. Phillips, seated, posed for this photograph with his children in 1944, a year before he died. Pictured here standing from left to right are Ed S. Phillips, Hettie Phillips, Essie Green, Mack Phillips, Jim Phillips, Nelle Deyton, and Kate Wills. (Courtesy of the Phillips family.)

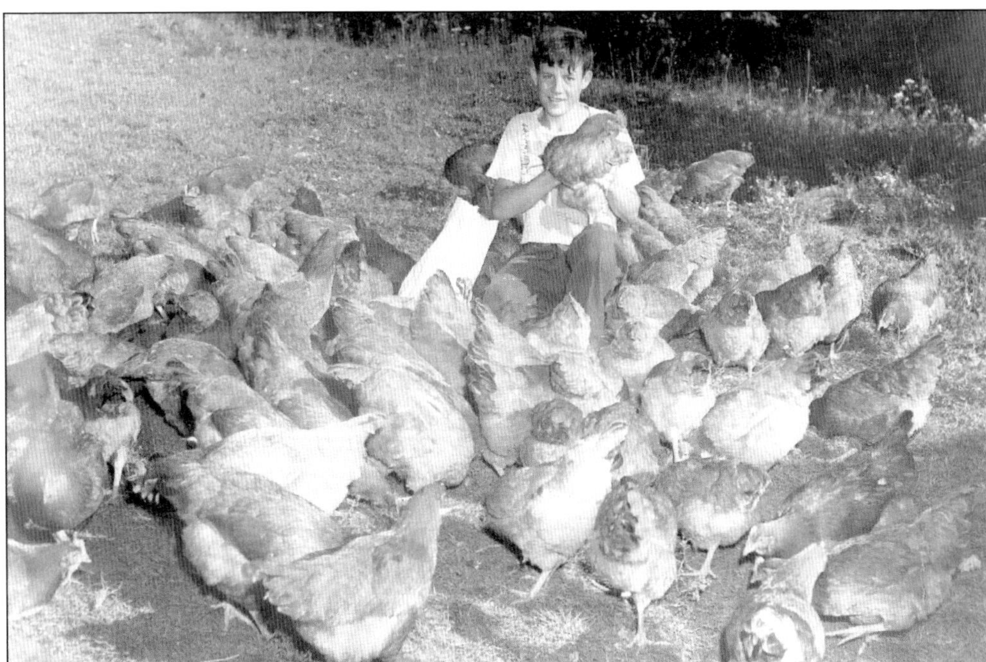

Tommy Vance's 4-H project was quite a flock. For many rural children, 4-H continues to provide opportunities to learn about and raise livestock. (Courtesy of the Avery County Historical Museum.)

Glenn Causey, who portrayed Daniel Boone in the historical drama *Horn in the West* in Boone for 41 seasons, is shown here at the Mile High Swinging Bridge on Grandfather Mountain. Although the raccoon does not seem bothered by Causey's headgear, the historical Daniel Boone might have been since he never owned a coonskin cap. (Courtesy of Hugh Morton/Grandfather Mountain.)

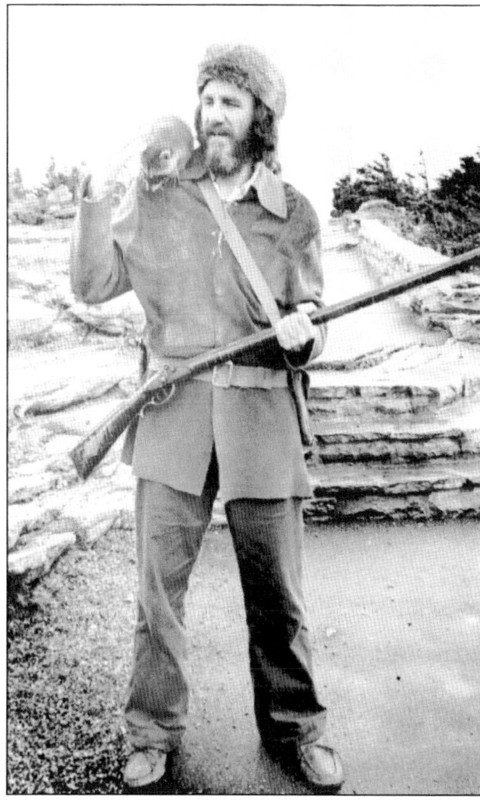

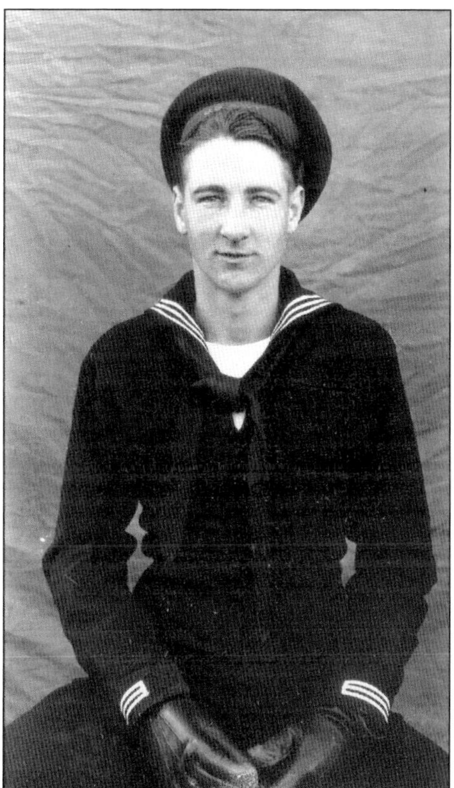

Ray Harmon, like many Avery County veterans, posed for a photograph in his World War II naval uniform. (Courtesy of the W. R. Trivett Collection.)

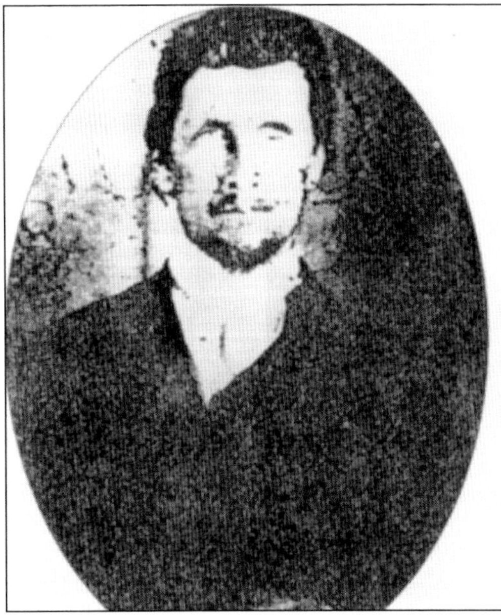

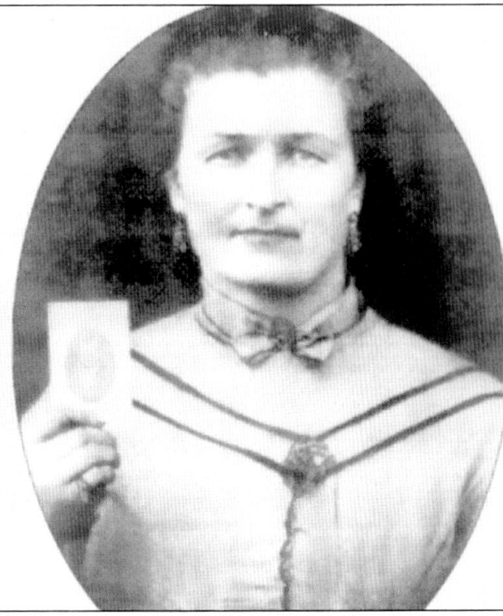

William M. "Keith" and Malinda Pritchard "Sam" Blalock both served in the Union and Confederate armies. A Union sympathizer, Keith joined the 26th North Carolina to avoid conscription. Malinda also went, disguised as a man, and they hoped to desert to the Union. When it did not seem they would be able to do so, Keith rolled in a patch of poison plants, giving himself a nasty rash that worried the army surgeon and earned him a medical discharge. Although her gender was never discovered by her fellow soldiers or officers, Malinda revealed that she was a woman in order to leave the army. After returning to present-day Avery County, they served as guides for escaped Union prisoners and as recruiters for the Union army. (Keith: courtesy of the William Eury Appalachian History Collection, Appalachian State University; Malinda: courtesy of the Southern Historical Collection, University of North Carolina, Chapel Hill.)

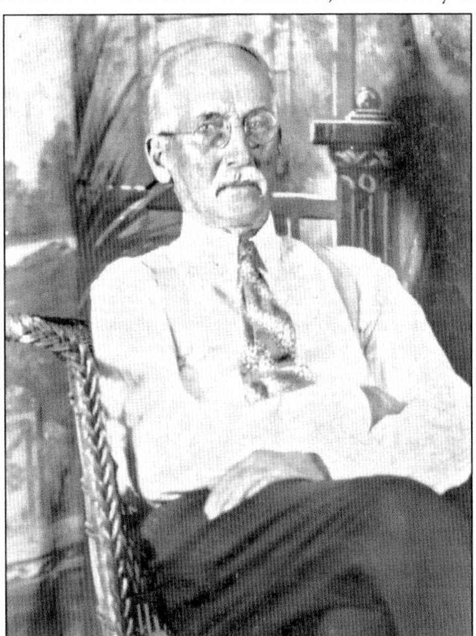

William Berry Norris (1861–1947) was an early settler on Beech Mountain. One of the first schools on Beech Mountain was known as the Norris School and was on his property. He was also one of the early leaders of the Fall Creek Baptist Church. (Courtesy of Naomi Houston.)

Horton Cooper was an educator, postmaster, justice of the peace, and author who penned the only history of Avery County. (Courtesy of the Avery County Historical Museum.)

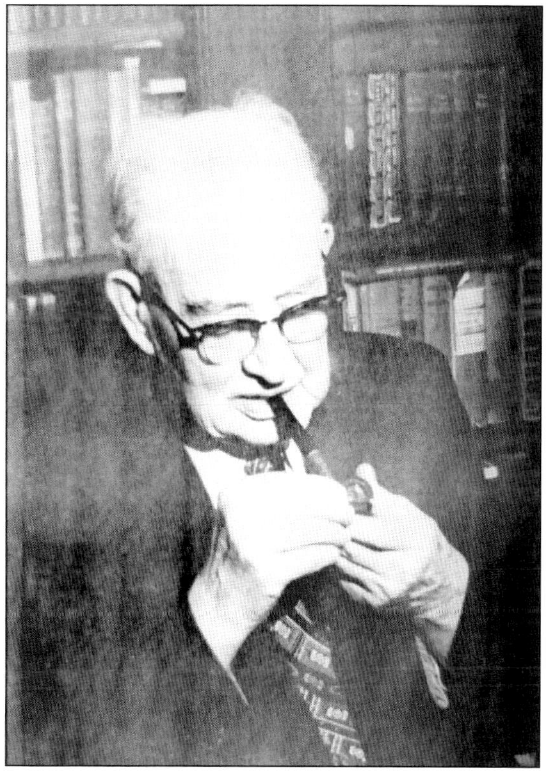

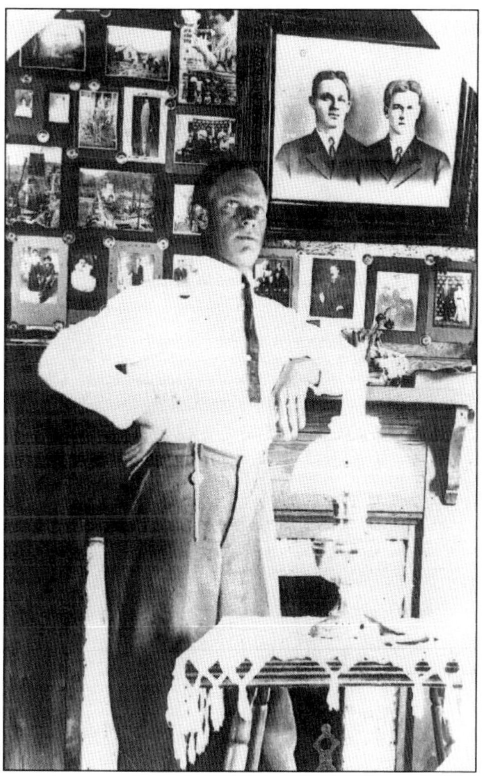

C. Gordon Davenport took this self-portrait. Davenport was, among other things, a well-known cabinet maker. He spent his later years helping his daughter Vivian operate the Parkway Junction Store in Linville Falls. (Courtesy of Tense Banks.)

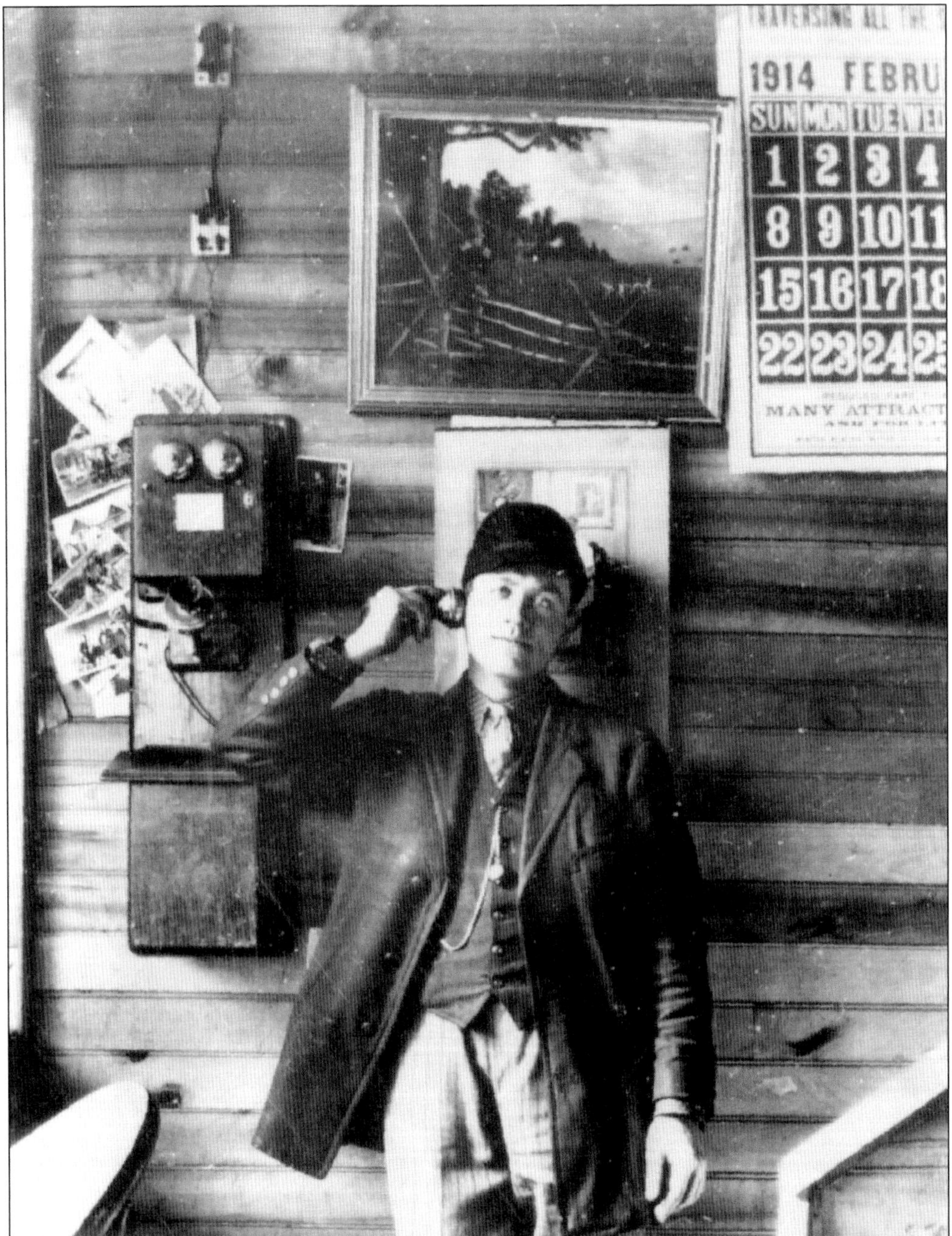

Cy Crumley was a conductor and photographer of the Eastern Tennessee and Western North Carolina Railroad (ET&WNC) and was a Pineola resident for a number of years. He is here demonstrating some of the modern technology inside the Newland Depot. (Courtesy of the Cy Crumley Collection/Johnny Graybeal.)

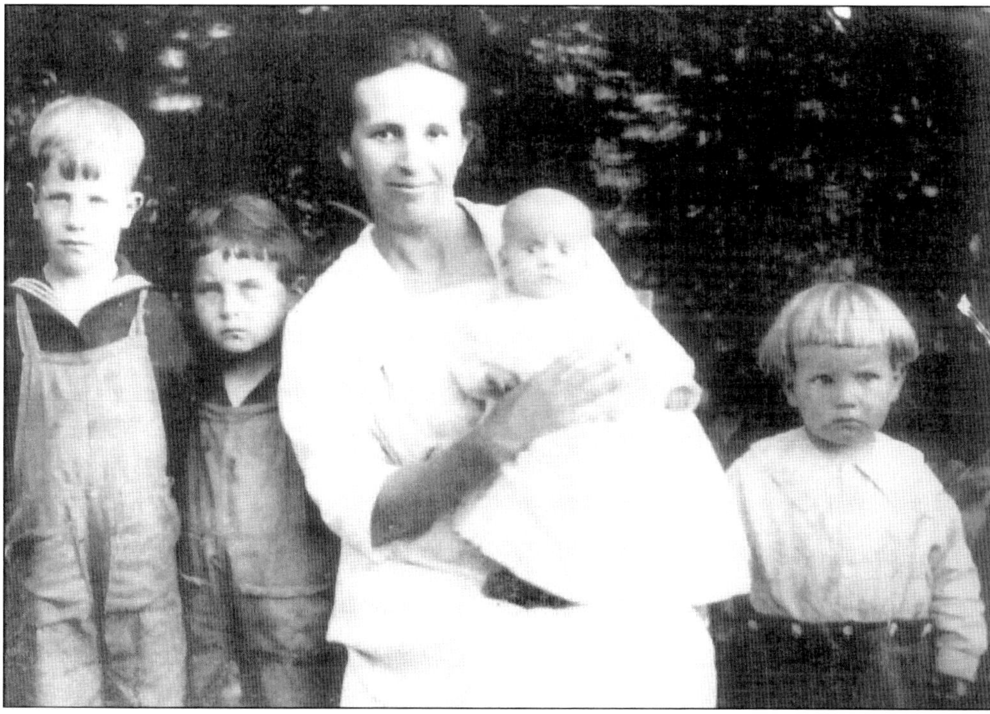

Jodie Vance of Pineola is seen here with her children, from left to right, Ray, Harry, Elwanda, and Sam. (Courtesy of Heidi Ellis.)

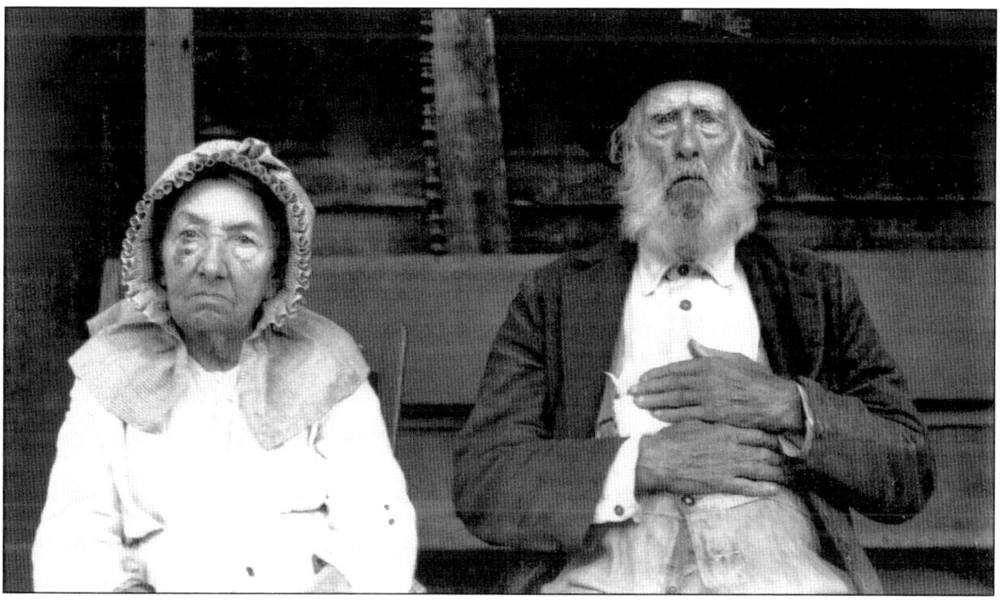

Eventton Mitchell and his wife had their image struck by W. R. Trivett. Though this photograph resembles some taken by outsider photographers, Trivett's customers chose their own clothing, poses, and backdrops, unlike the subjects of photographers who came looking for typical mountain folk. These photographers sometimes asked people to pose in old clothes or in front of abandoned buildings in order to enforce the stereotypes of mountain people. Though the Mitchells appear quaint, they do so by choice. (Courtesy of the W. R. Trivett Collection.)

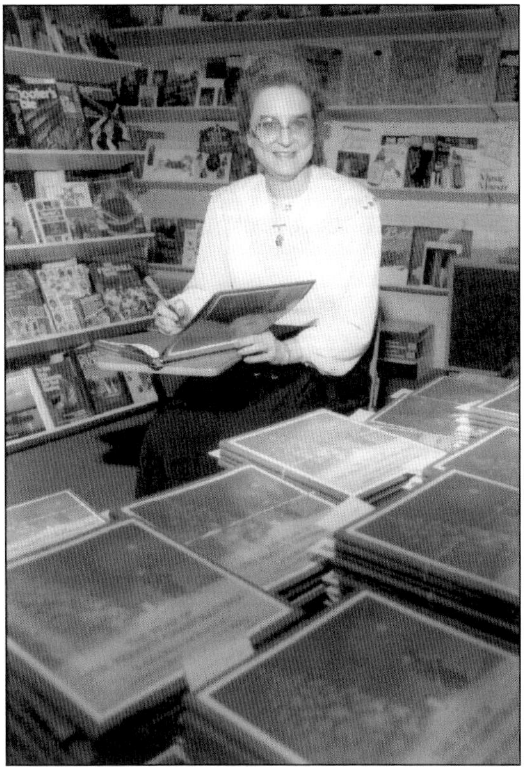

Dr. Gloria Houston signs copies of her popular children's book *The Year of the Perfect Christmas Tree*. A frequently honored author and educator, Houston grew up in the Ingalls community and draws upon childhood and family history to create her beloved and award-winning books. (Courtesy of Avery County Historical Museum.)

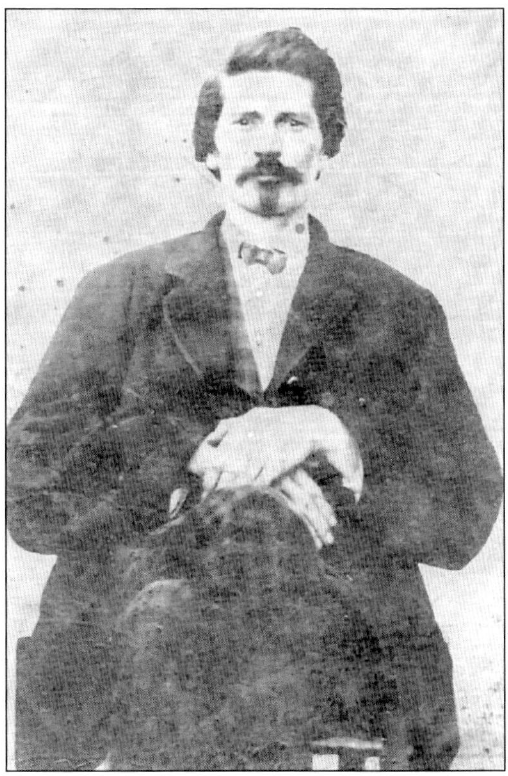

Confederate veteran John Wise (1834–1931) is here pictured in an 1860s photograph. He was a schoolteacher at Owl Den School both before and after the war and was well known for his hunting antics and storytelling. He attended the 50th anniversary of the Battle of Gettysburg with his two brothers, Tom and Newton. (Courtesy of Tense Banks.)

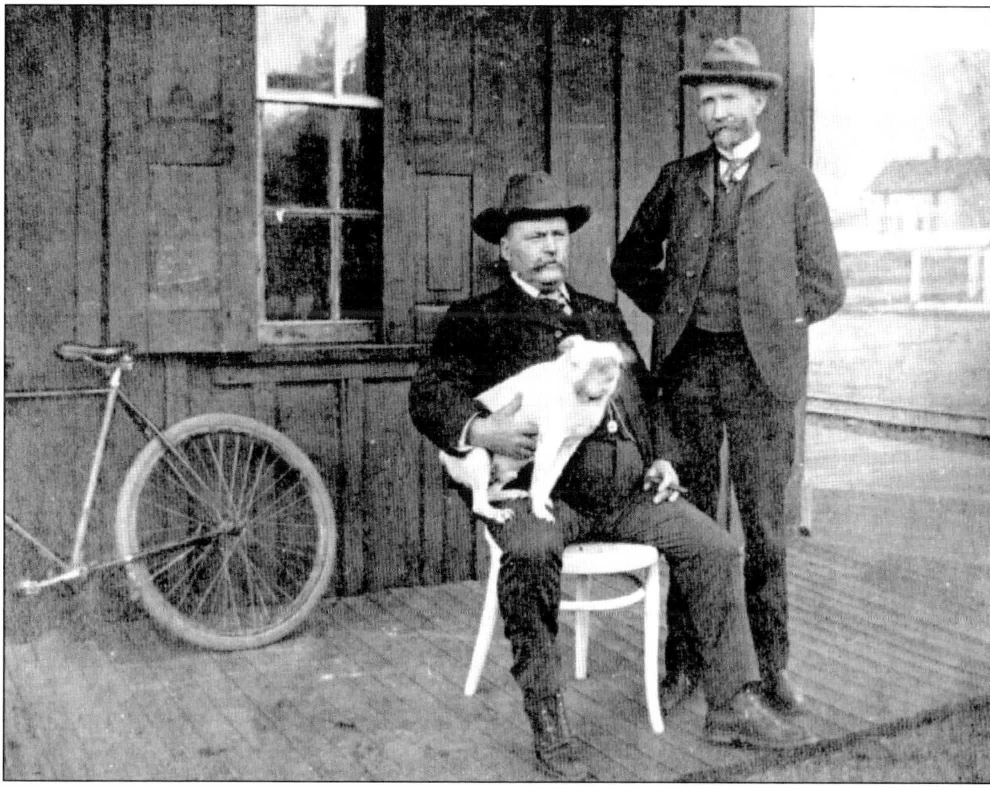

James Lawton (left) and J. E. Vance pose outside the charming Cranberry Depot, *c.* 1900. (Courtesy of the Cy Crumley Collection/Johnny Graybeal.)

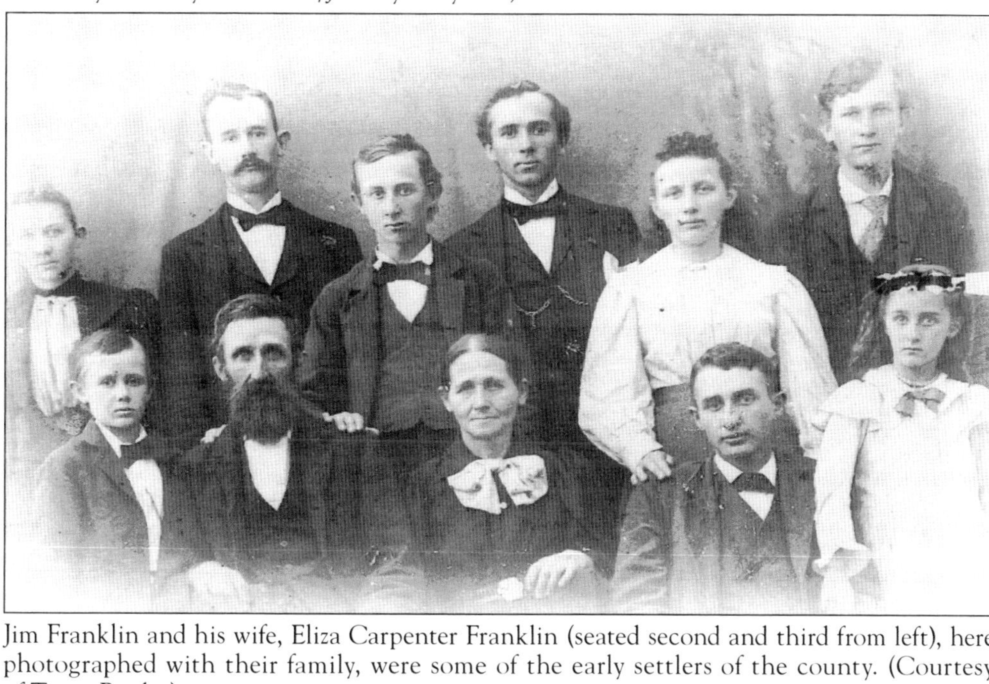

Jim Franklin and his wife, Eliza Carpenter Franklin (seated second and third from left), here photographed with their family, were some of the early settlers of the county. (Courtesy of Tense Banks.)

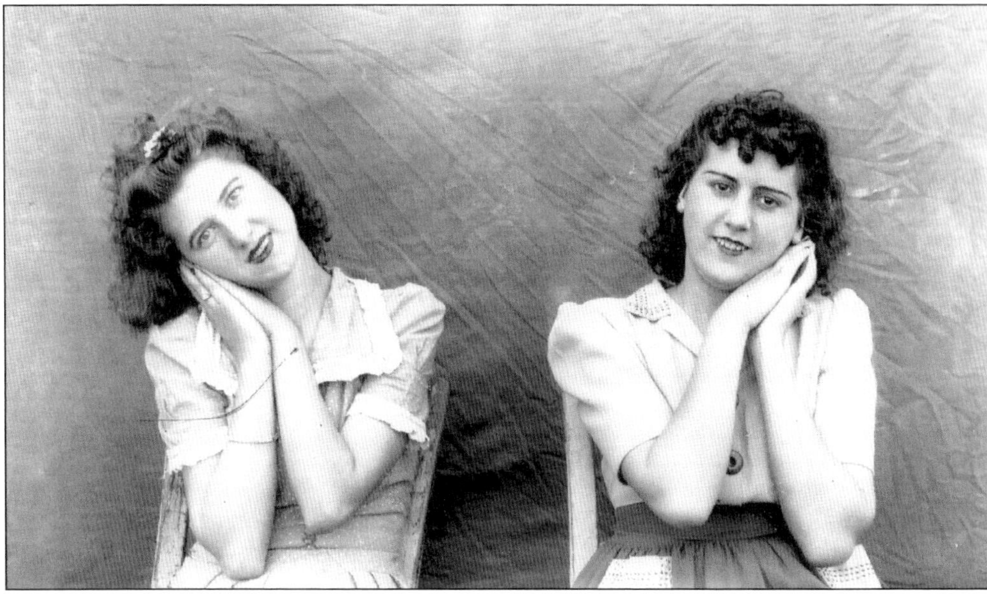

Juanita Estep (left) and Ruby Guy Estep strike a dreamy pose. (Courtesy of the W. R. Trivett Collection.)

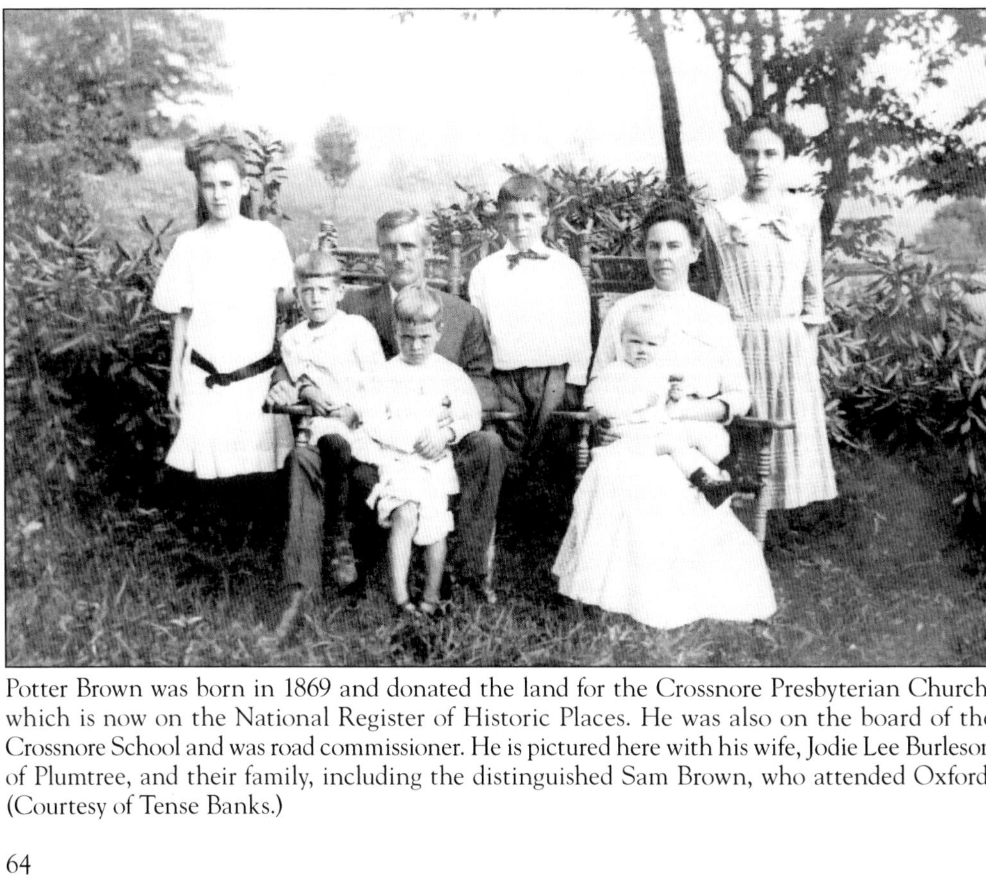

Potter Brown was born in 1869 and donated the land for the Crossnore Presbyterian Church, which is now on the National Register of Historic Places. He was also on the board of the Crossnore School and was road commissioner. He is pictured here with his wife, Jodie Lee Burleson of Plumtree, and their family, including the distinguished Sam Brown, who attended Oxford. (Courtesy of Tense Banks.)

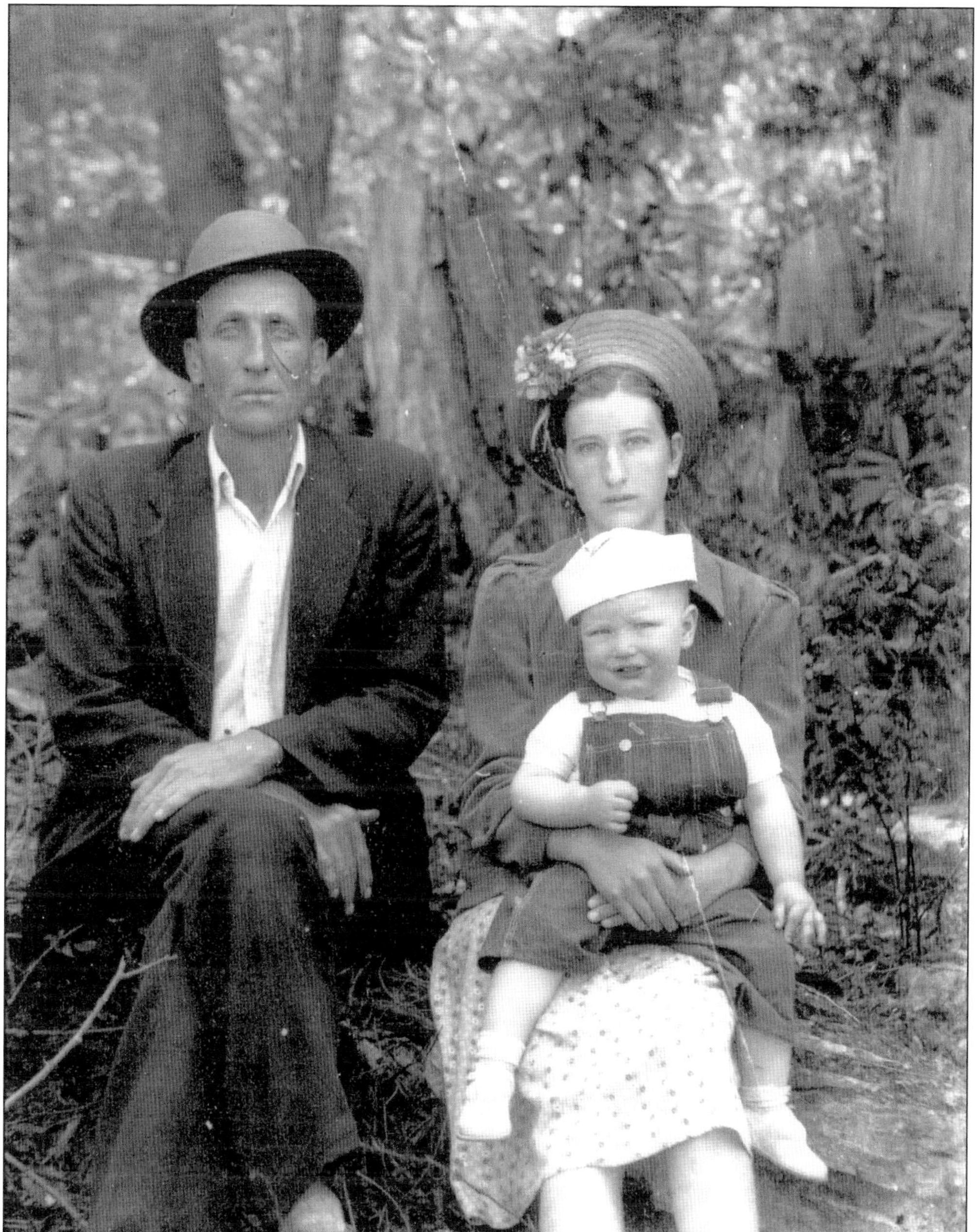

John W. Phillips and Betty Dugger Phillips had this photograph taken with their son, Wade W. Phillips, all of whom are wearing stylish hats they likely obtained by mail order. (Courtesy of the W. R. Trivett Collection.)

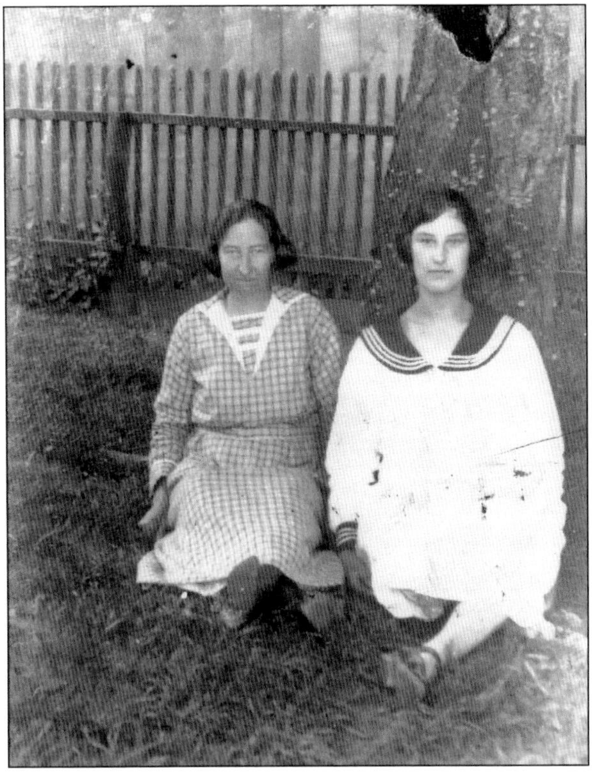

Polly Presnell (left) and Leon Presnell sit under a tree in Flat Springs. (Courtesy of the W. R. Trivett Collection.)

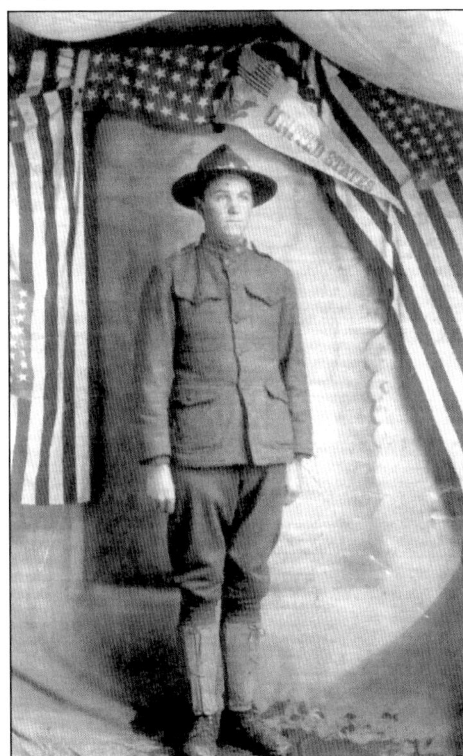

Elbert E. Stamey served as a private in the 120th Infantry Regiment of the 30th Division during World War I. He died July 4, 1940. (Courtesy of Doyle Ollis.)

Grady Hall "Pap" Norris (1896–1970) was a life-long resident of the area. He never owned a car, nor drove, and was a faithful member of the Fall Creek Baptist Church, where he is buried. (Courtesy of Naomi Houston.)

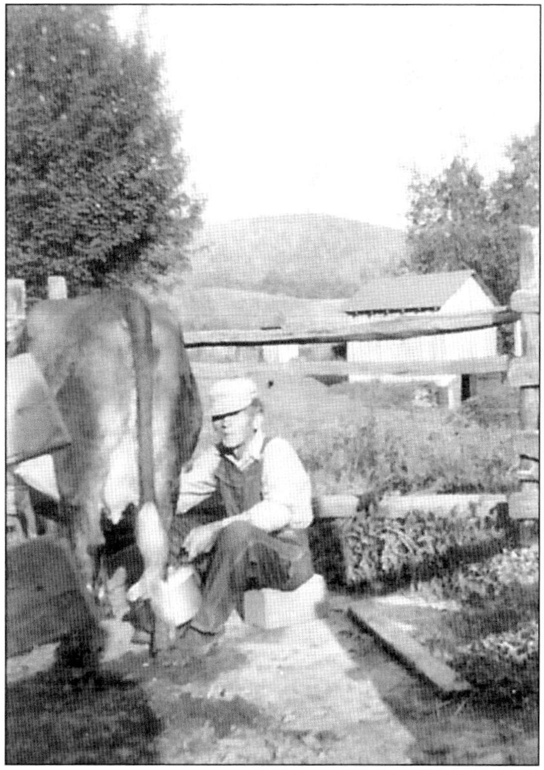

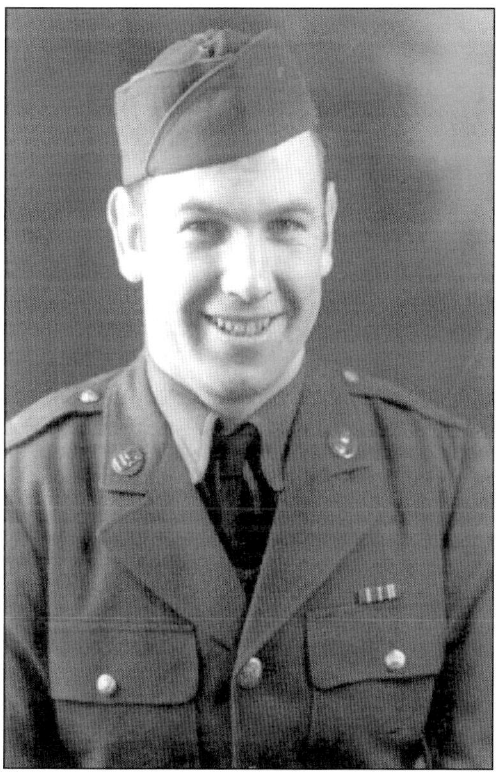

Jesse Glenn Ollis was a veteran of World War II. (Courtesy of Doyle Ollis.)

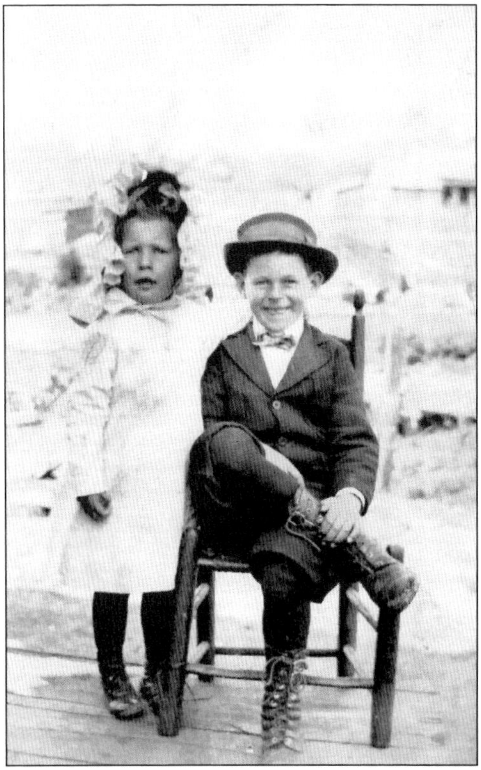

Harold McGrath, who served as Linville postmaster, is here seen with his sister, Elizabeth McGrath. (Courtesy of the Avery County Historical Museum.)

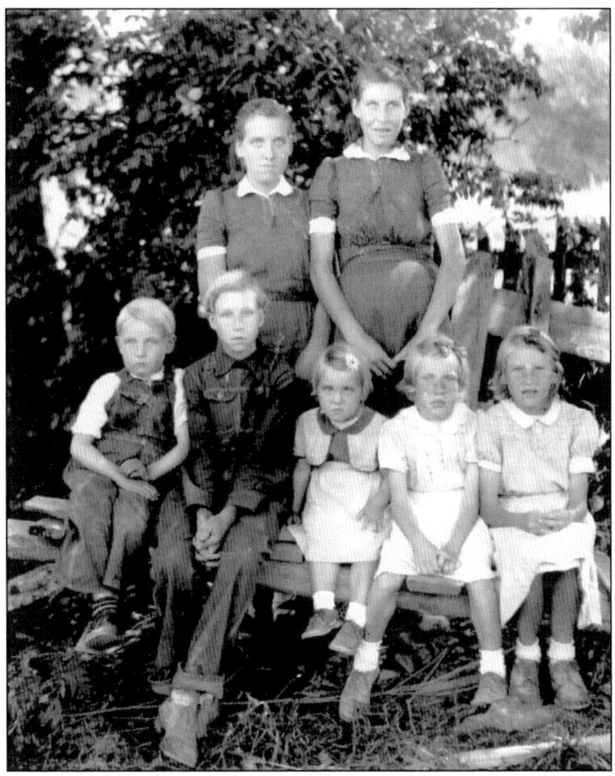

These children, part of the Henson family, were residents of the Poga community. Shown here from left to right are (first row) Clay Henson, Hub Henson, Dale Henson, Majjie Henson, and Berniece Henson; (second row) Vergie Henson and Bina Henson. (Courtesy of the W. R. Trivett Collection.)

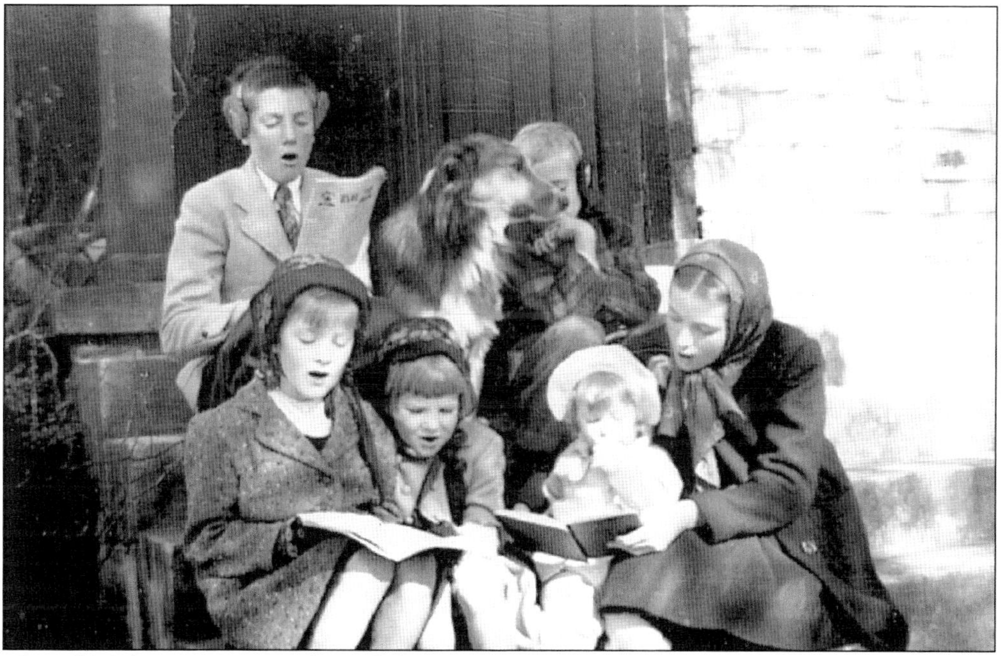

The cold didn't seem to stop these children (and their dog) from making a joyful noise. Pictured here from left to right are (first row) Delrita Phillips, Emma Jane Phillips, Susie Phillips, and Patsanna Phillips; (second row) Bud Phillips, Tippy (dog), and Tony Phillips. (Courtesy of the Phillips family.)

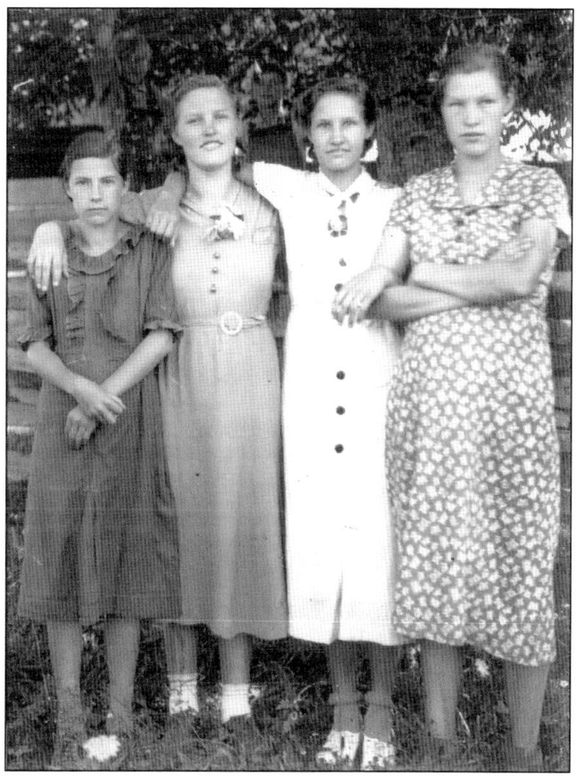

From left to right, Kallie Hicks Dugger poses with an unidentified friend, Rainey Dugger Trivett, and Sylvia Harmon Dugger. (Courtesy of the W. R. Trivett Collection.)

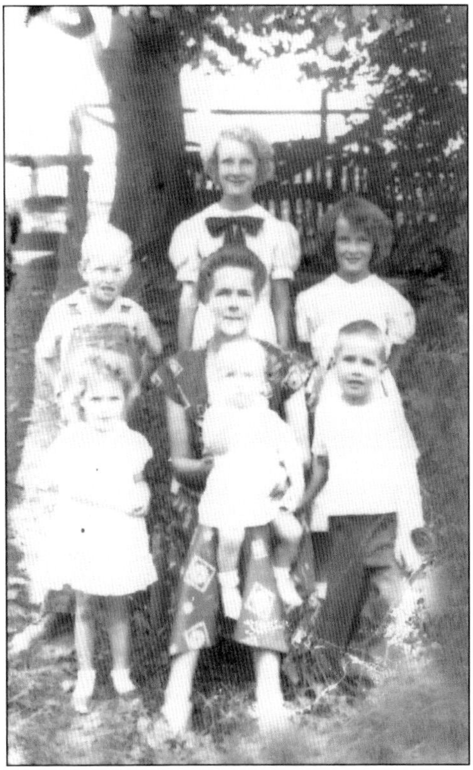

The Smithsonian Institute has a quilt made by this woman, Elsie Trivett, in its collection. Shown here from left to right are (first row) June Trivett Taylor, Elsie Trivett with Lester on her lap, and Reed Trivett; (second row) Jene Trivett, Eva Nell Trivett, and Lean Vell Trivett. (Courtesy of the W. R. Trivett Collection.)

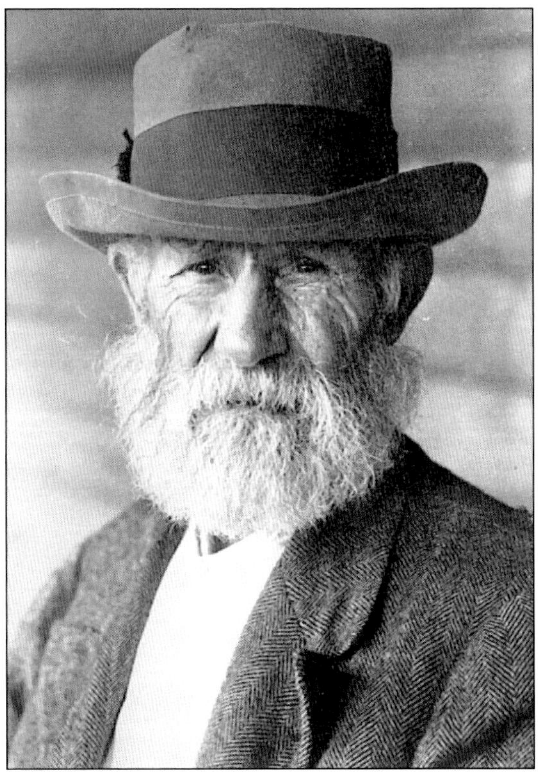

"Joe," Joseph Taylor Ollis, was born in 1847 on Brushy Creek and had 20 children who lived to adulthood. (Courtesy of Doyle Ollis.)

Col. John B. Palmer commanded the 58th North Carolina Troops in the Civil War. A native of New York, Palmer made his home in present-day Avery County and was the wealthiest man in the area. During the war, his beautiful home, Grasslands, was raided and burned by Union soldiers. The estate is now the site of a new real estate and business development. (Courtesy of the North Carolina Department of Archives and History.)

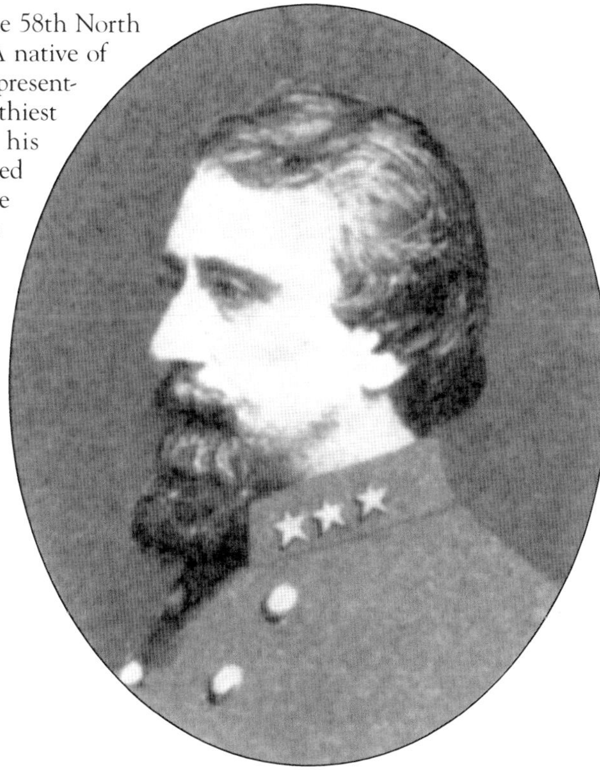

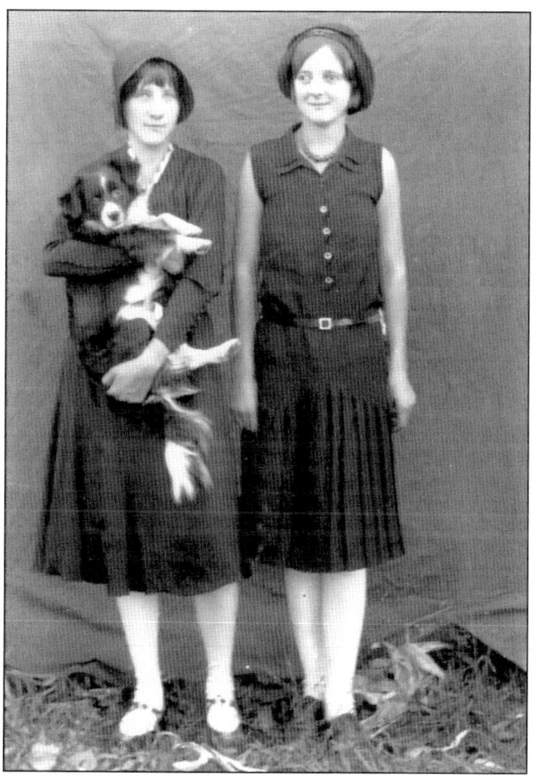

Flossie Stout (left), Ardith Harmon, and a friend model fashionable flapper wear. (Courtesy of the W. R. Trivett Collection.)

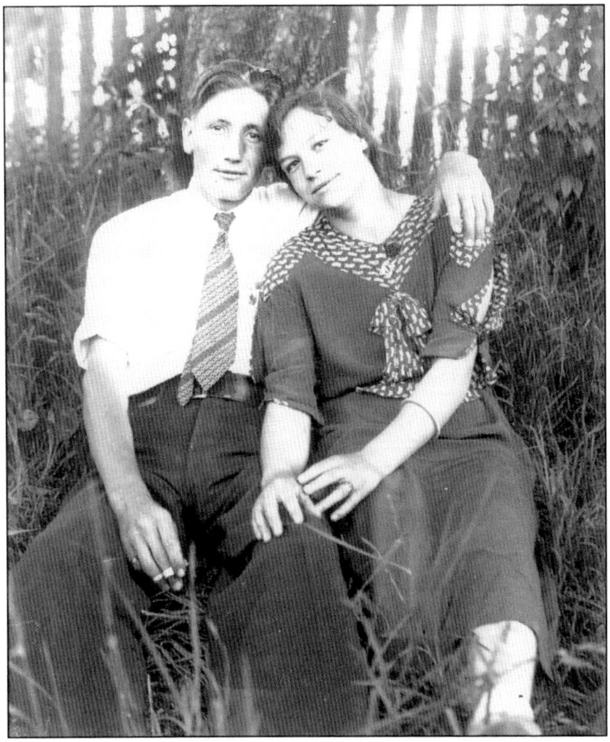

These charming sweethearts are Dana Guy and Ruth Stout Guy. The prominently displayed ring may indicate that this is an engagement or wedding photo. Dana's cigarette is also a nice touch. (Courtesy of the W. R. Trivett Collection.)

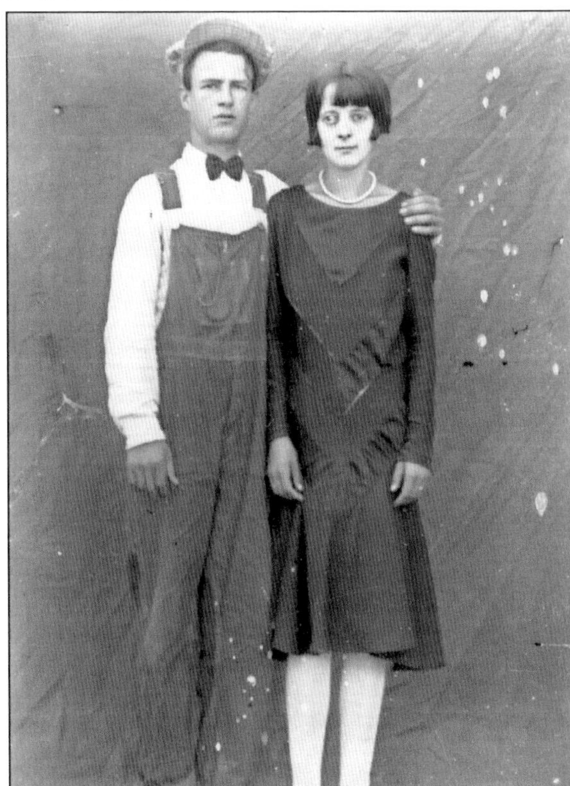

Jarvis Stout and Ortha Harmon Oaks appear to be quite a stylish pair. Note his bow tie and overalls. (Courtesy of the W. R. Trivett Collection.)

From left to right, Cherie Greene, Linia Greene, an unidentified friend, and Edith Guy are dressed warmly and fashionably in this 1920s image. (Courtesy of the W. R. Trivett Collection.)

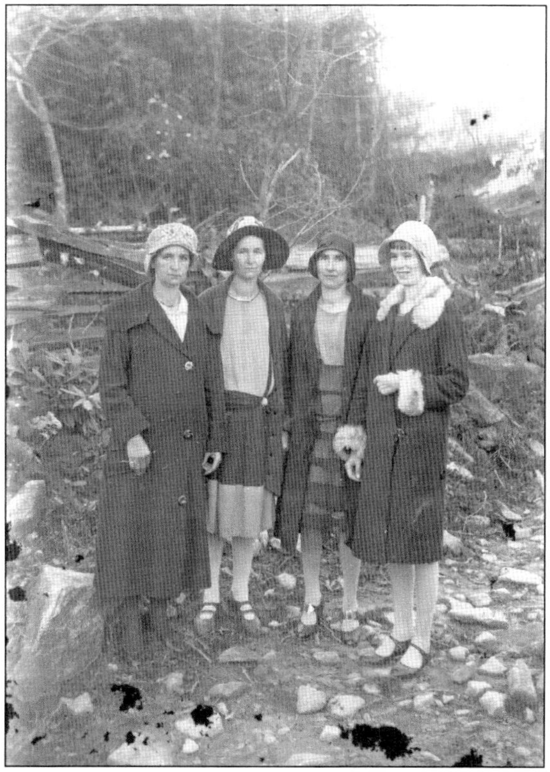

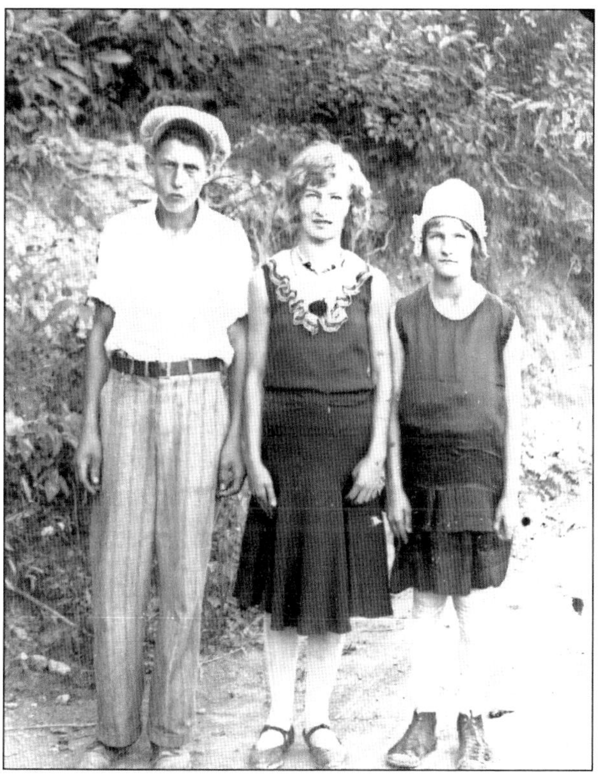

Sherman Hicks (left), Addie Estep (center), and Vertie Stines stood by the roadside for this photograph. (Courtesy of the W. R. Trivett Collection.)

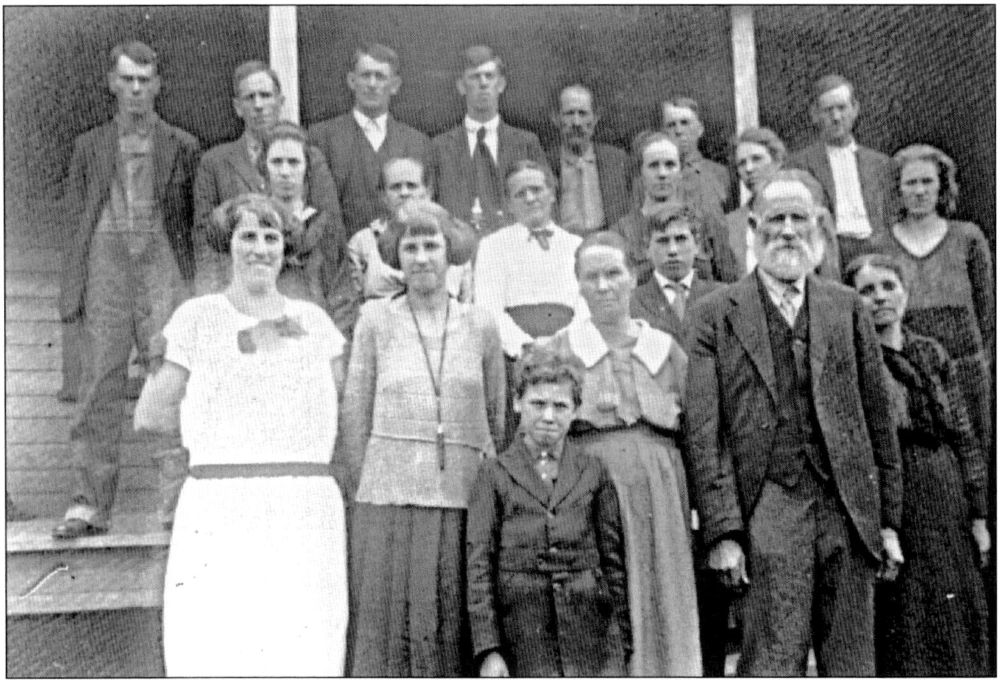

Joe Ollis of Brushy Creek is here pictured with his large family. He had 20 children who lived to adulthood. Pictured here from left to right are (first row) Lula Ollis Pyatte, Mae Ollis Vance, Don Ollis, Delzie Mace Ollis, Peter Ollis (behind Delzie), Joe Ollis, and Annie Ollis Weatherman; (second row) Carrie Ollis Riddle, Myra Ollis Ledford, Gusty Ollis Riddle, Lovie Ollis Gouge, Sadie Ollis Wiseman, and Berta Ollis Stamey Vance; (third row) Clate Ollis, Ade Ollis, Jess Ollis, Jim Ollis, John Ollis, Baxter Ollis, and Dock Ollis. (Courtesy of Doyle Ollis.)

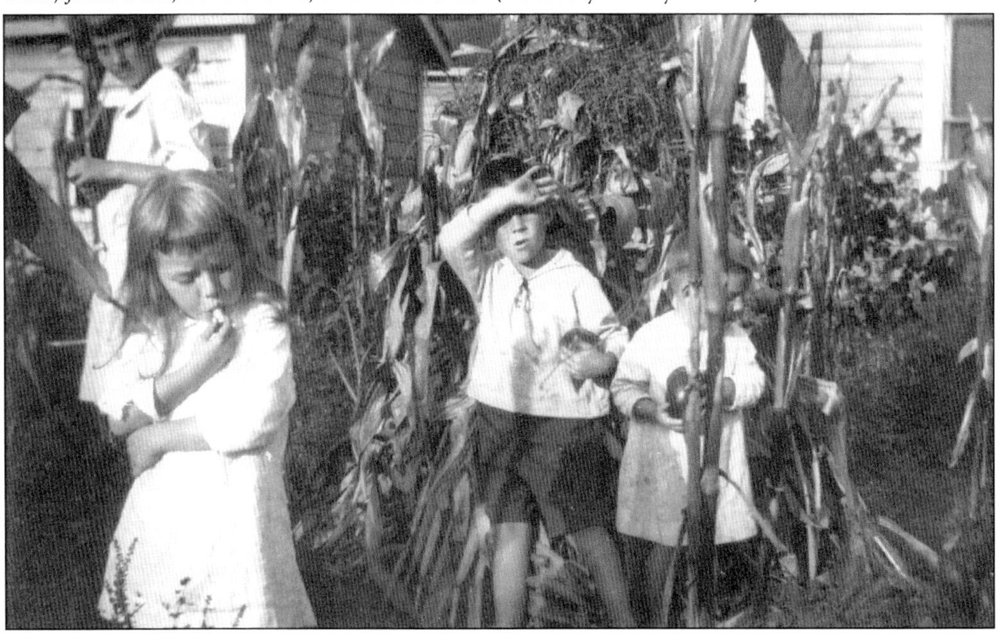

Henrietta Thompson, Sara Coleman, Sam Thompson, and Matthew Thompson play around a "foddershock" made of corn stalks. (Courtesy of the Phillips family.)

"Gusty," Augusta Ollis Riddle (1871–1946), was the wife of John Riddle. (Courtesy of Doyle Ollis.)

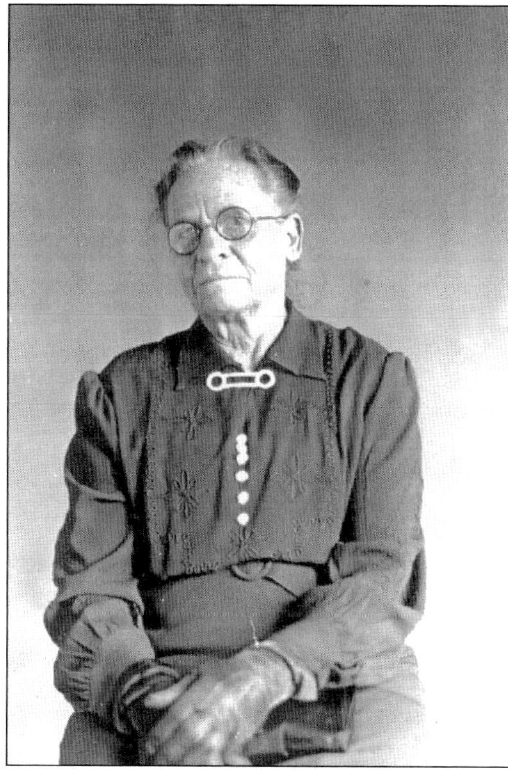

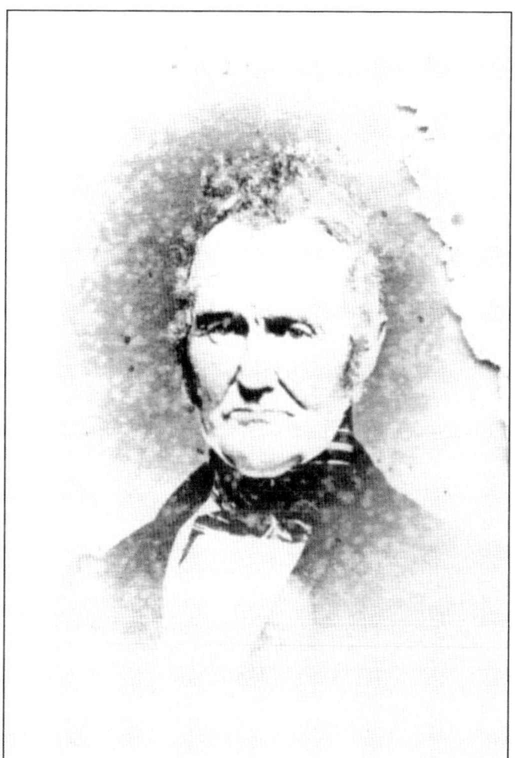

Dr. Ebenezer Childs, a native of Shelburne, Massachusetts, was born in 1784. He was a physician and surgeon in present-day Avery County in the 1850s. He died in 1862. His body was placed in an alcohol-filled lead coffin in a brick mausoleum in Childsville. His remains were later moved to Elmwood Cemetery in Columbia, South Carolina. (Courtesy of Claudia Childs McGough.)

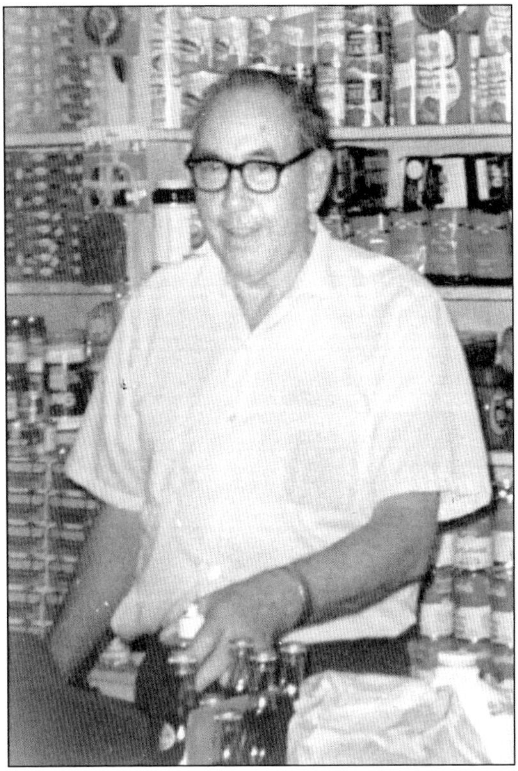

Carl Stewart was proprietor of Stewart's General Store in Pineola. Many local families claim that they would have gone hungry if it had not been for his generosity, as he allowed needy customers to charge their groceries during hard times. (Courtesy of the Stewart family.)

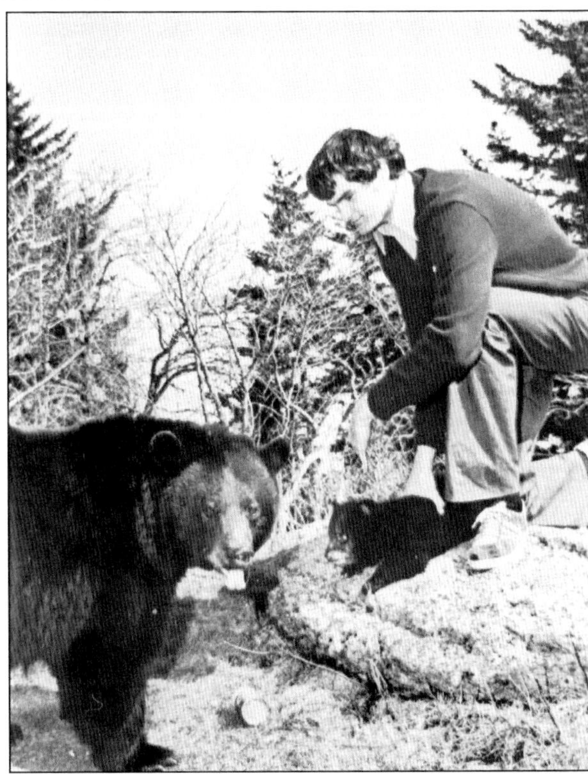

Avery County native Tommy Burleson, a professional basketball player, spent a summer working on Grandfather Mountain and is here seen with the beloved Mildred the Bear and one of her many cubs. (Courtesy of Hugh Morton/Grandfather Mountain.)

Shepherd Monroe Dugger was a teacher, mining engineer, farmer, tourism promoter, co-owner with J. Erwin Calloway of the Grandfather Hotel, and author of *War Trails of the Blue Ridge* and *The Balsam Groves of Grandfather Mountain*. (Courtesy of the Avery County Historical Museum.)

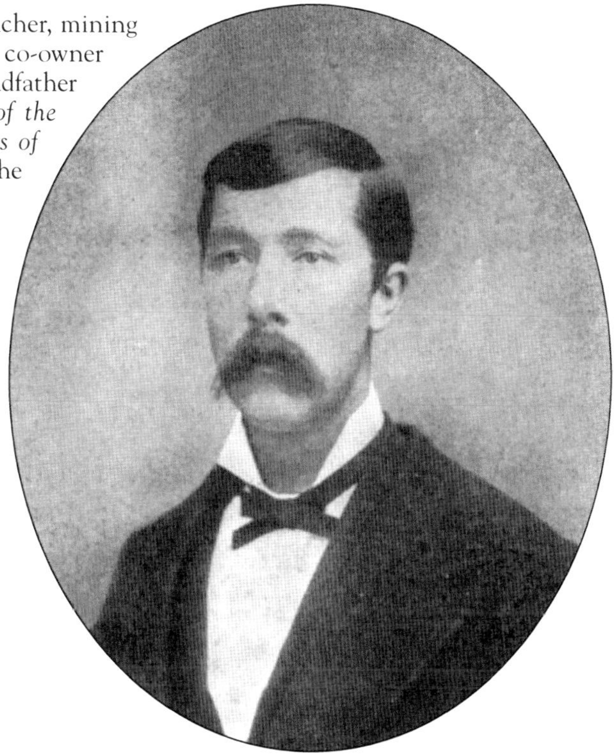

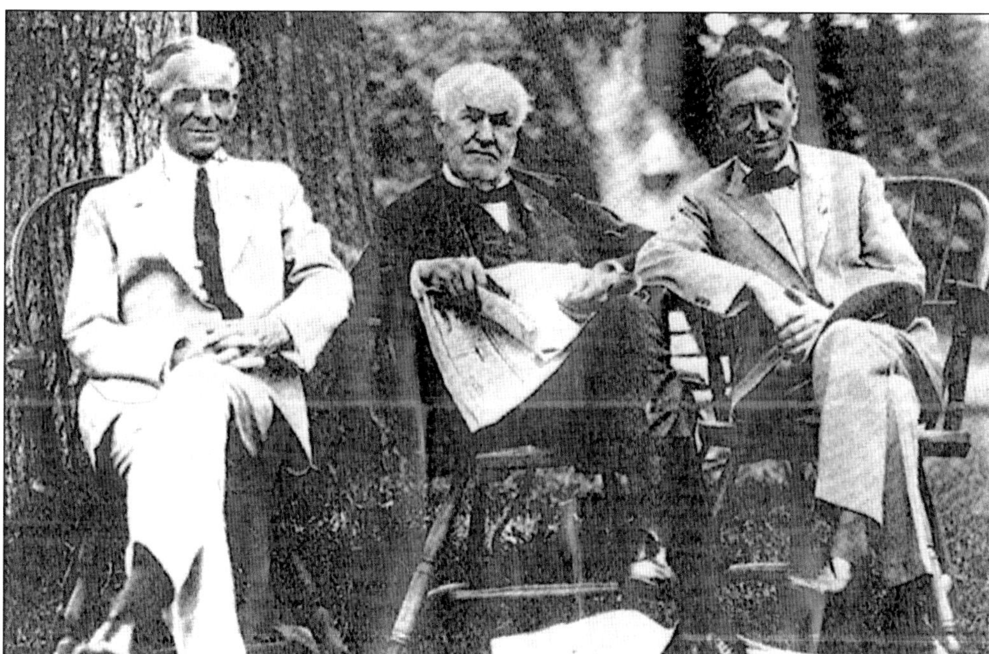

Henry Ford (left), Thomas Edison (center), and Harvey Firestone enjoyed a visit at the summer home of Howard Marmon, Hemlocks. This image has been labeled one of America's most famous photographs. The distinguished trio had come to Avery County to visit Marmon, an automotive visionary who designed the car that won the first Indianapolis 500. (Courtesy of Dallas Gragg.)

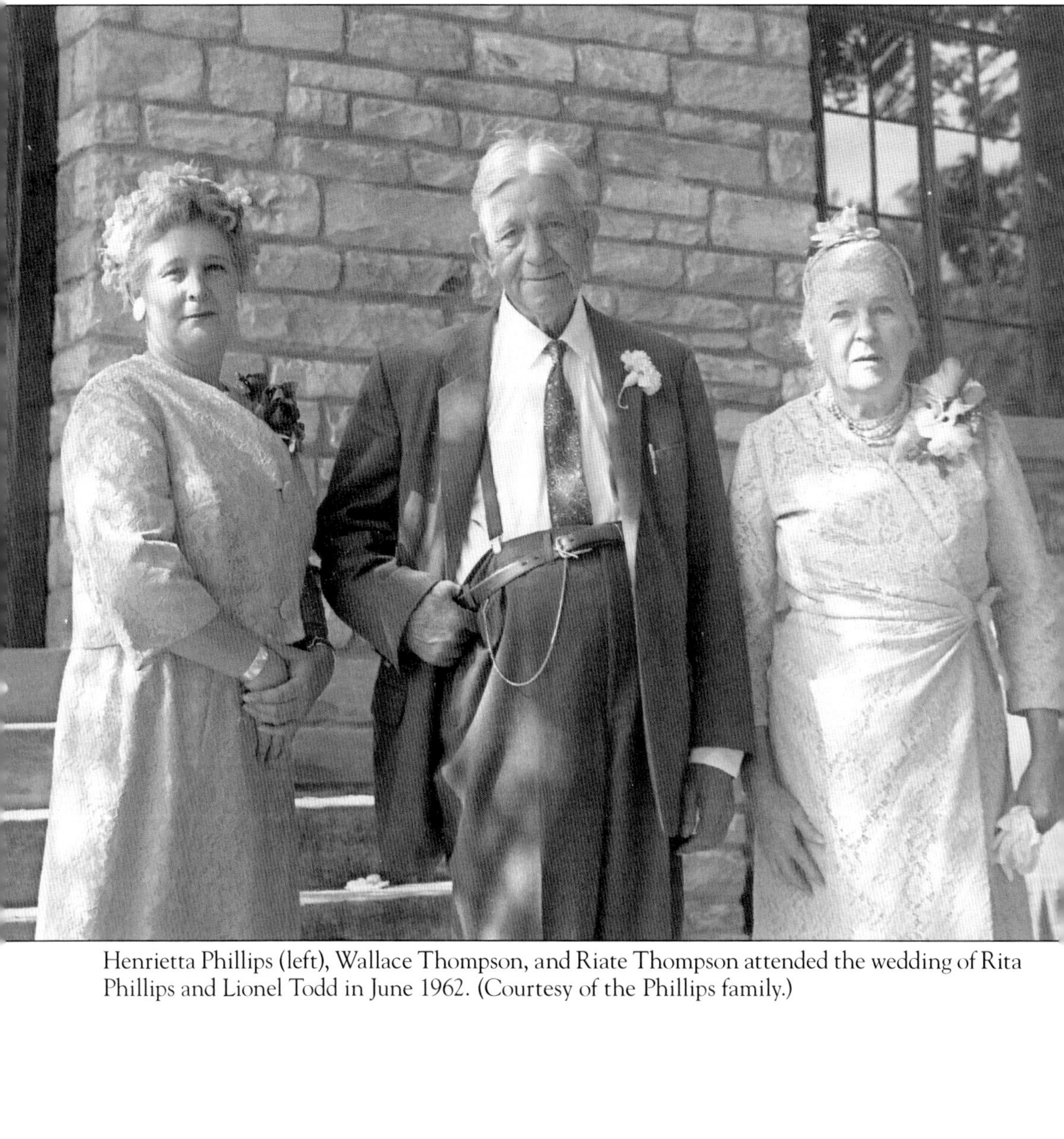

Henrietta Phillips (left), Wallace Thompson, and Riate Thompson attended the wedding of Rita Phillips and Lionel Todd in June 1962. (Courtesy of the Phillips family.)

Four

Business, Commerce, and Work

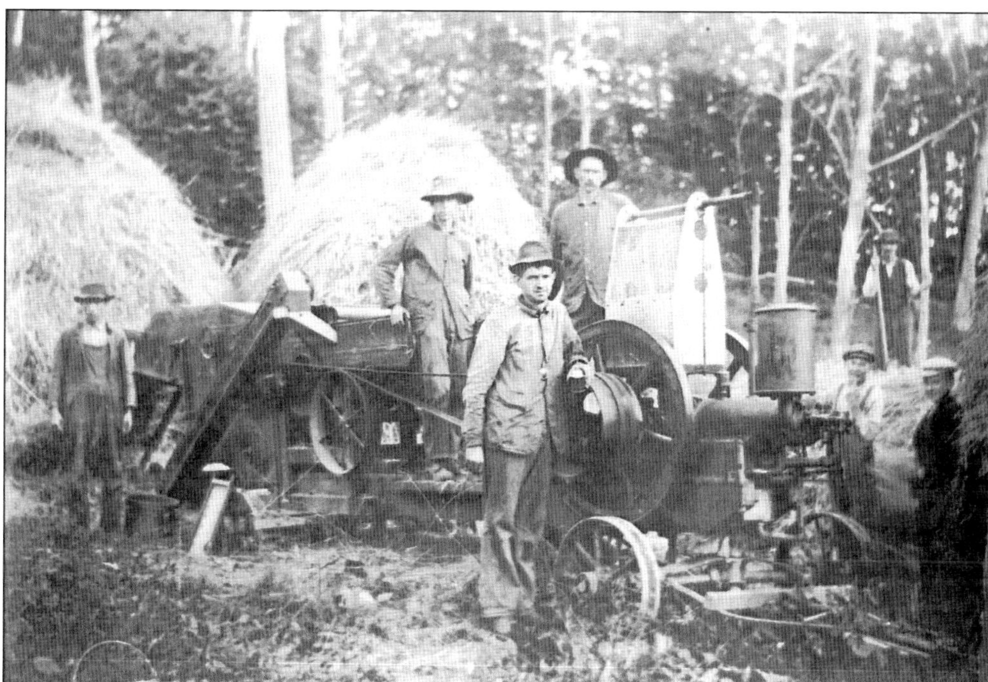

A member of the Wise family is standing in front of the flywheel of a rye threshing machine, and Claude Franklin is on the far right, c. 1910. Often neighbors or relatives who owned expensive machinery would loan out their equipment to friends, receiving in payment a portion of the harvest. (Courtesy of Tense Banks.)

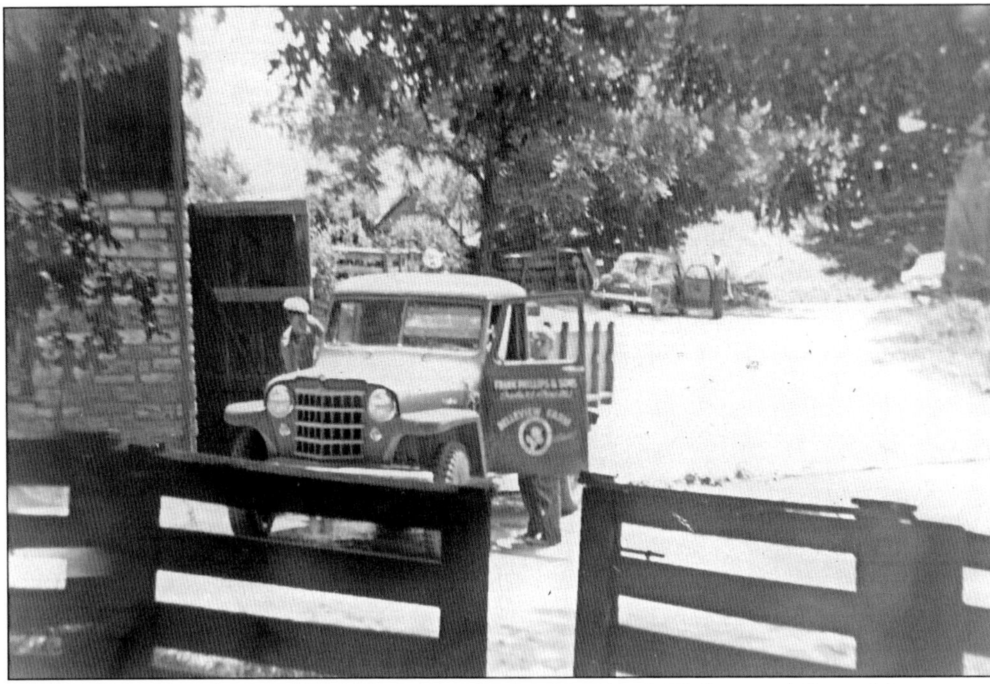

This truck was used on Belleview Farms and owned by Frank Phillips and Sons. (Courtesy of the Phillips family.)

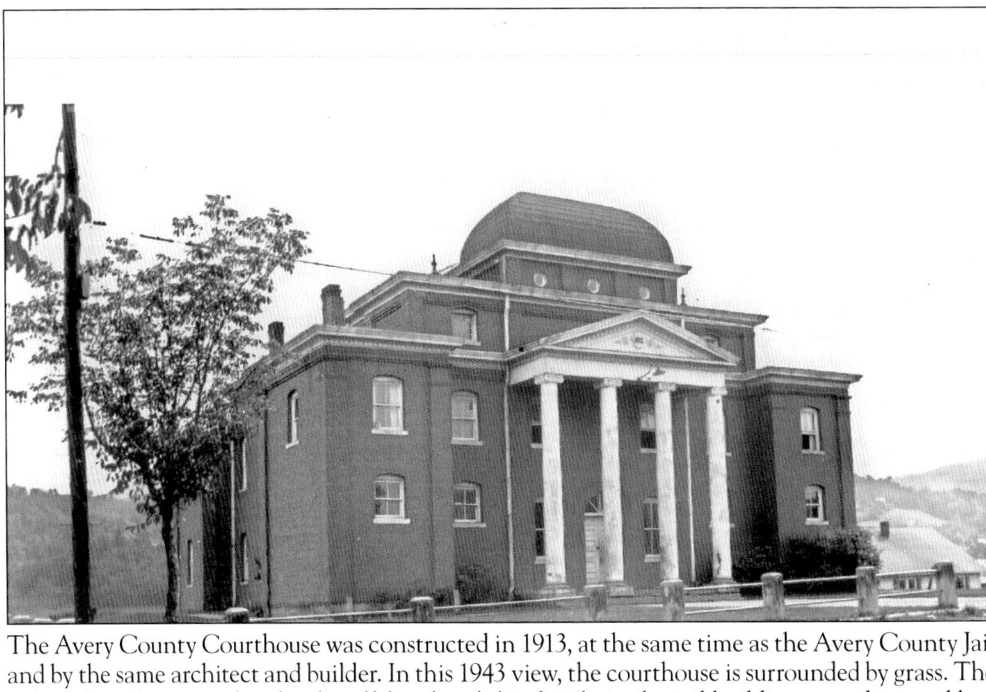

The Avery County Courthouse was constructed in 1913, at the same time as the Avery County Jail and by the same architect and builder. In this 1943 view, the courthouse is surrounded by grass. The jailer, who often was also the sheriff, lived with his family in the jail building next door and had livestock and a large garden behind both structures. This entire area, now in the heart of downtown Newland, is paved. (Courtesy of the North Carolina Division of Archives and History.)

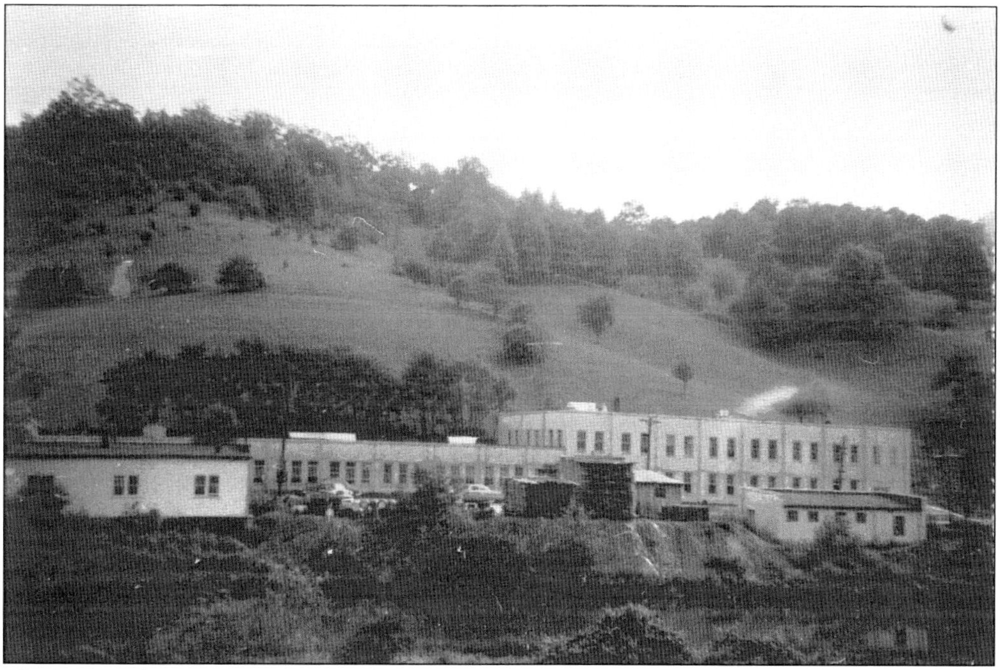

The Tar Heel Mica Company was founded by David T. Vance in 1901 and is still mining mica today. (Courtesy of David C. Vance Sr.)

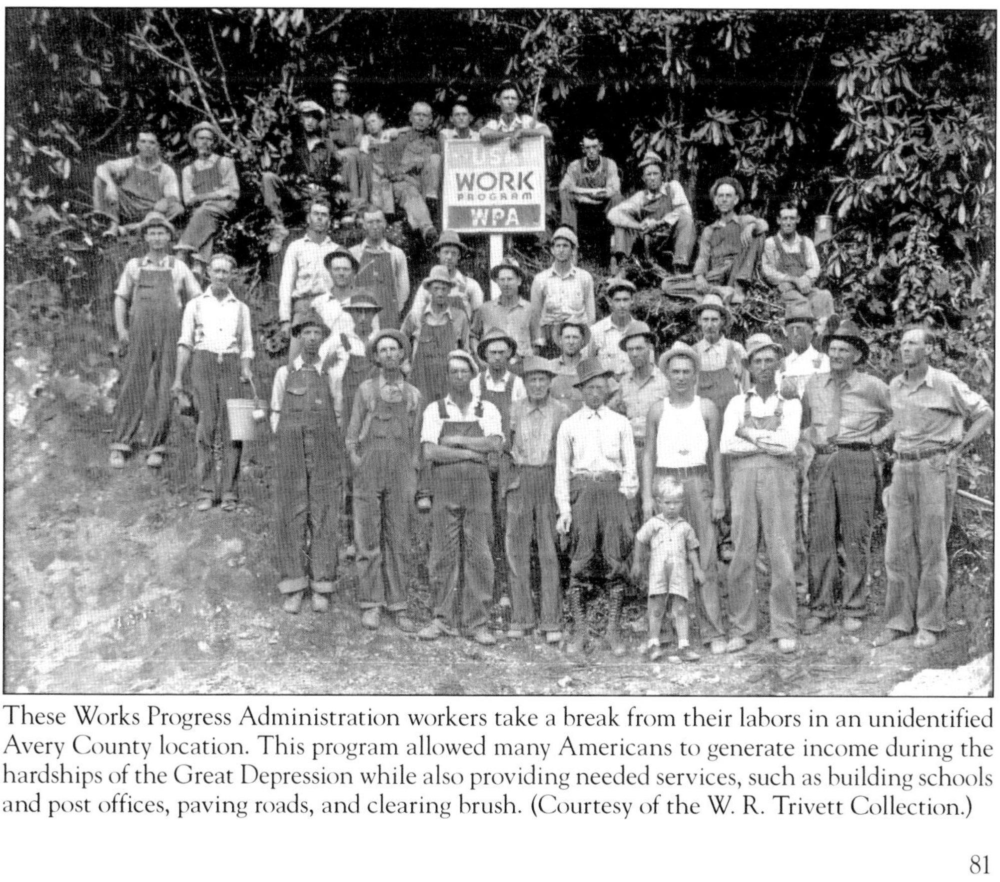

These Works Progress Administration workers take a break from their labors in an unidentified Avery County location. This program allowed many Americans to generate income during the hardships of the Great Depression while also providing needed services, such as building schools and post offices, paving roads, and clearing brush. (Courtesy of the W. R. Trivett Collection.)

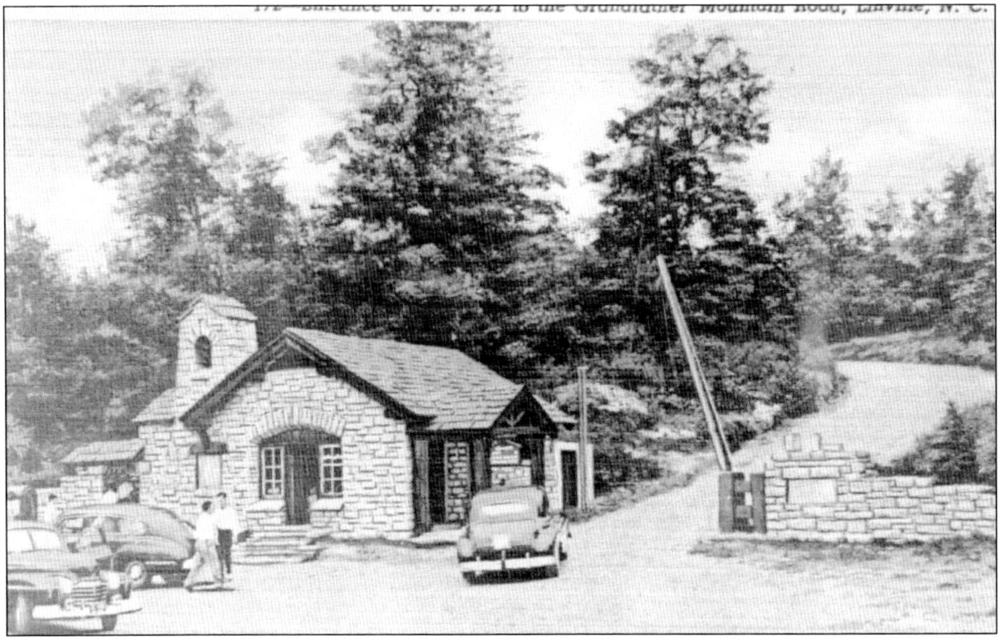

An early postcard depicts visitors at the entrance to Grandfather Mountain. Many early postcards were either photographs or, like this linen sample, paintings copying real photographs. (Courtesy of Pack Memorial Library.)

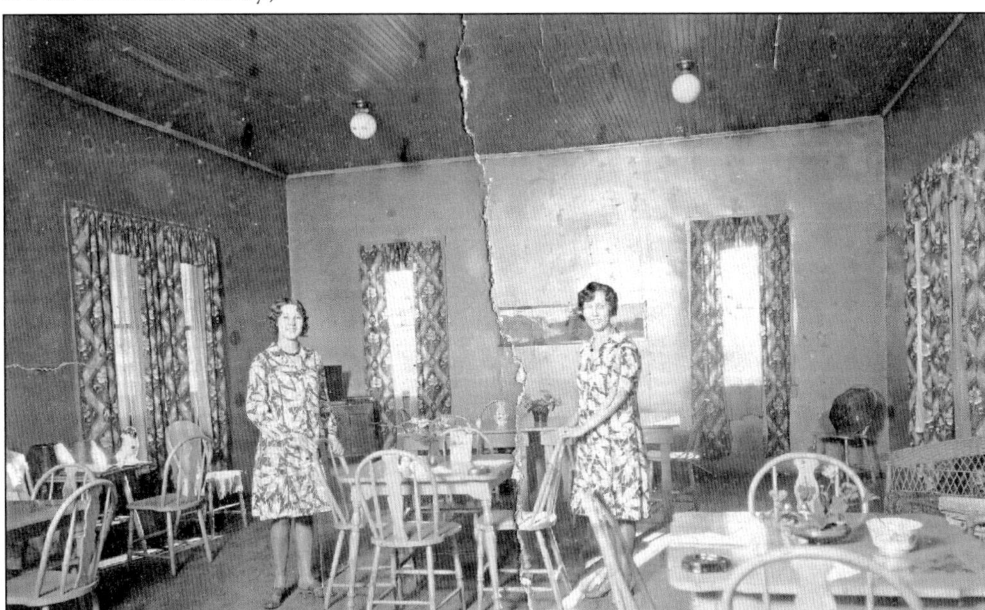

The Pineola Tea Room was one of many successful businesses that sprang up to cater to the railroad and tourism clientele. Originally known as Saginaw, Pineola got its name from Everett Camp, a timber investor and railroad owner. Camp built a prosperous hotel in the community, and named it after a combination of the word "pine" and "Ola" after the daughter of the hotel's manager. The name stuck and spread to the entire village, which became a railroad hub with rails branching out in five directions. (Courtesy of the Avery County Historical Museum.)

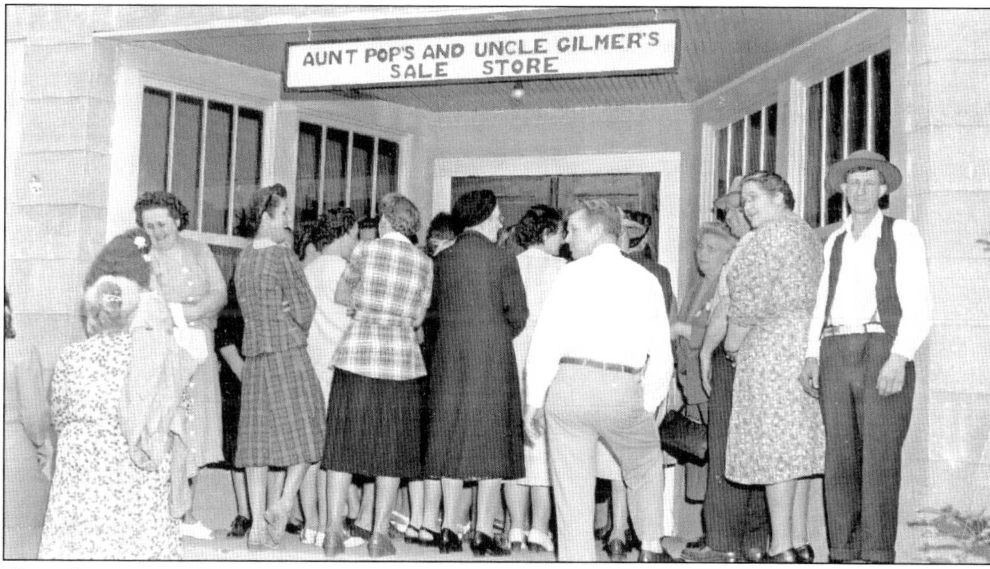

The sales store in Crossnore, known to locals as the "Rag Shakin' " was begun when Dr. Mary M. Sloop, hoping to provide a young woman with an education instead of an early marriage to a shiftless man, asked her cousins to send clothes that might be suitable to outfit the young lady for college. Dr. Sloop was horrified when the requested clothes arrived: they were all mourning dresses. When a local woman offered to buy one of the dresses, Dr. Sloop decided to sell them all and soon had plenty of money to outfit the young student, who went off to college. The sales store was born, as more people donated unneeded clothes. Crossnore's thrift store is still a thriving business that helps in the support of the Crossnore School. (Courtesy of the Avery County Historical Museum.)

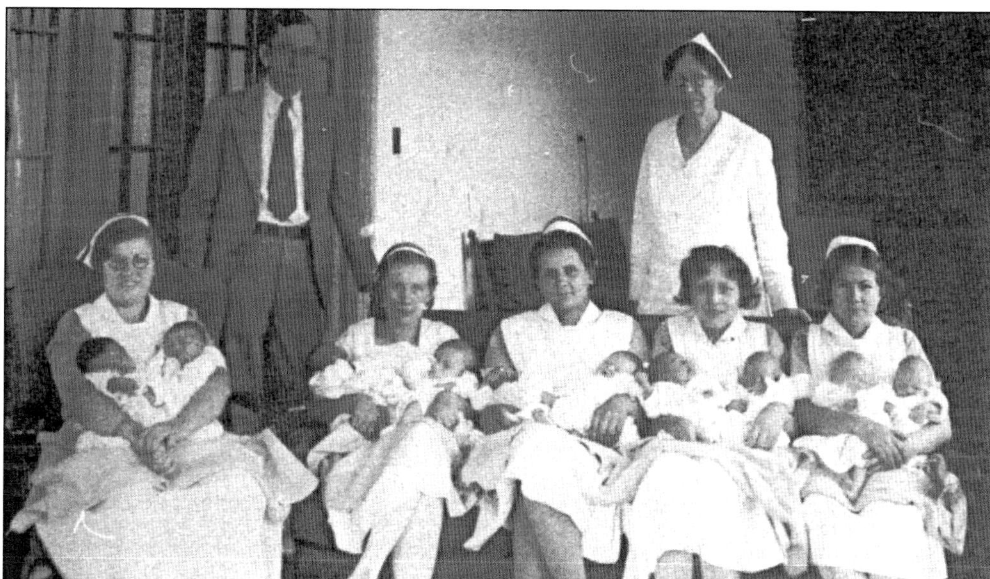

These nurses with infants were photographed in Banner Elk, possibly at the Grace Hospital, which served both as a hospital and as a training facility for nurses. While some of these nurses stayed in Banner Elk, others took their knowledge to help patients around the world. (Courtesy of Lees-McRae College.)

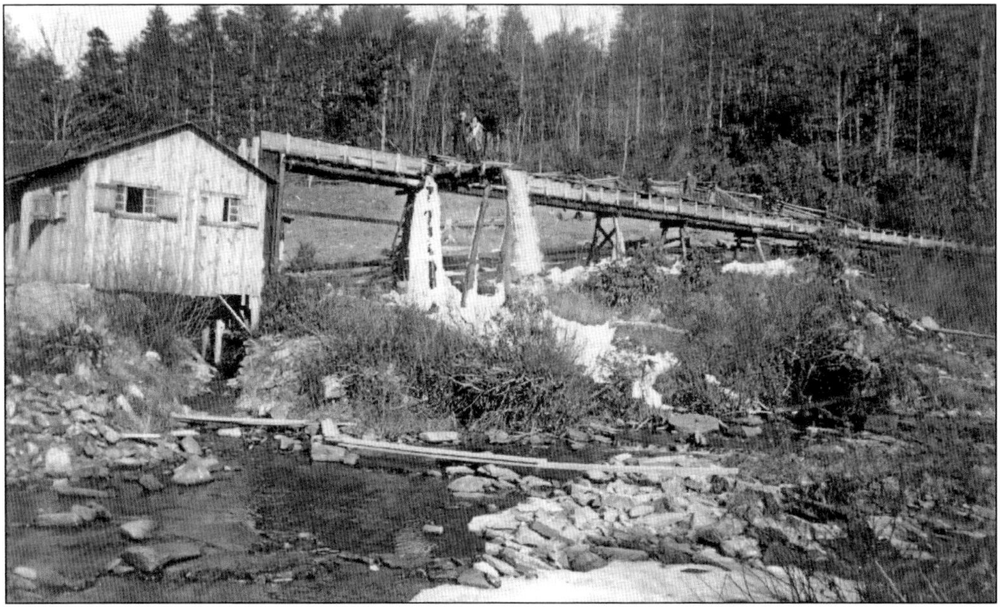

The Camp Creek Mill, owned by Frank Bicknell, was located in what is today the Altamont section of Avery County. The area was known as Grasslands in the 1860s, when Col. John Palmer owned the property, and was later called Trout (1883–1892). In the 1890s, the name became Altamont. This photograph was taken on January 1, 1920. (Courtesy of the North Carolina Division of Archives and History.)

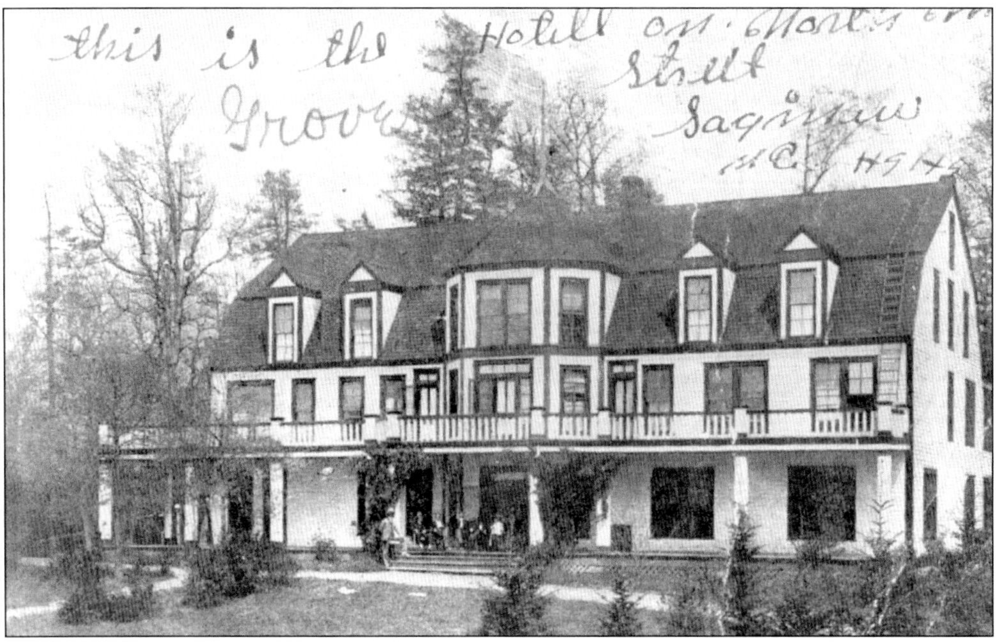

This photo-postcard, dated January 1912, shows the Pineola Inn in Saginaw, North Carolina. The 25-room hotel was operated by Mrs. Lewellen Penland. As the story goes, Mrs. Penland had a daughter named Ola. Everett Camp, who built the Linville River Railroad that ran through Saginaw, providing an outlet for timber, combined "pine" and "Ola" to form Pineola. Saginaw was officially changed to Pineola on July 21, 1914. (Courtesy of the Avery County Historical Museum.)

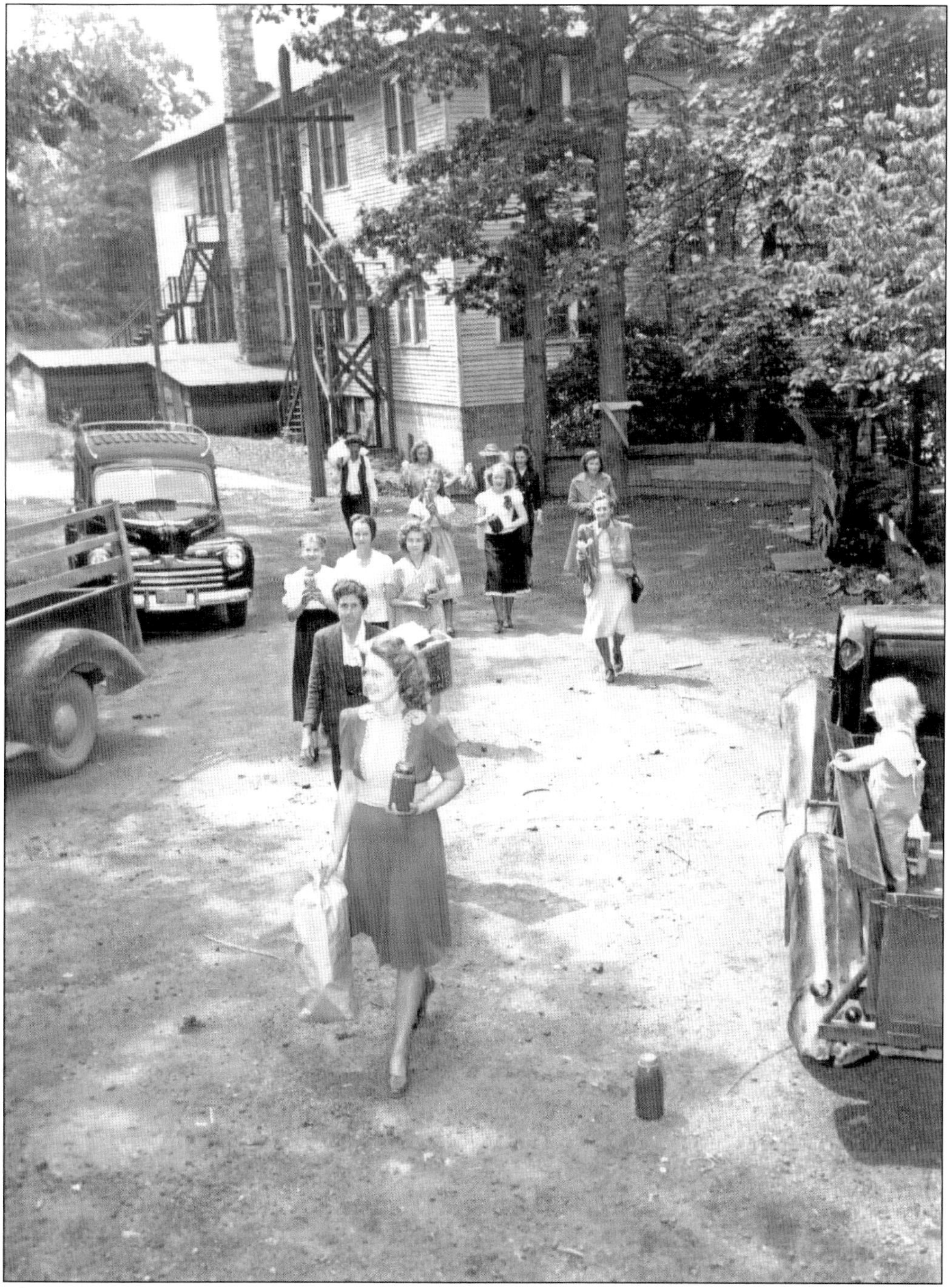

These women in Crossnore were photographed in 1949 as they left a local canning factory. It is interesting to note the young person standing the bed of the truck while his mother carries out her jars of food and other goods. (Courtesy of the North Carolina Division of Archives and History.)

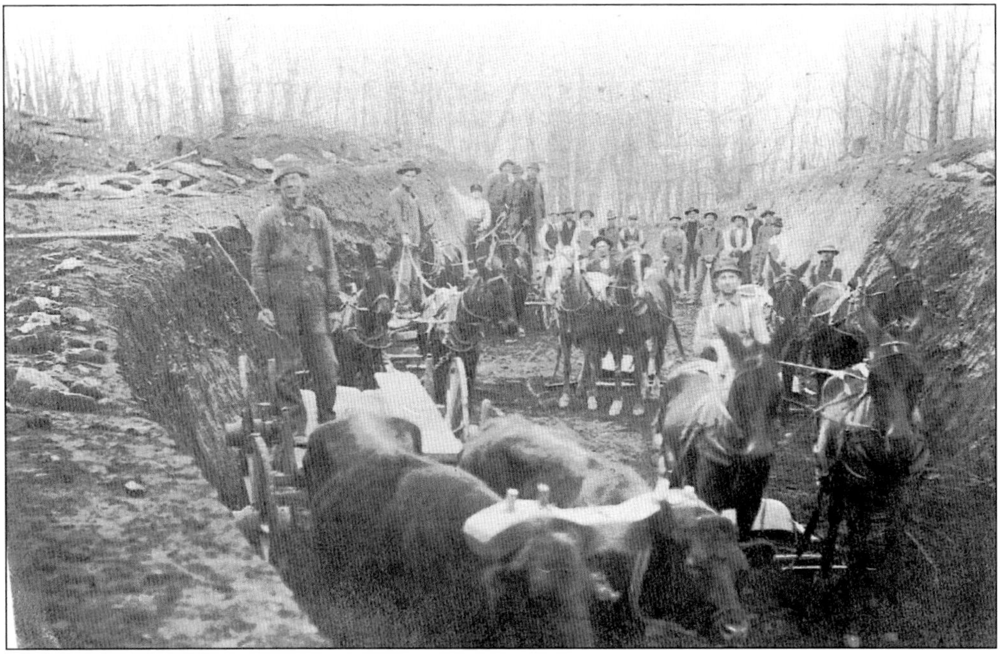

In 1912, a team of men began work on the Linville-to-Altapass section of the Appalachian Highway, an early scenic road project instigated by State Geologist Dr. Joseph Hyde Pratt. The ambitious project was to link up several existing roads and was designed to bring tourists to view the scenery and stay in local inns. World War I brought a halt to the project, and it was never resumed. (Courtesy of Tense Banks.)

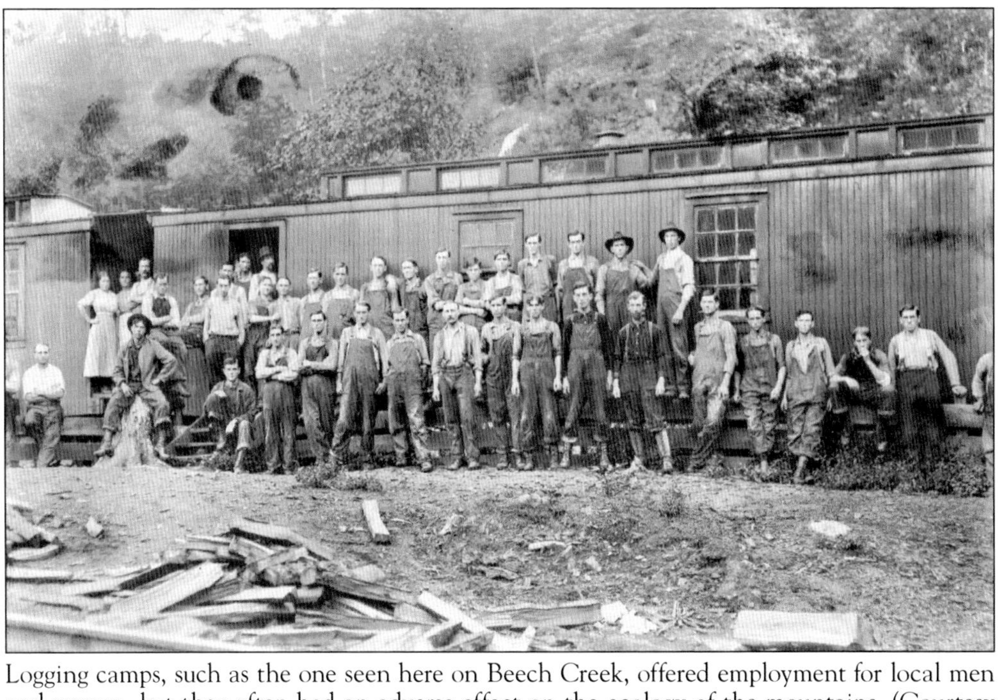

Logging camps, such as the one seen here on Beech Creek, offered employment for local men and women, but they often had an adverse effect on the ecology of the mountains. (Courtesy of Naomi Houston.)

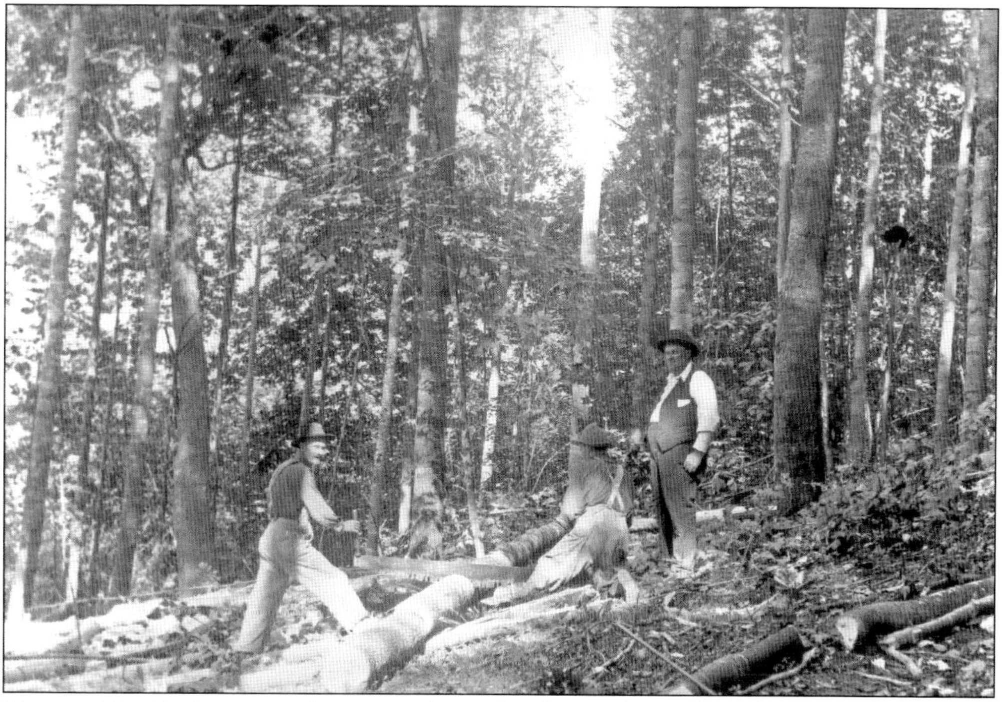

These unidentified men are thinning pulpwood and second growth timber on property owned by the Cranberry Iron and Coal Company in September 1920. (Courtesy of the North Carolina Division of Archives and History.)

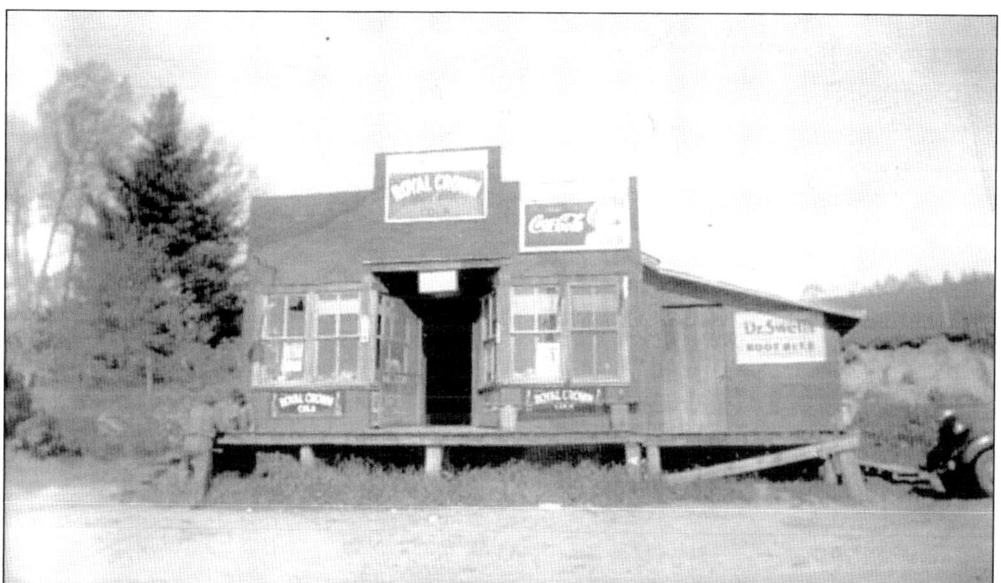

The Sally Wiseman Store was owned by Aunt Sally Dellinger Wiseman, a postmistress and storekeeper who was known to sneak candy to children unable to pay for it. (Courtesy of Doyle Ollis.)

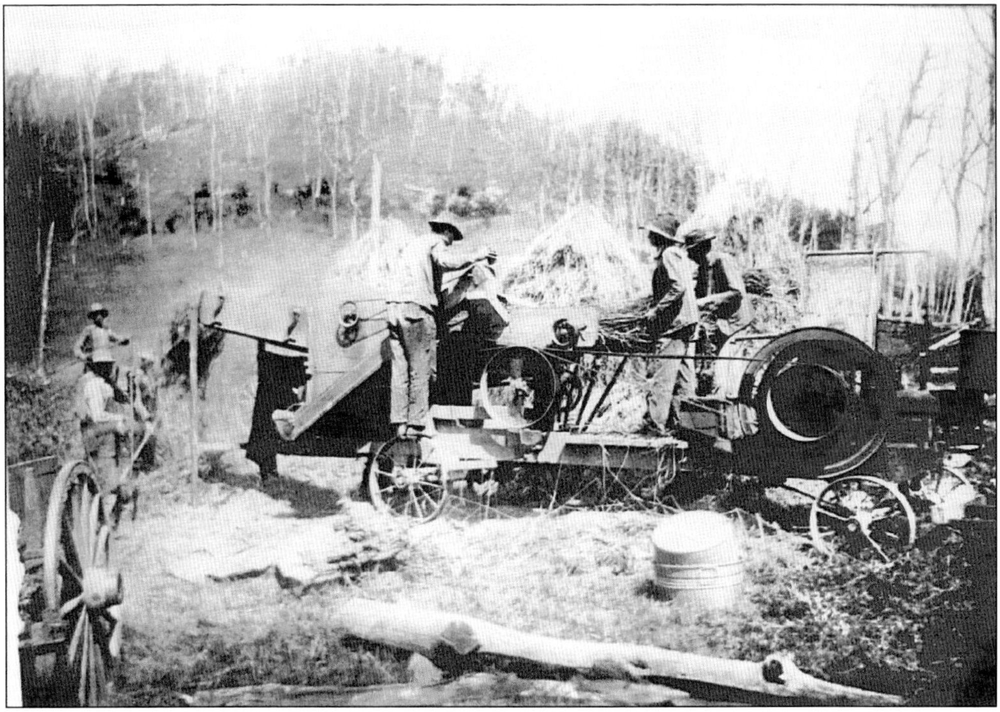

This rye threshing machine is being operated by an unidentified group of men, *c.* 1912. (Courtesy of Tense Banks.)

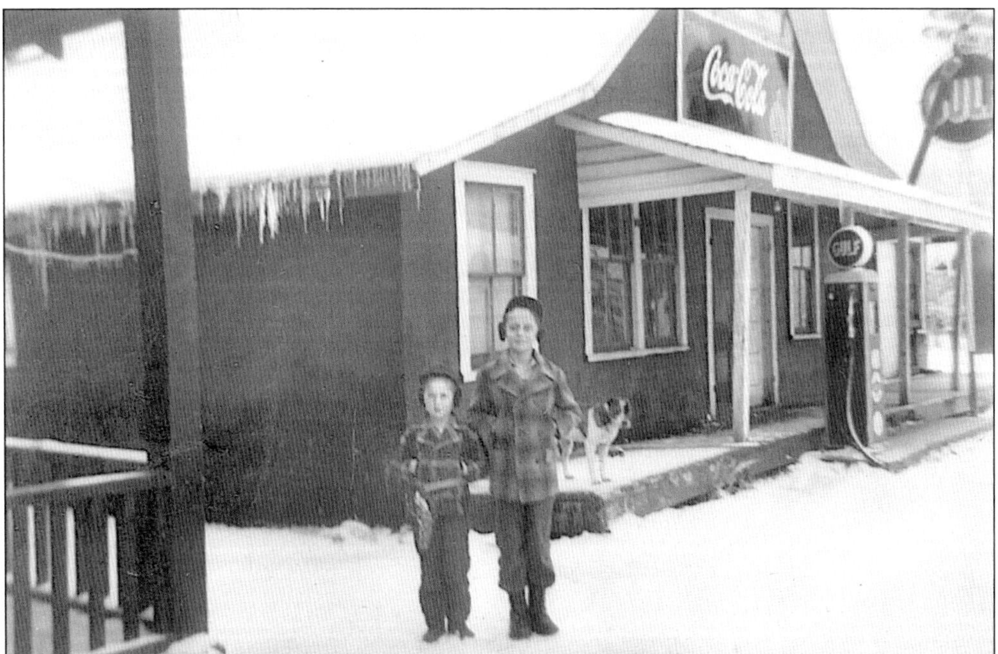

Carl Stewart (left) and his brother, Neil, are standing in front of the general store in Pineola. (Courtesy of the Stewart family.)

Women are here seen working at the Weaving Room at Lees-McRae College. Weaving was an important industry that allowed mountain people, particularly women, to preserve a cultural practice, produce beautiful goods, and generate income. (Courtesy of Lees-McRae College.)

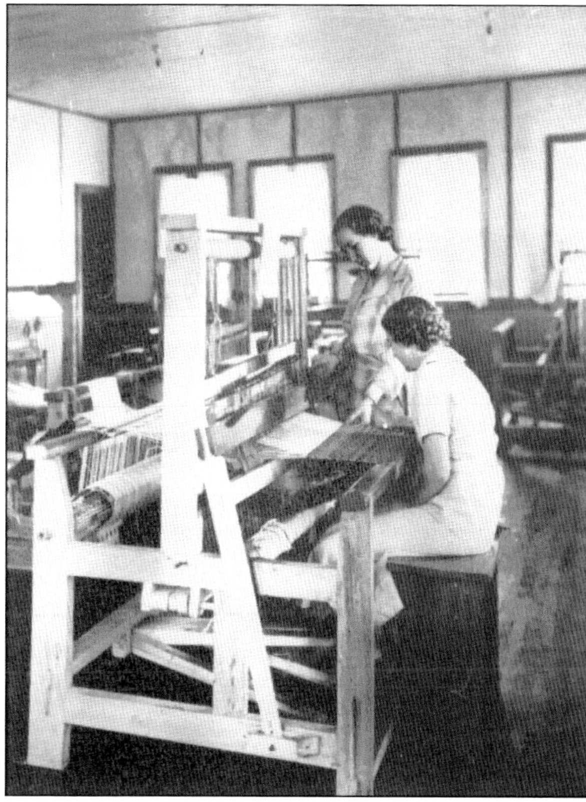

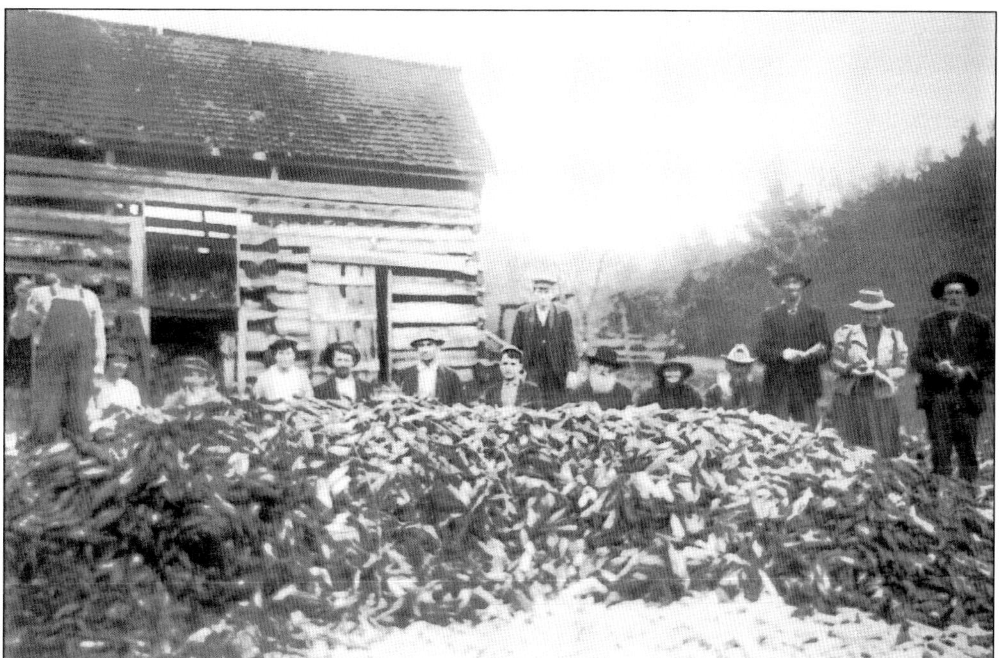

Occasions like this corn shucking at Jim Franklin's on October 27, 1910, were important social functions as well as part of the labor performed on farms. (Courtesy of Tense Banks.)

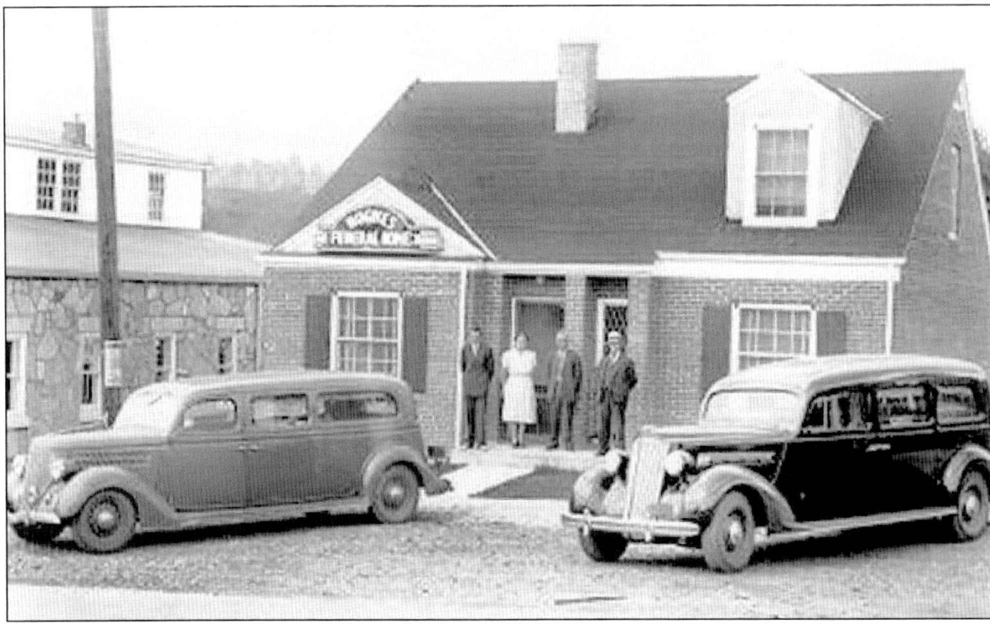

The Hughes Funeral Home in Newland was founded by Ronald Hughes in 1946 and later purchased by Reins-Sturdivant. Until funeral homes became common, mountain people prepared the dead for burial themselves. Women made shrouds and washed and dressed the body for burial, while men dug graves and built caskets. Caskets could also be purchased from a store along with other necessary goods. (Courtesy of the Reins-Sturdivant Funeral Home.)

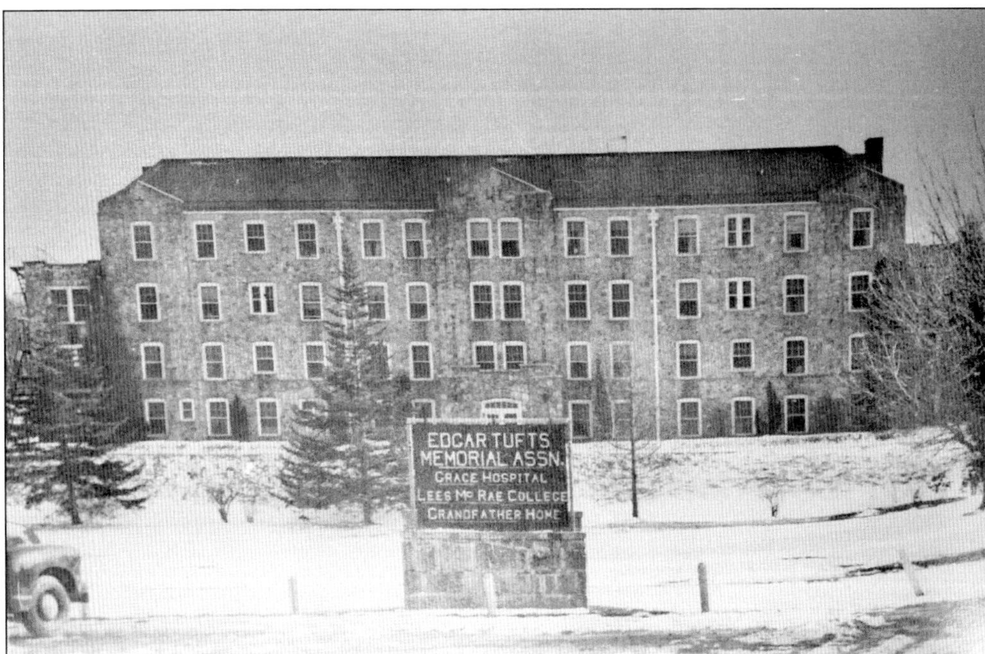

One of the many facilities sponsored by the philanthropic Edgar Tufts Memorial Association was Grace Hospital in Banner Elk. This is actually the third building to bear the name. (Courtesy of Lees-McRae College.)

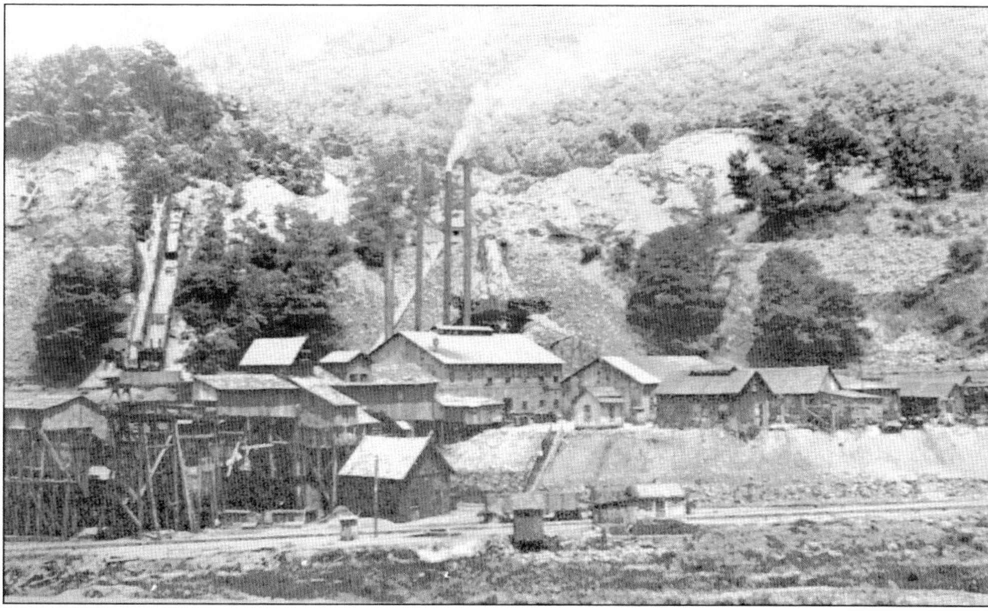

The Cranberry Iron Ore Mine was used from the 1820s up through the 20th century. Until 1828, the area, home of North Carolina's largest iron ore deposit, was called Cranberry Forge. The town of Cranberry was a company town created for the workers and their families. (Courtesy of the Avery County Historical Museum.)

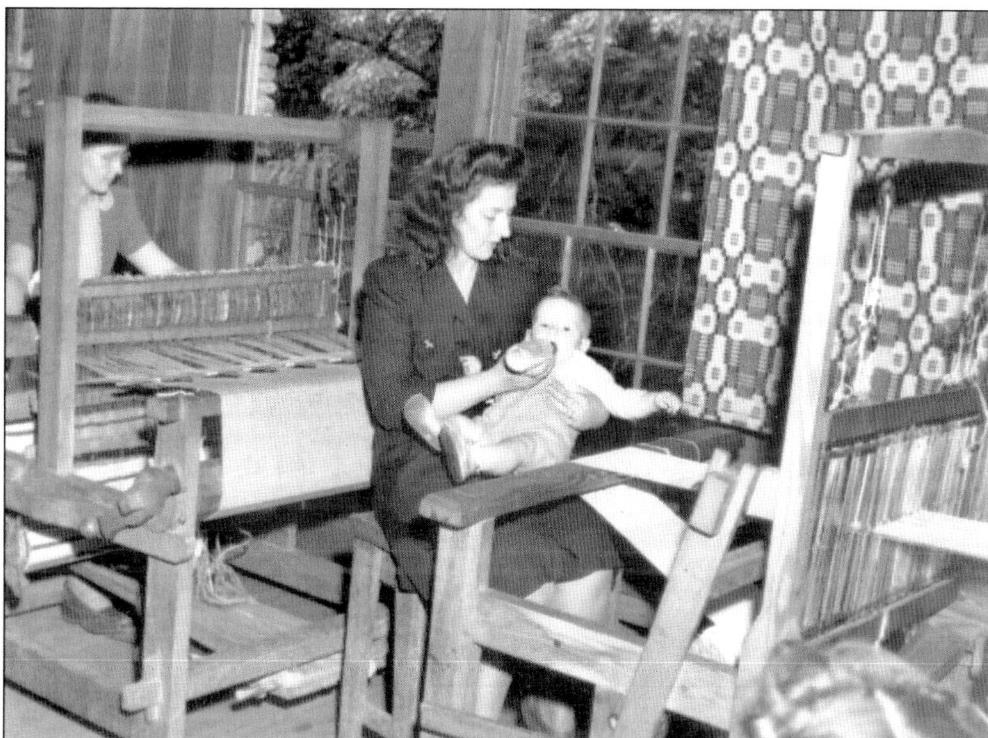

At the Crossnore Weaving Room in July 1948, this young woman was able to bring her child with her as she worked. (Courtesy of the North Carolina Division of Archives and History.)

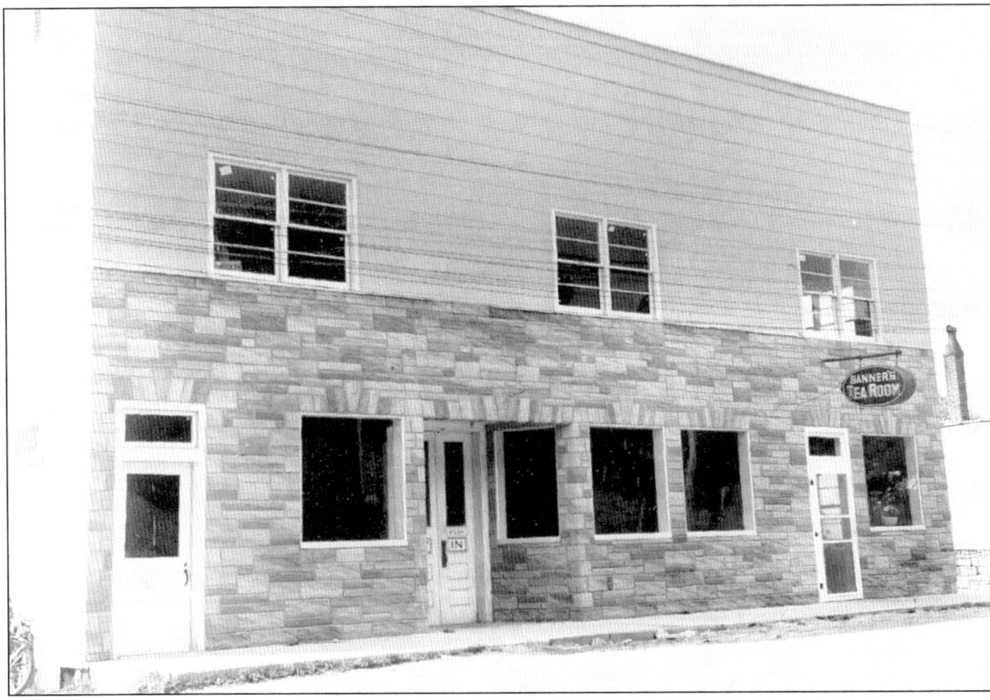

Tea rooms were a very popular type of business in 20th-century Avery County. While some were only semi-permanent, Banner's Tea Room in Newland was a more stable establishment. (Courtesy of the Avery County Historical Museum.)

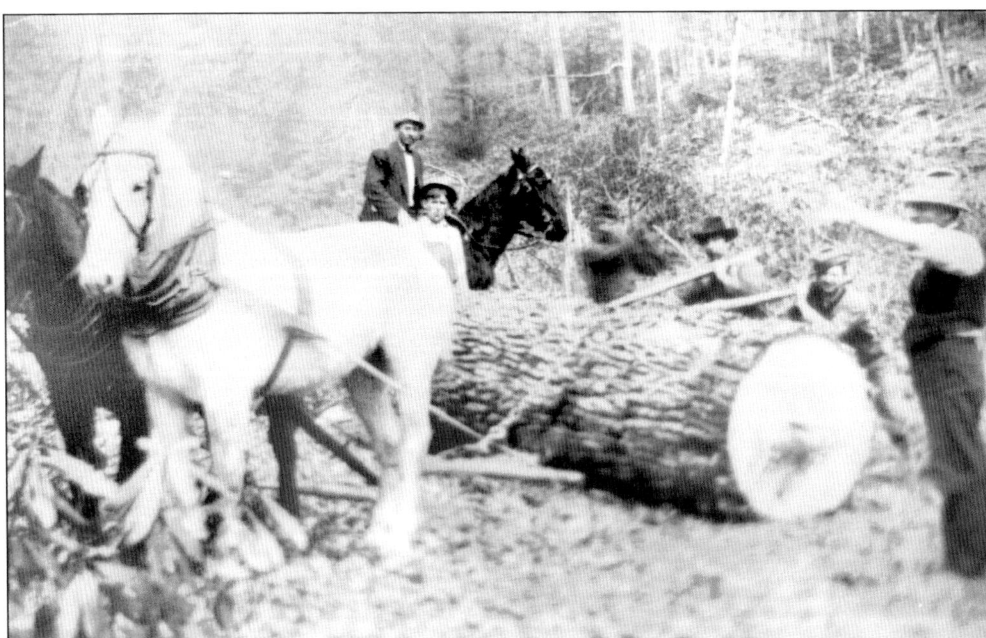

Mitch Burleson and his sons are here seen logging, a popular off-season occupation for farmers before becoming a full-fledged industry with the arrival of the railroads. (Courtesy of Tense Banks.)

In this image, the Drs. Sloop perform outdoor surgery in order to take advantage of ideal light and ventilation then unavailable indoors. Note the woman on the right, who appears to be covering her mouth with the bouquet of flowers. (Courtesy of the Avery County Historical Museum.)

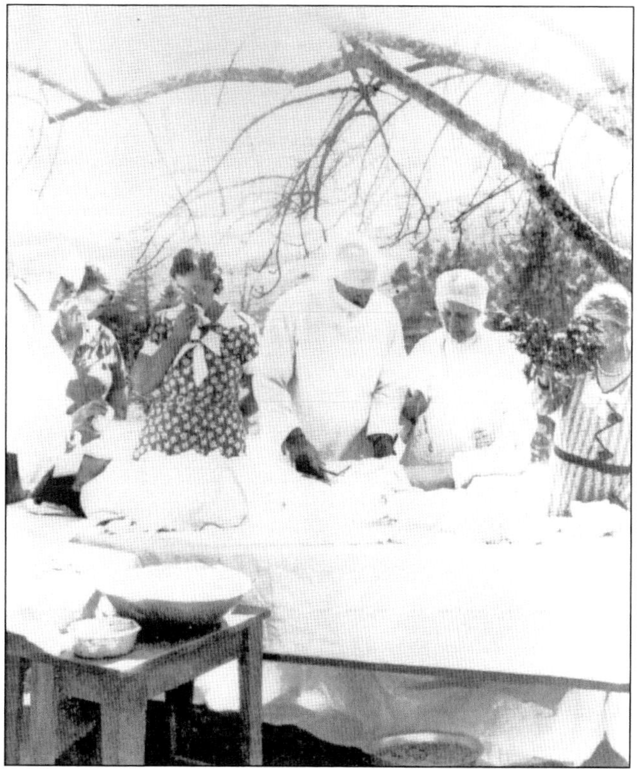

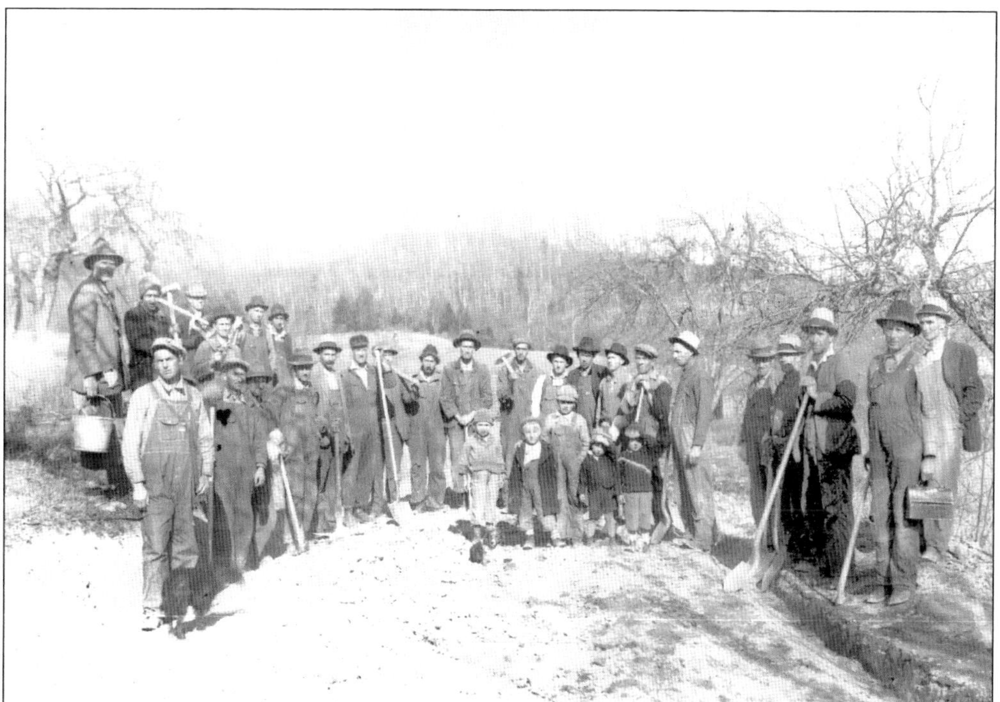

Men from the Works Progress Administration work on the Flat Springs Road in the late 1930s. (Courtesy of the W. R. Trivett Collection.)

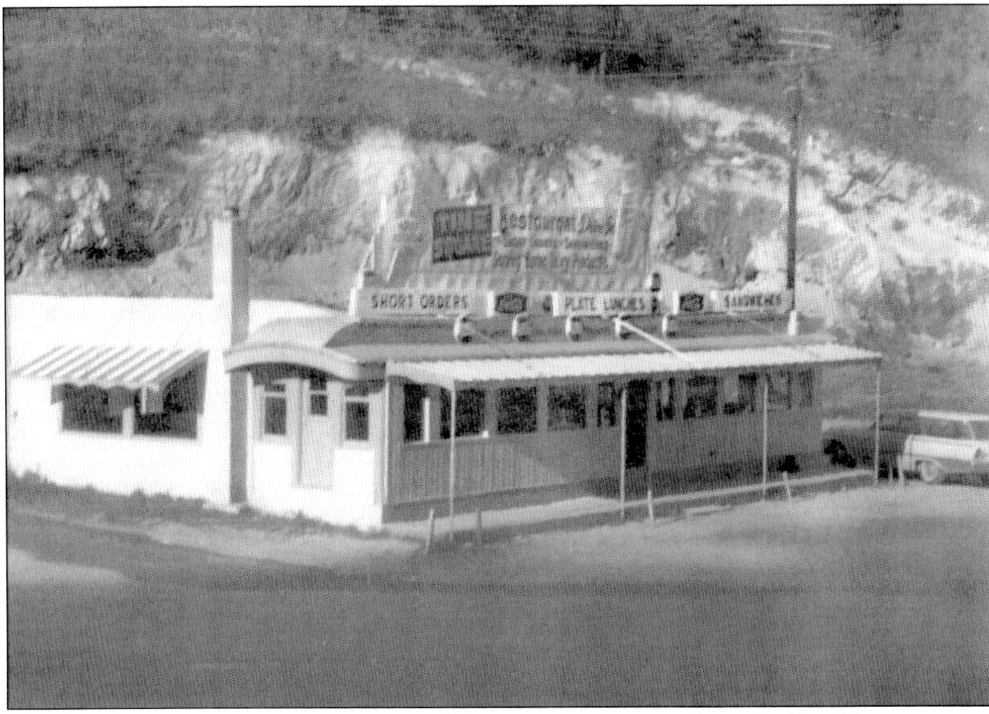

The Times Square Diner was constructed from a passenger car from the East Tennessee and Western North Carolina Railroad. Today the restaurant still utilizes part of this railroad car as a countertop. (Courtesy of the Avery County Historical Museum.)

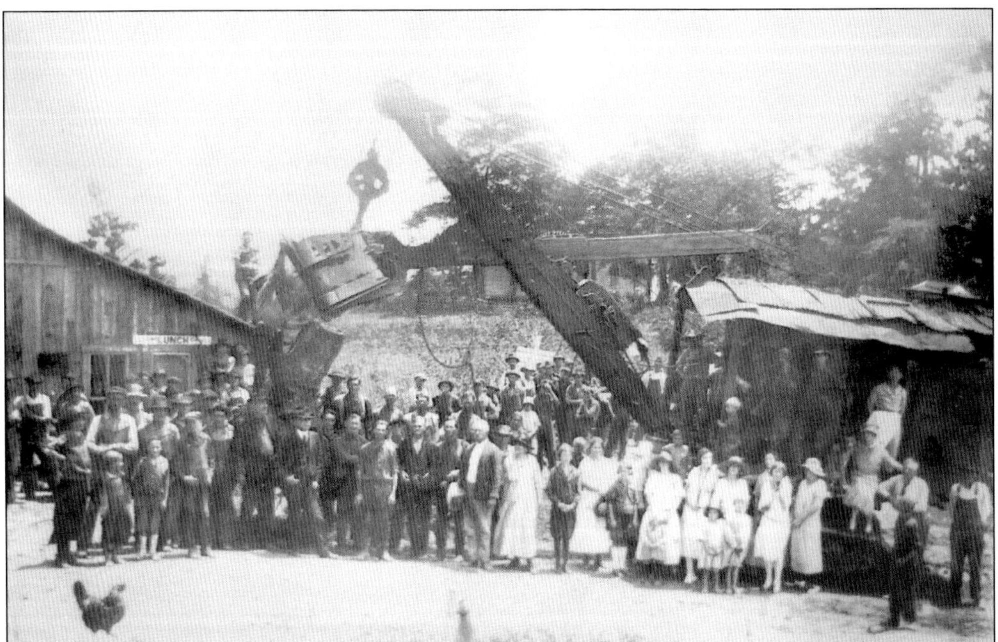

The construction of U.S. 221, *c.* 1925, brought a steam shovel to Linville Falls, which these workers and their friends and family used as a photographic backdrop. (Courtesy of Tense Banks.)

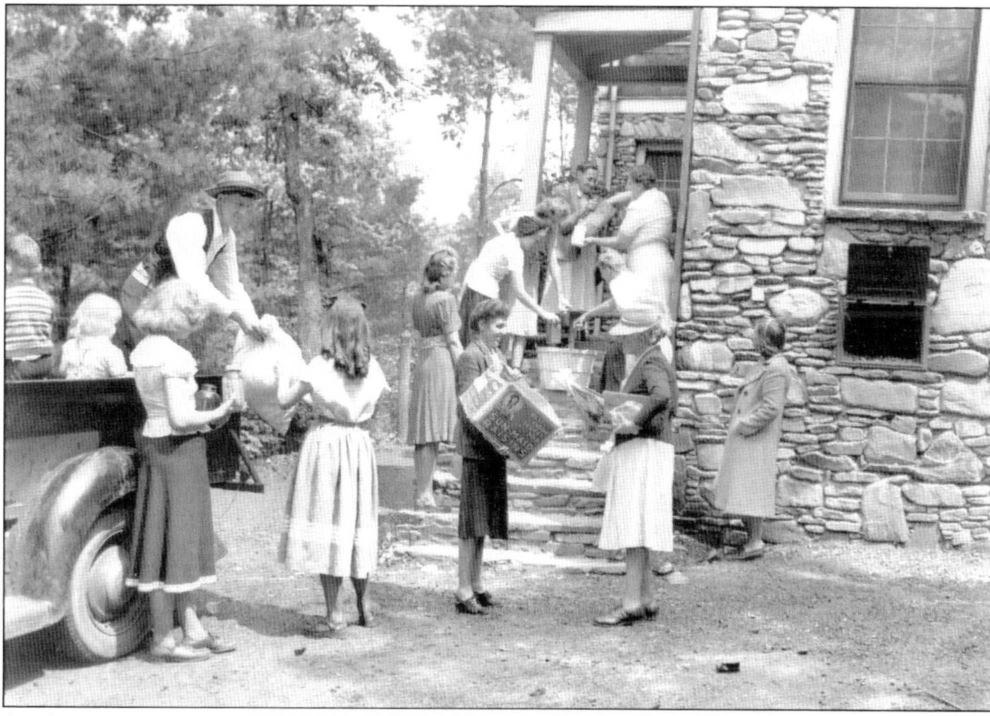

At the cannery in Crossnore, a truck is unloaded and used goods are brought in to be sold. (Courtesy of the North Carolina Division of Archives and History.)

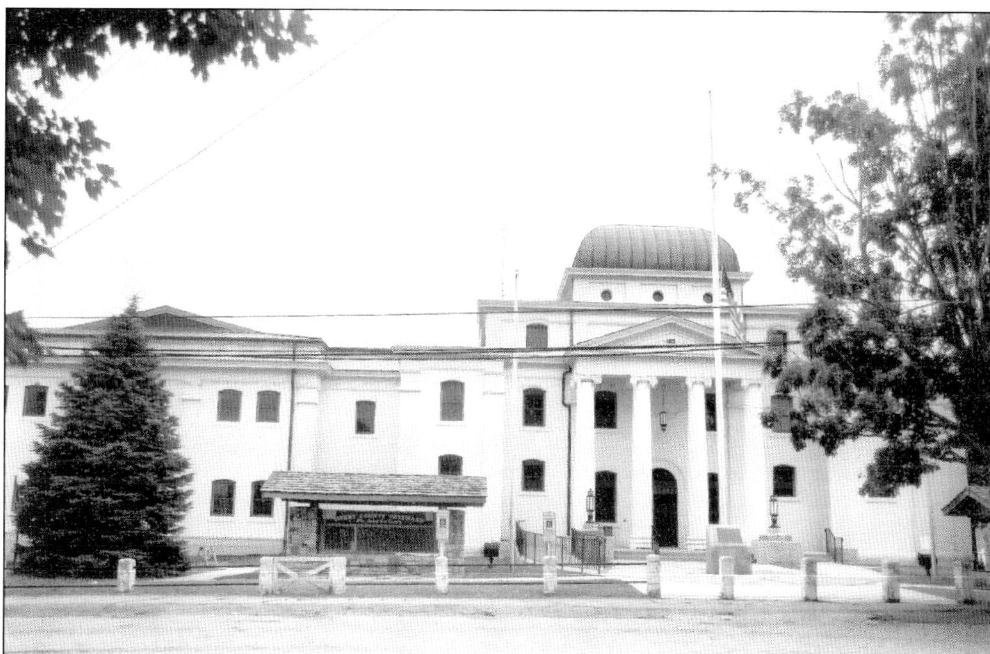

The historic 1913 Avery County Court House has undergone early-21st-century remodeling and extension. (Courtesy of Michael C. Hardy.)

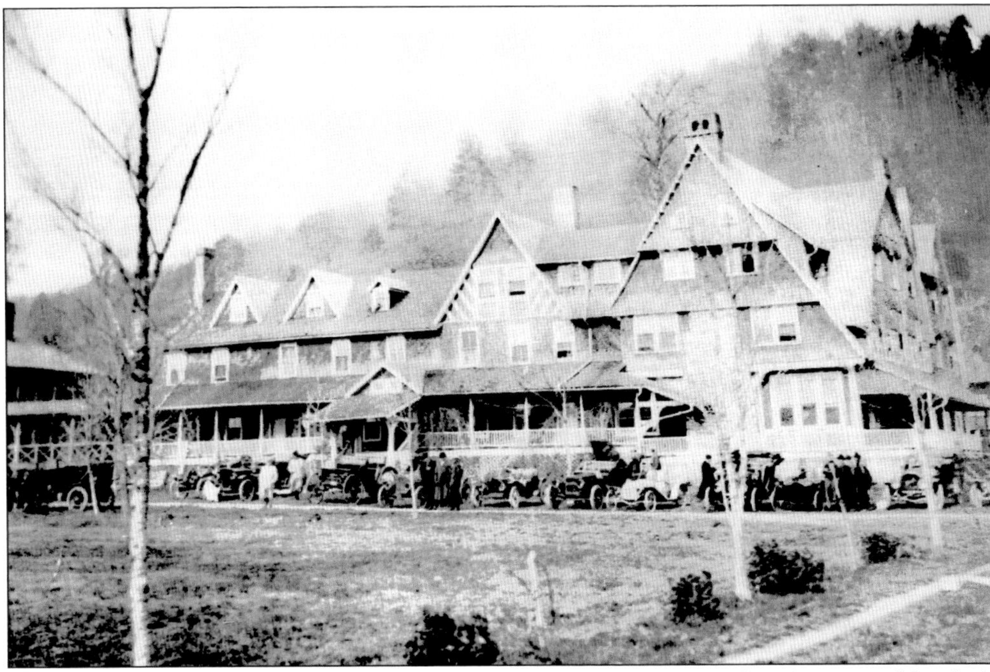

A group of early automobiles and their drivers gather at Eseeola in Linville. The original first hole of the Linville Golf Course lies in front of the hotel. (Courtesy of the Avery County Museum.)

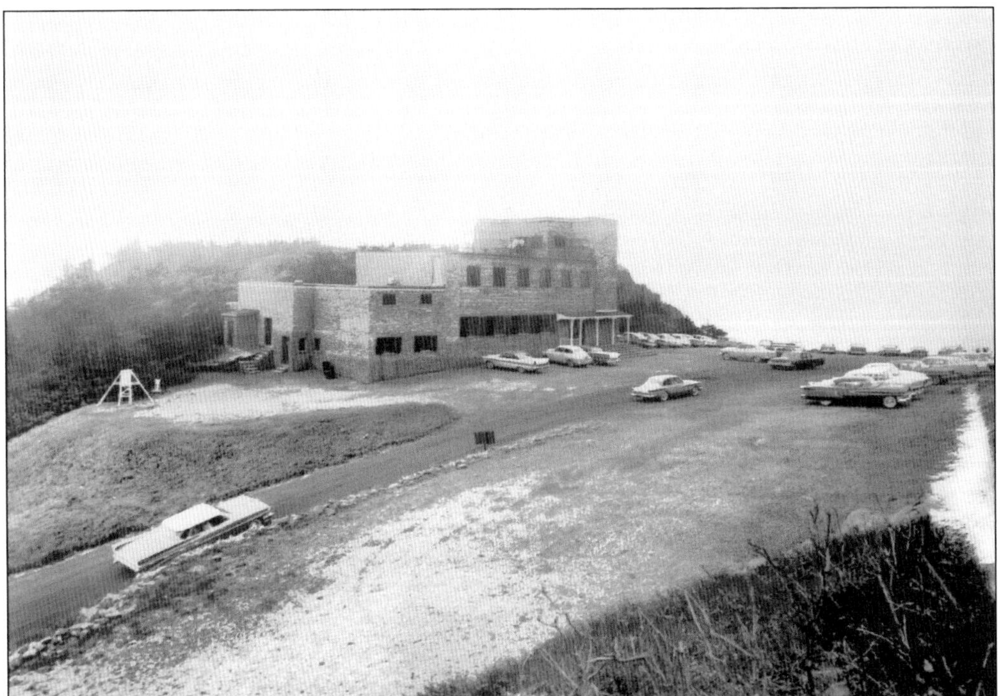

Visitors are shown here driving up to the swinging bridge at Grandfather Mountain. (Courtesy of Hugh Morton/Grandfather Mountain.)

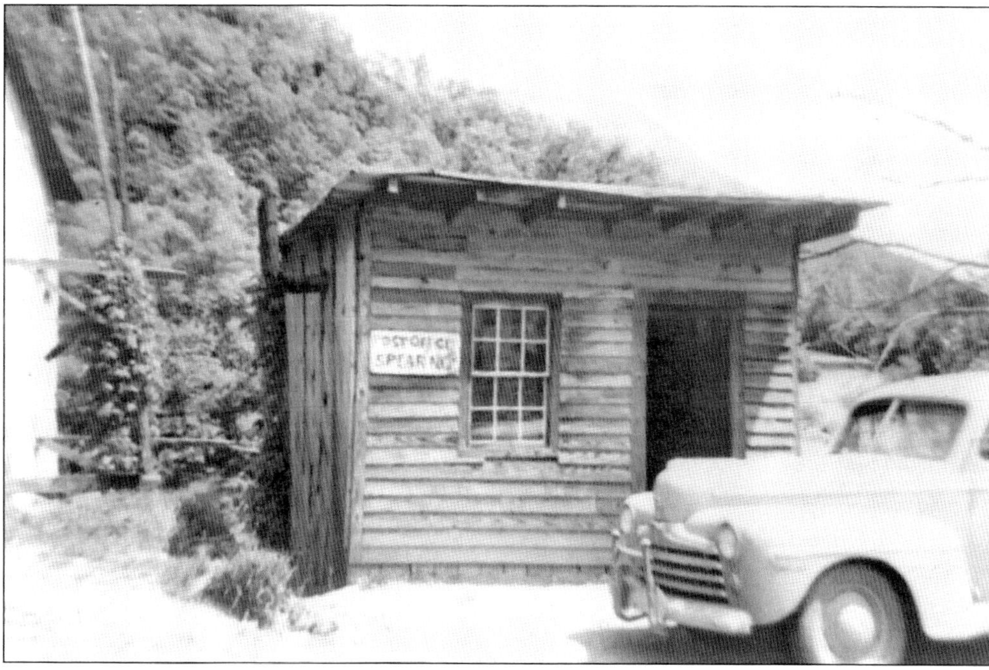

Many rural Avery County post offices, like this one in Spear, helped provide links to the rest of the world. The Spear Post Office was established on August 29, 1882, and discontinued on June 30, 1953. Postmasters and postmistresses included James P. Thompson, Minerva Greer, Mattie N. Bowman, Sliter B. Braswell, Juda E. Vance, Dont Buchanan, Nora A. Thompson, Mack A. Thompson, Baxter G. Franklin, Ethel Buchanan, Nellie Buchanan, and Hazel Thompson. (Courtesy of Naomi Houston.)

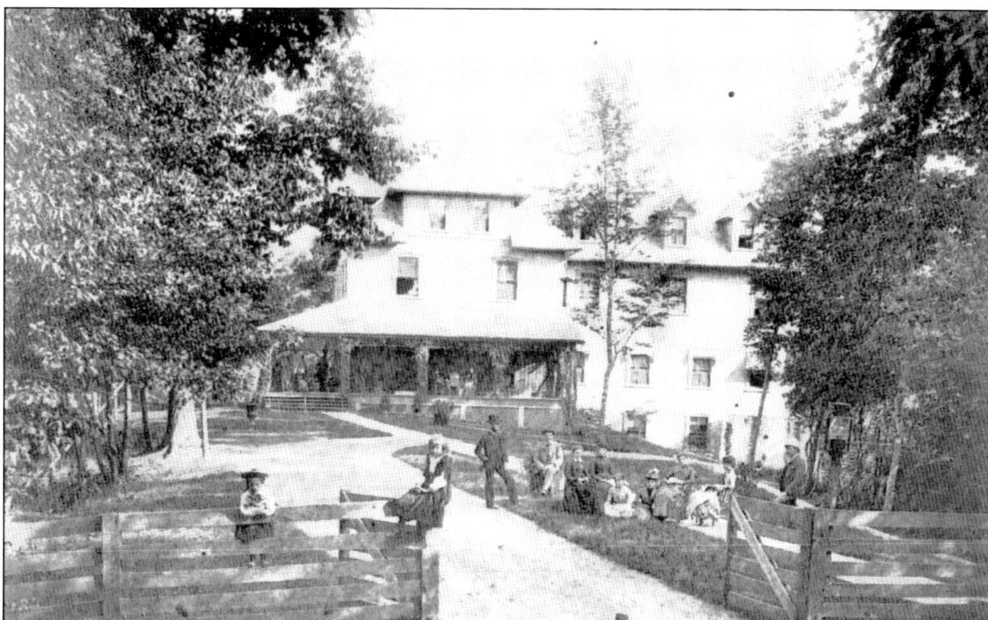

The Cranberry Hotel served visitors to the area as well as men from the railroad. (Courtesy of the Avery County Historical Museum.)

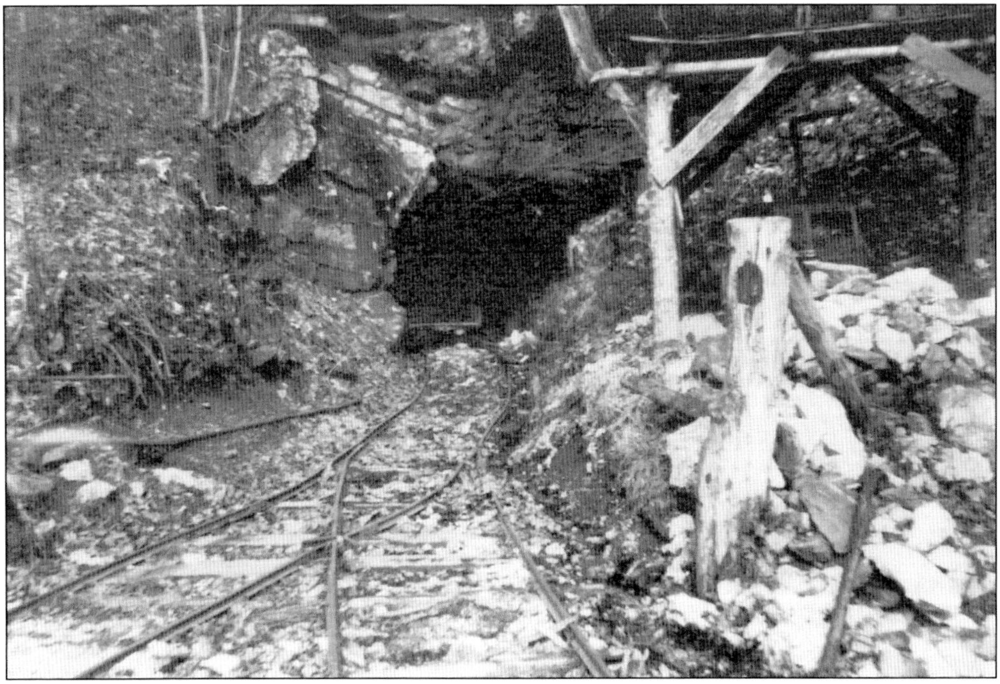

Slippery Elm Mica Mine on Plumtree Creek was just one of the many mines in the Cranberry area. (Courtesy of David C. Vance Sr.)

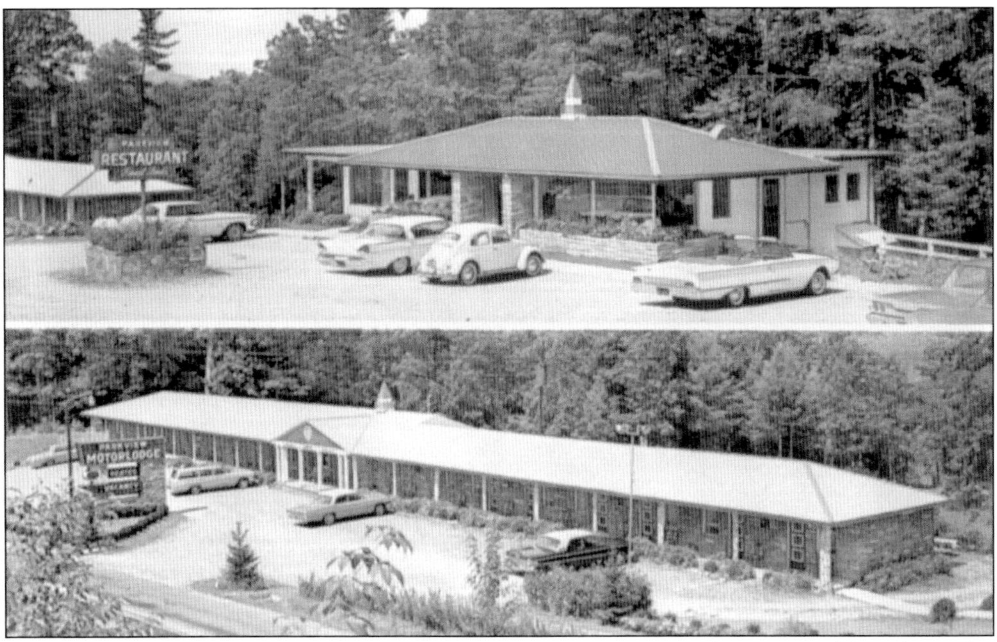

Parkview Lodge in the Linville Falls area was advertised as being in the center of the Blue Ridge Mountains and "Naturally Air Conditioned." The lodge continues to be a thriving business and tourist destination. (Courtesy of Cindy Peters.)

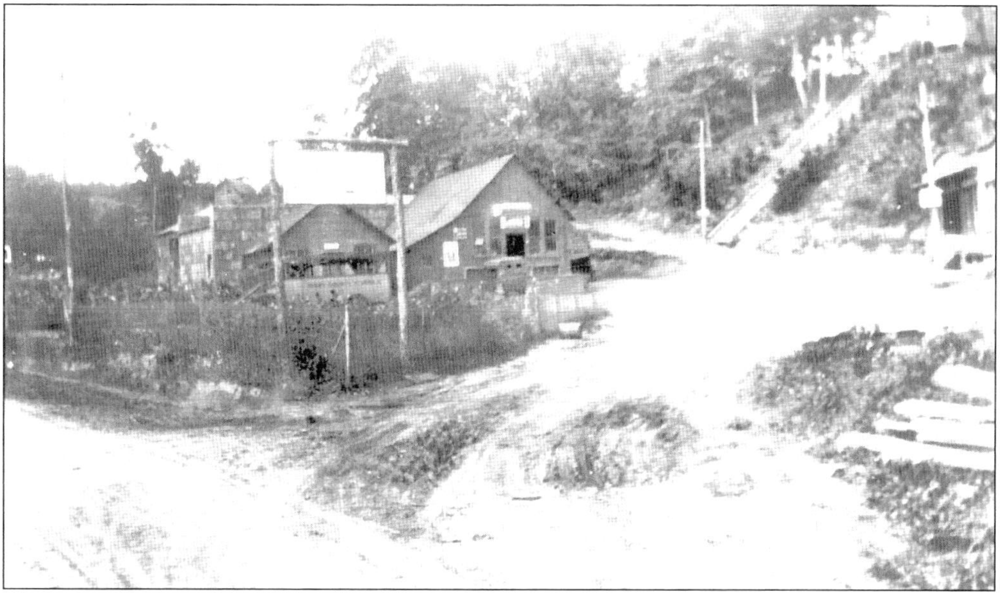

At a crossroads in the town of Crossnore, the steps to the Baptist church can be seen on the right. The post office is below the sign in the center. (Courtesy of the Clark family.)

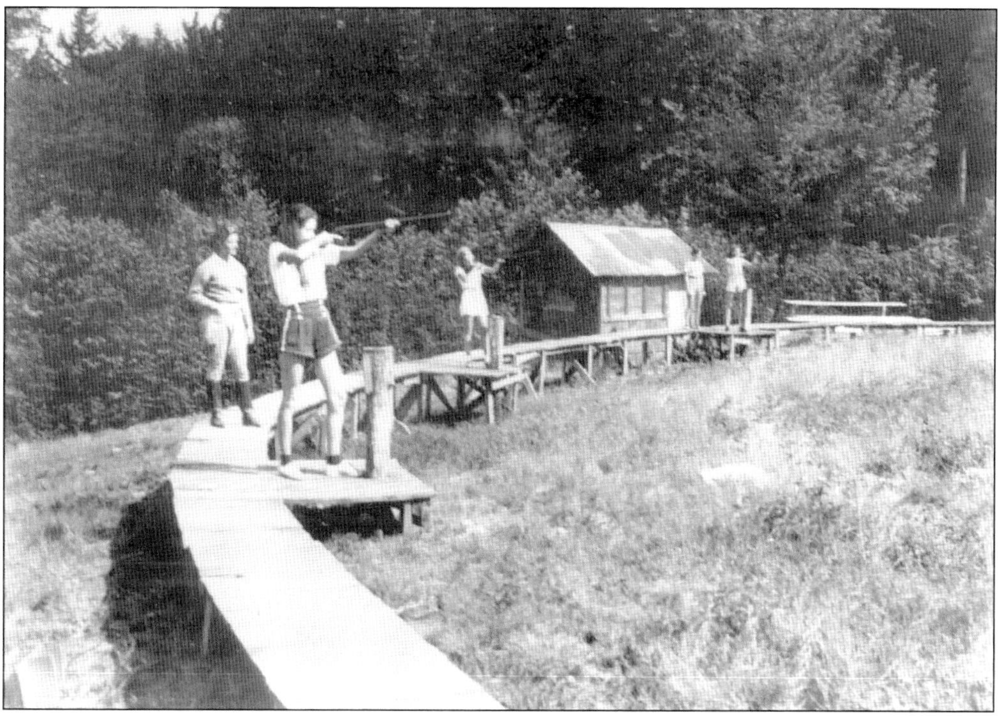

Avery County saw the formation of several successful resort businesses, including summer camps like the Banner Elk camp seen here. Activities such as skeet shooting, archery, and horseback riding were popular. This photograph of skeet-shooting young ladies was taken in 1938. (Courtesy of the Avery County Historical Museum.)

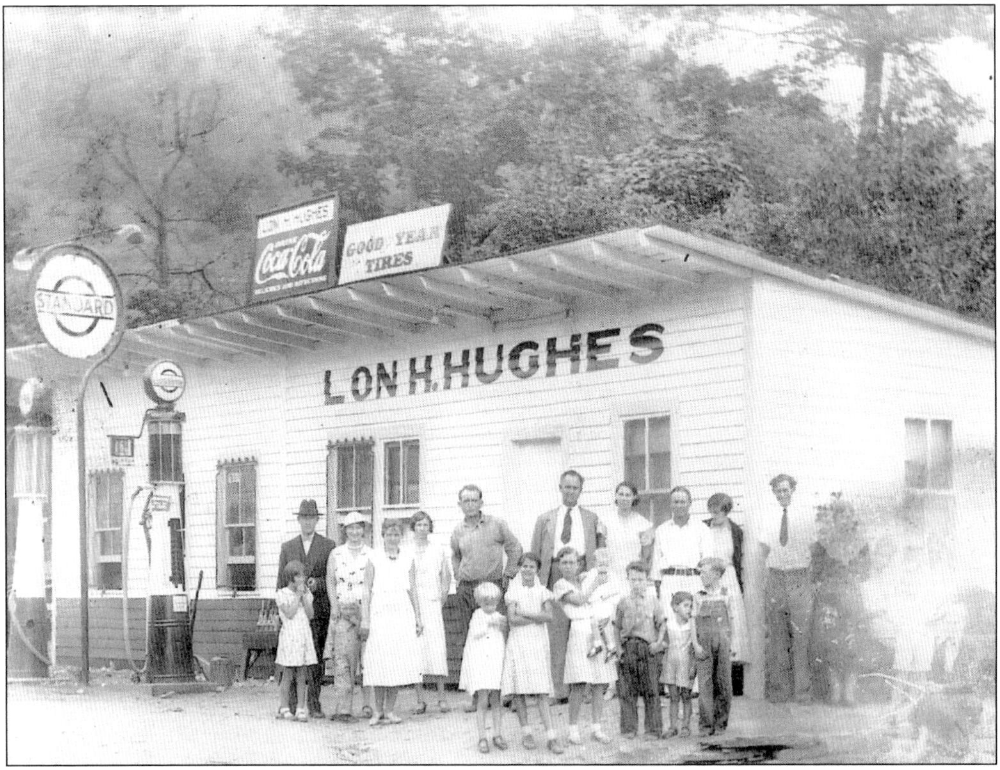

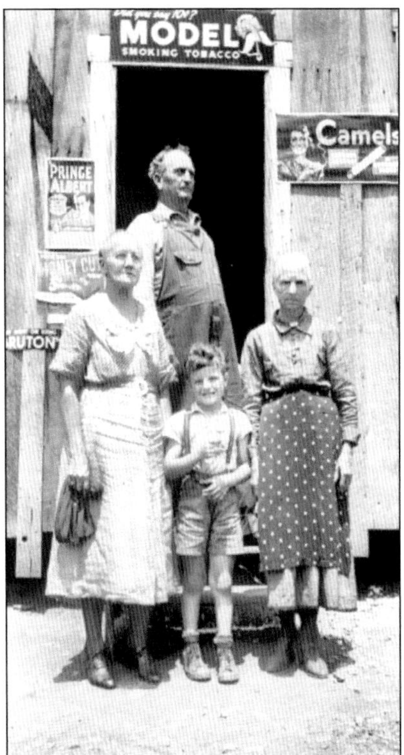

Hughes's General Store was operated by Lon Hughes, who lived between 1901 and 1963. (Courtesy of the Avery County Historical Museum.)

At the Old Stafford Store in the Hughes community, Cull Chappell stands behind Frankie Chappell (left), Jack Chappell (center), and Mrs. Stafford (right). This photograph was nearly lost. A museum visitor brought a box of negatives that had been thrown in the trash when the store was being cleaned out. This photograph, along with the one from Squirrel Creek School, was developed from the negatives. (Courtesy of the Avery County Historical Museum.)

Five

Transportation

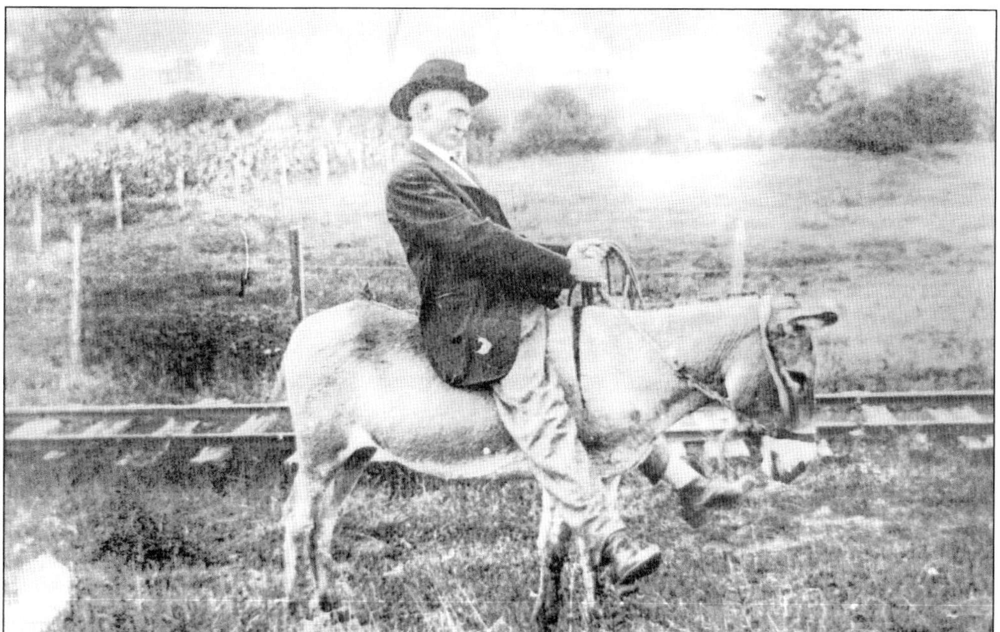

This photograph illustrates two different modes of transportation. The man, possibly W. B. Clay, rides a donkey. Just behind him are recently laid railway tracks. The town of Newland can be seen in the background. (Courtesy of the Avery County Historical Museum.)

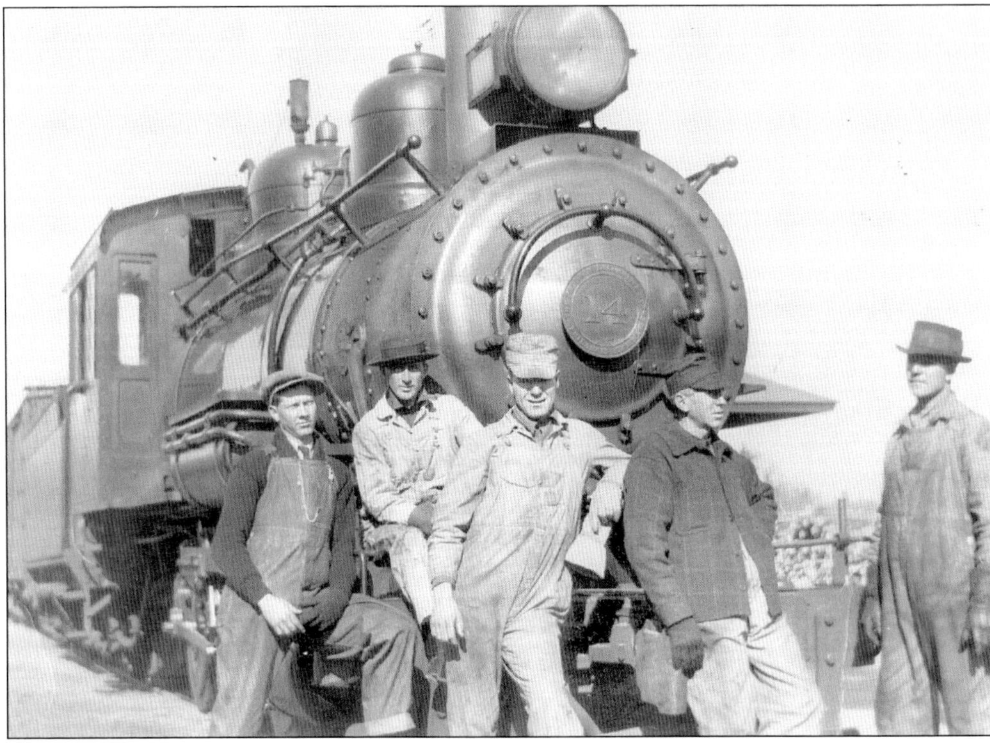

From left to right, Chick Farrell, Frank Angel, Ted Blalock, Engineer C. E. Miller, and Bill Johnston pose in front of Locomotive Number 14 of the East Tennessee and Western North Carolina Railroad. Built by the Baldwin Company, Number 14 was the last new locomotive purchased by the East Tennessee and Western North Carolina Railroad on July 21, 1919. This photograph was taken Thanksgiving Day 1924 in Pineola. (Courtesy of the Stewart family.)

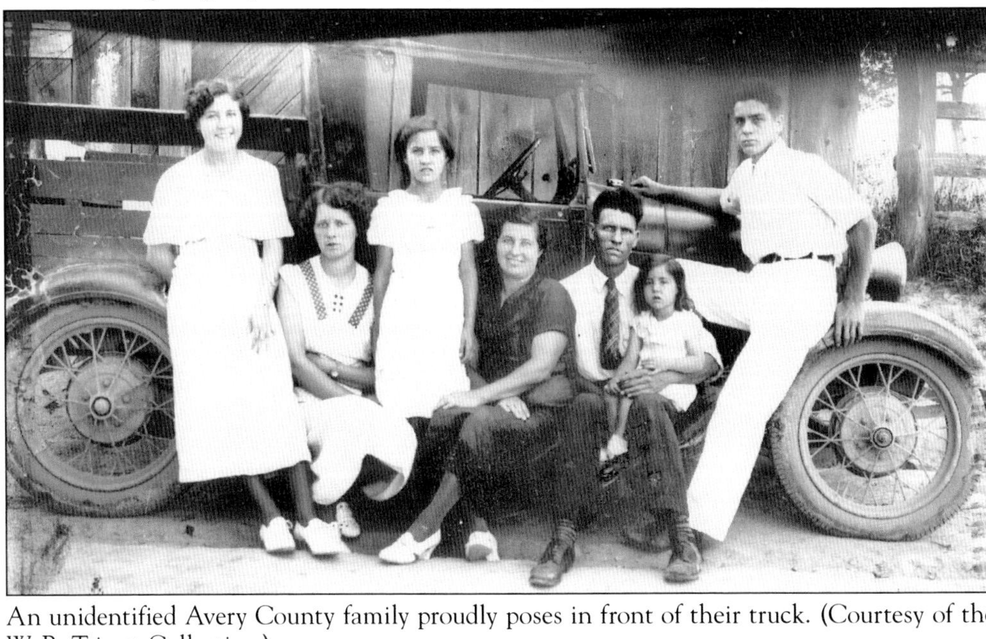

An unidentified Avery County family proudly poses in front of their truck. (Courtesy of the W. R. Trivett Collection.)

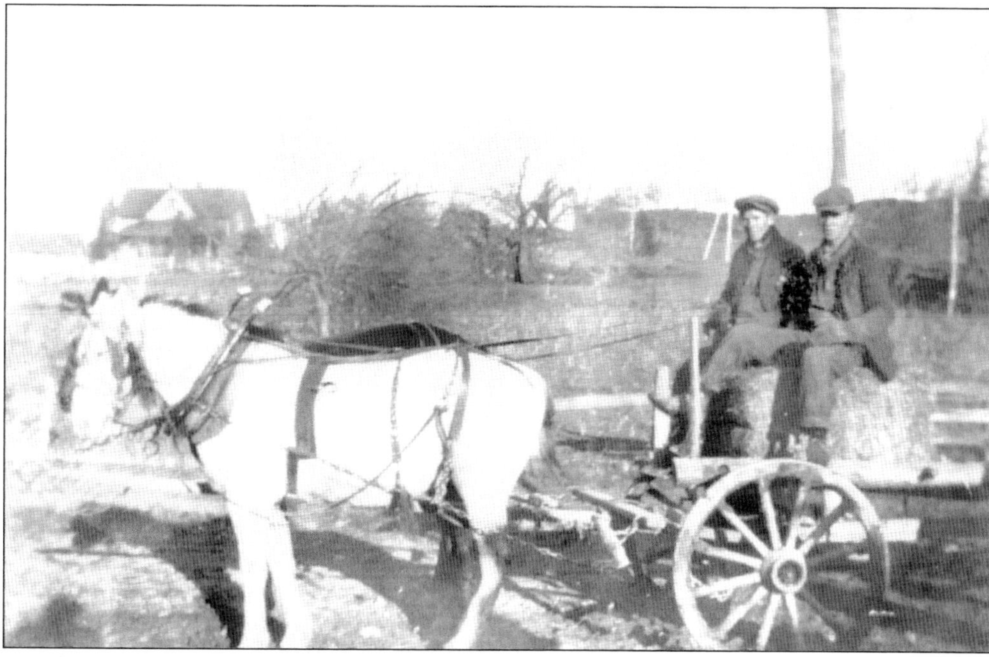

Members of the McGrath family use their horses and wagon, a form of transportation that remained important until well unto the mid-20th century. (Courtesy of the Avery County Historical Museum.)

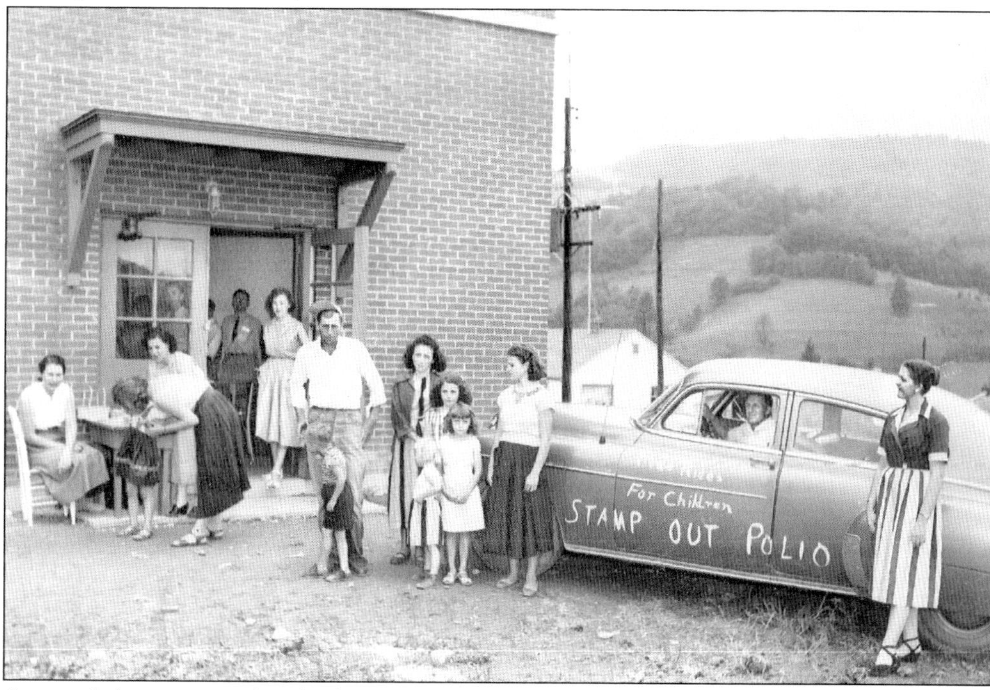

Automobiles were used as both as modes of transportation and as entertainment. In this photograph, taken at the Newland Elementary School, an automobile is being used to give children free rides if they would come and be vaccinated for polio. (Courtesy of the Avery County Historical Museum.)

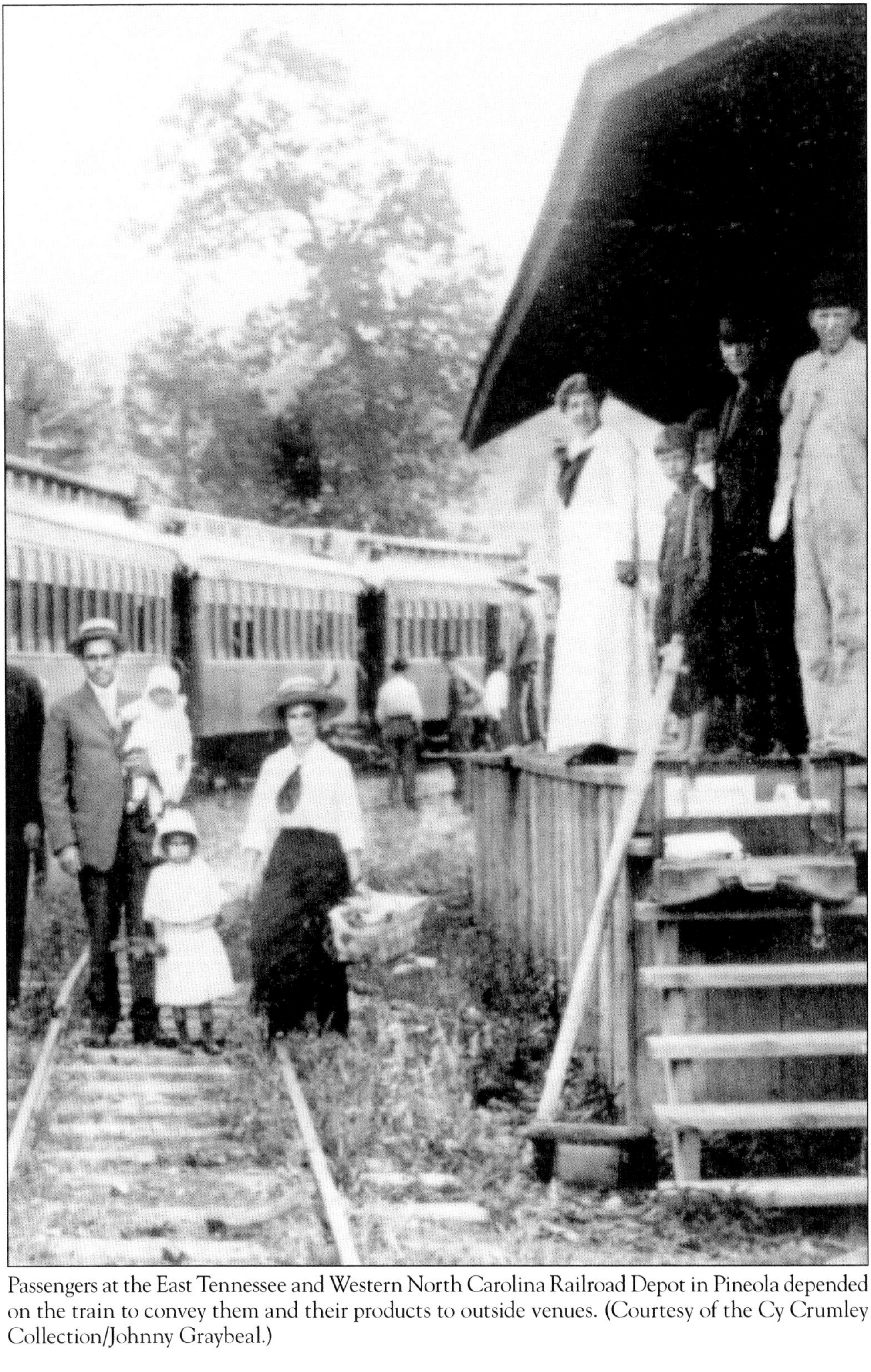

Passengers at the East Tennessee and Western North Carolina Railroad Depot in Pineola depended on the train to convey them and their products to outside venues. (Courtesy of the Cy Crumley Collection/Johnny Graybeal.)

Once the viaduct was completed around Grandfather Mountain in 1987, Gov. James G. Martin led a group of cars across the bridge in celebration. (Courtesy of Hugh Morton/Grandfather Mountain.)

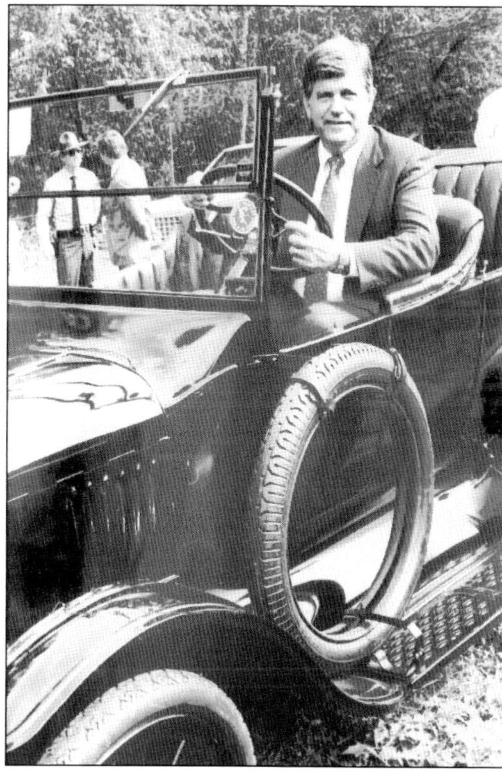

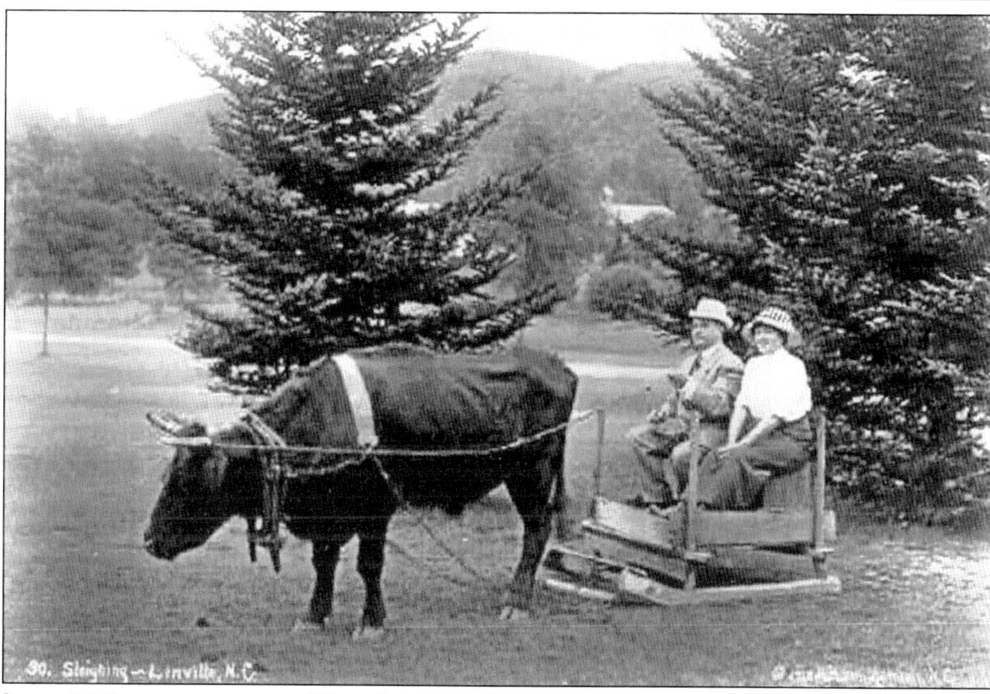

James P. Vinning, manager of Eseeola Inn, and a friend, Anne Watkins, strike a pose in an ox-pulled sled. In the early days of the resort, a sled race was a popular form of recreation. (Courtesy of the Library of Congress.)

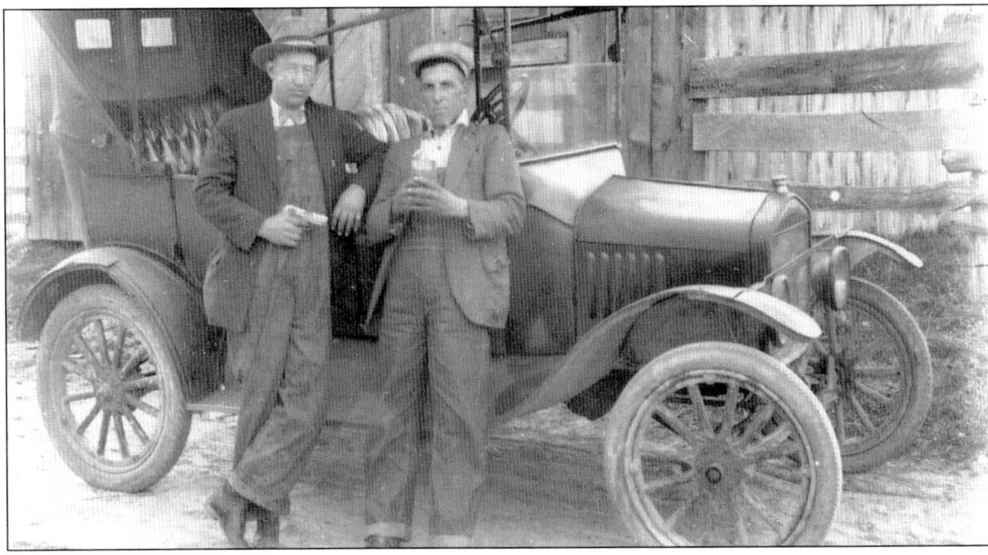

Posing with an automobile as a backdrop was a common practice in Avery County. In this W. R. Trivett photograph, it appears that a "law man" (with pistol) has possibly captured a "moonshiner" with his product, or these two gentlemen could just be imitating a scene they had seen in a movie. (Courtesy of the W. R. Trivett Collection.)

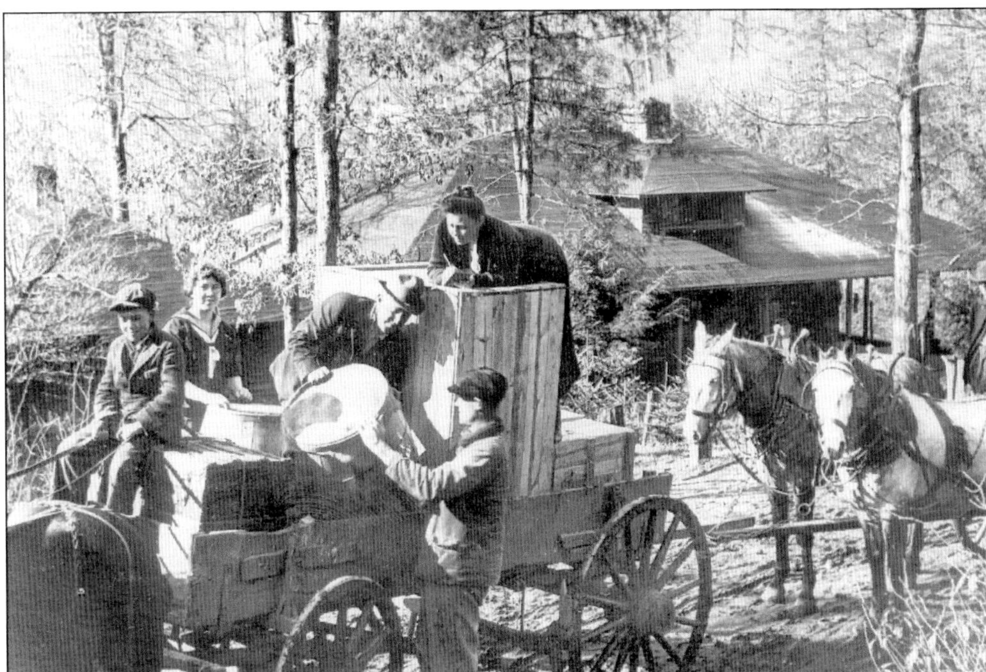

Before the arrival of automobiles, a horse-drawn wagon was the only way to ship and receive goods. Here Dr. Mary Sloop checks on the unloading of goods for the Sales Store in Crossnore. (Courtesy of the Avery County Historical Museum.)

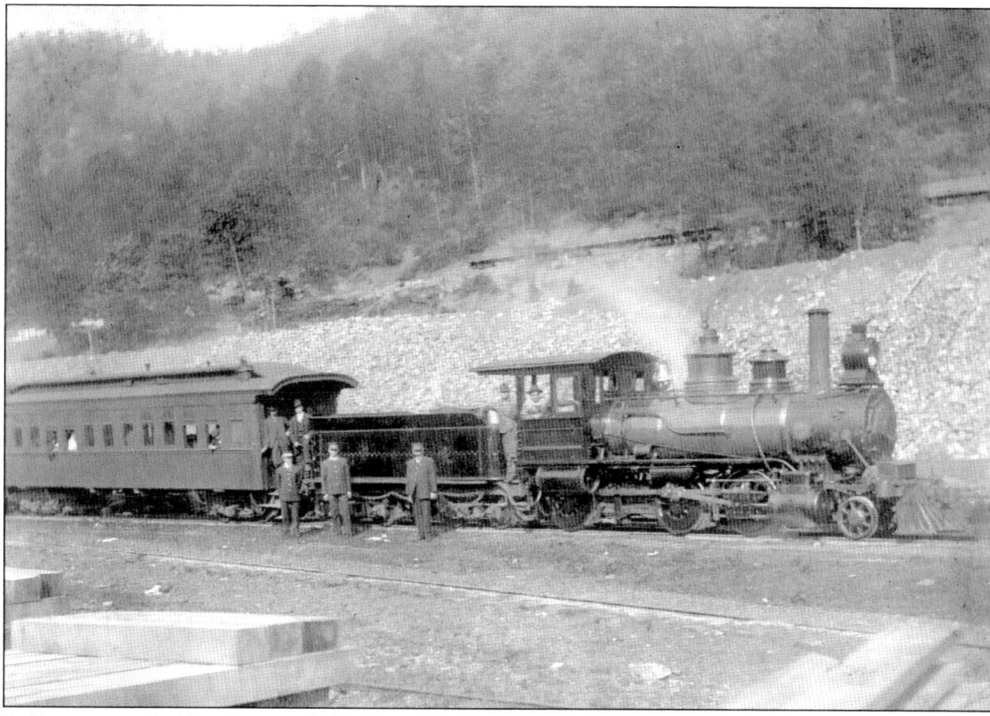

Pulling a coach, Number 1 of the East Tennessee and Western North Carolina Railroad waits at Cranberry, *c.* 1904. Arthur Allison is the engineer in the cab. (Courtesy of the Cy Crumley Collection/Johnny Graybeal.)

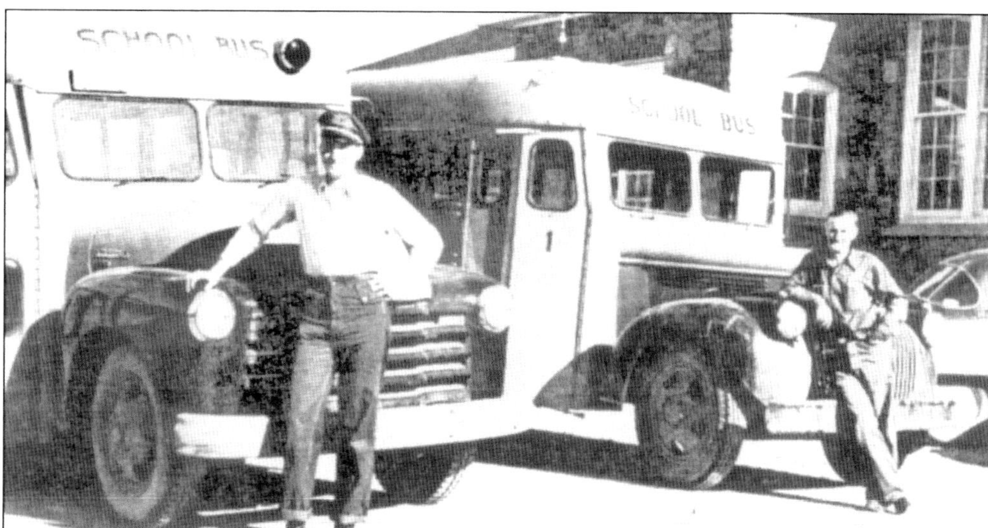

Jack Guy and Lance Cook were Beech Mountain school bus drivers *c.* 1953. Drivers were often required to put chains on the bus when the weather turned nasty, and they had to get students to school or home in hazardous weather, as classes were seldom cancelled. (Courtesy of Ralph E. Lentz II.)

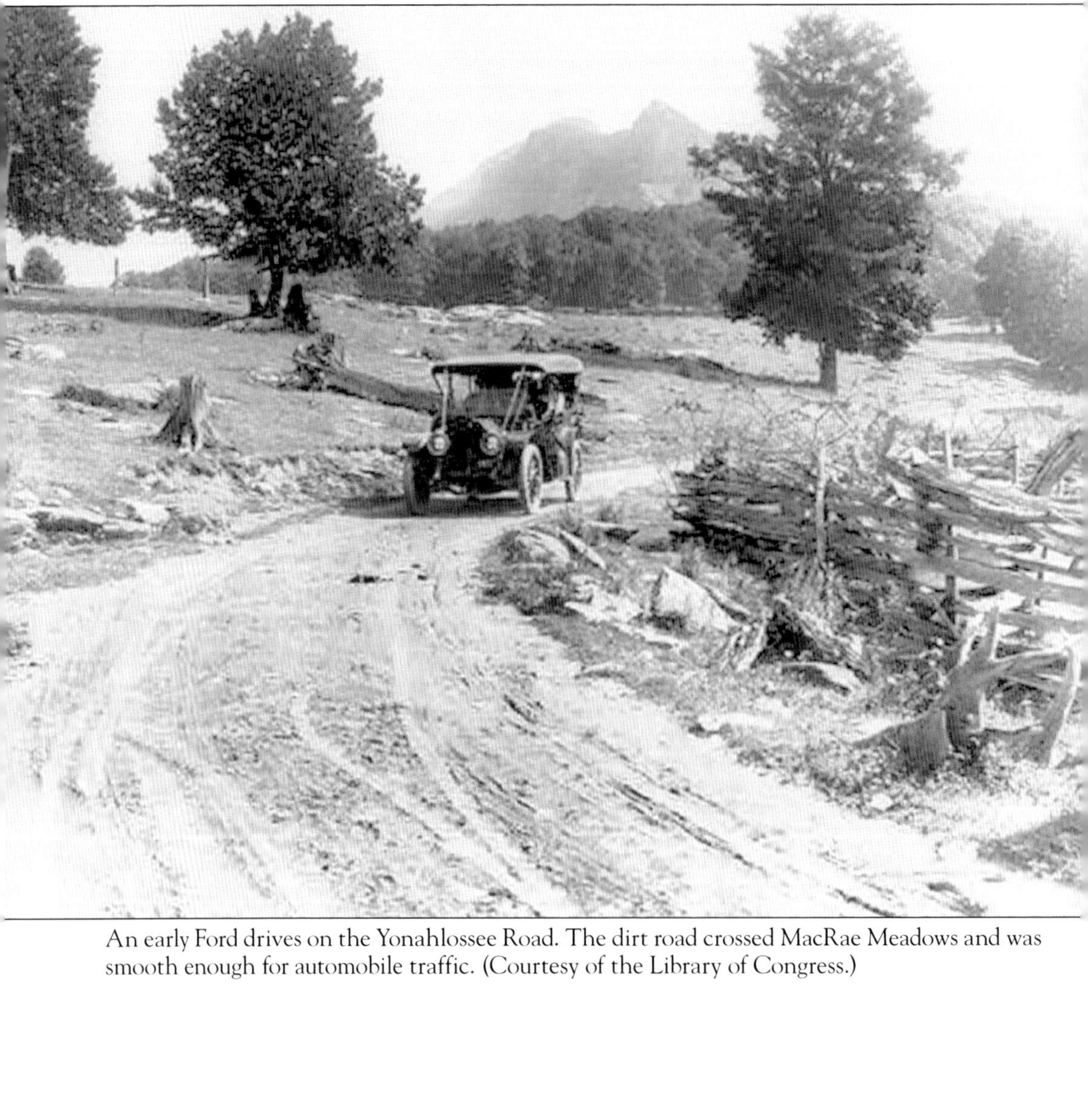

An early Ford drives on the Yonahlossee Road. The dirt road crossed MacRae Meadows and was smooth enough for automobile traffic. (Courtesy of the Library of Congress.)

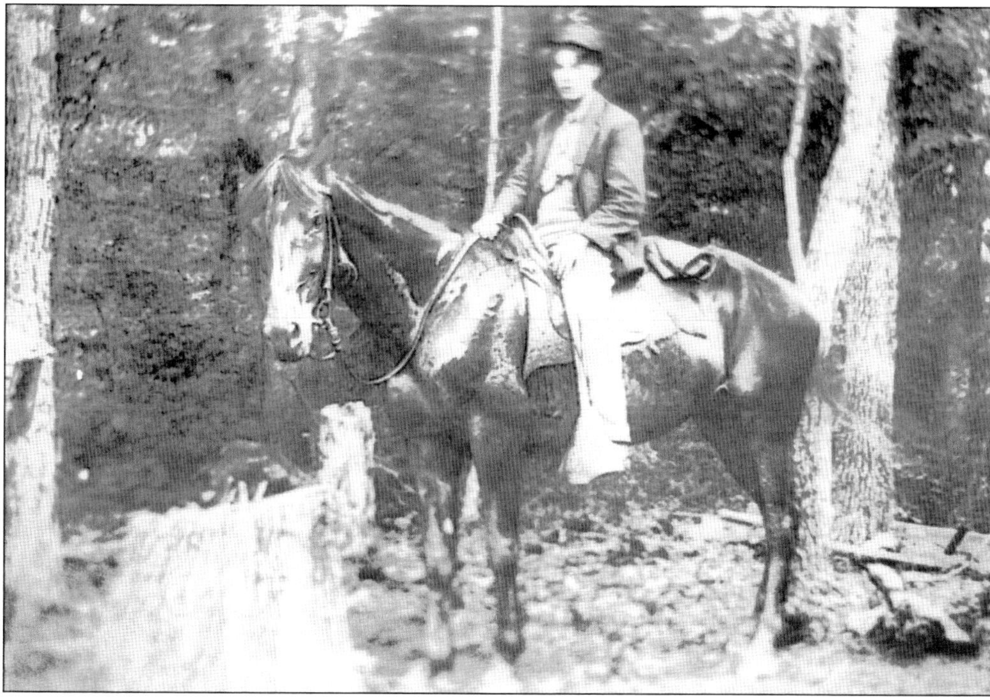

Aaron Teams employs an early mode of transportation, his horse. (Courtesy of Tense Banks.)

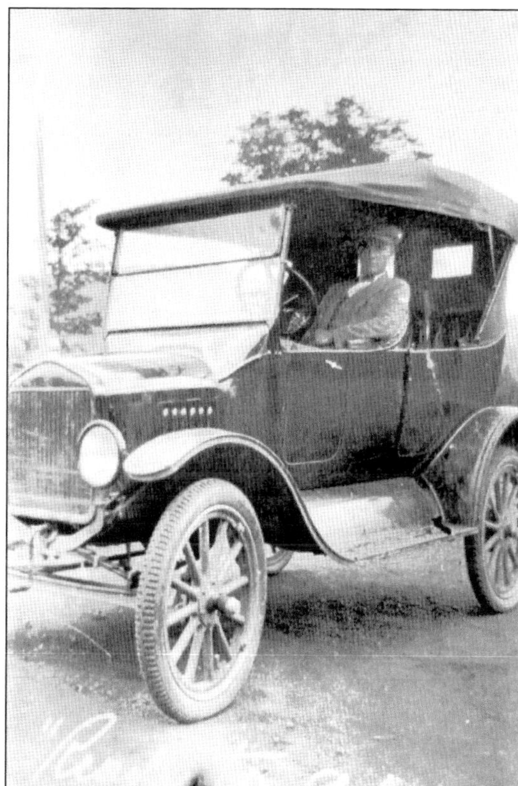

This early photograph of William Burleson in his automobile is entitled "Ready to go." (Courtesy of Beatrice Buchanan.)

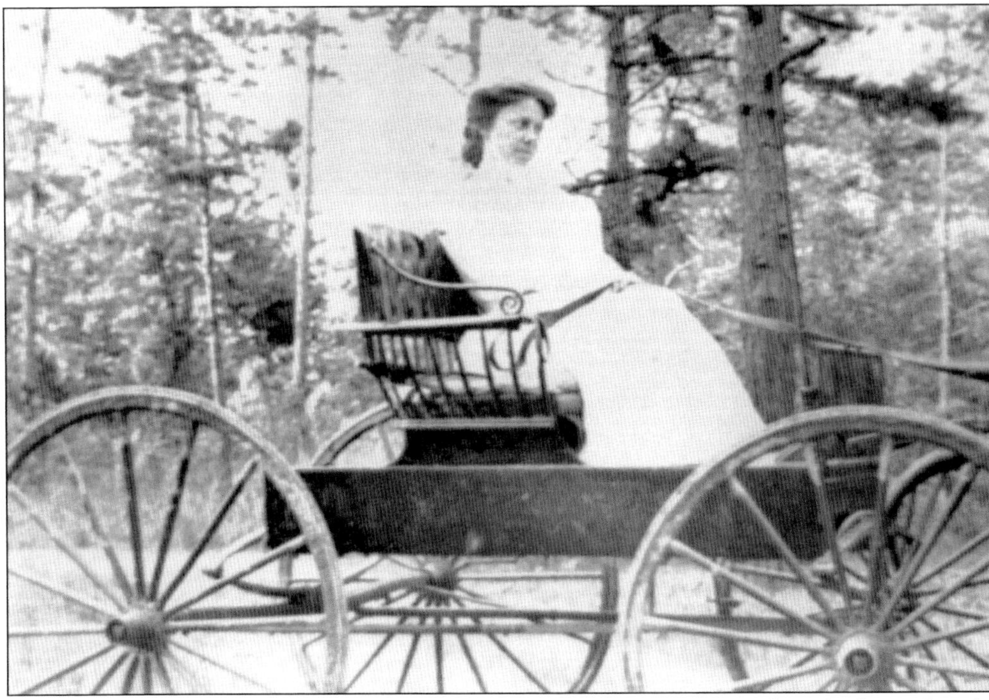

A young Mary Sloop is here seen in her carriage. She and Dr. Eustace Sloop both employed a variety of transportation methods in order to reach their patients. Her side-saddle is on display in the Avery County Historical Museum. (Courtesy of the Avery County Historical Museum.)

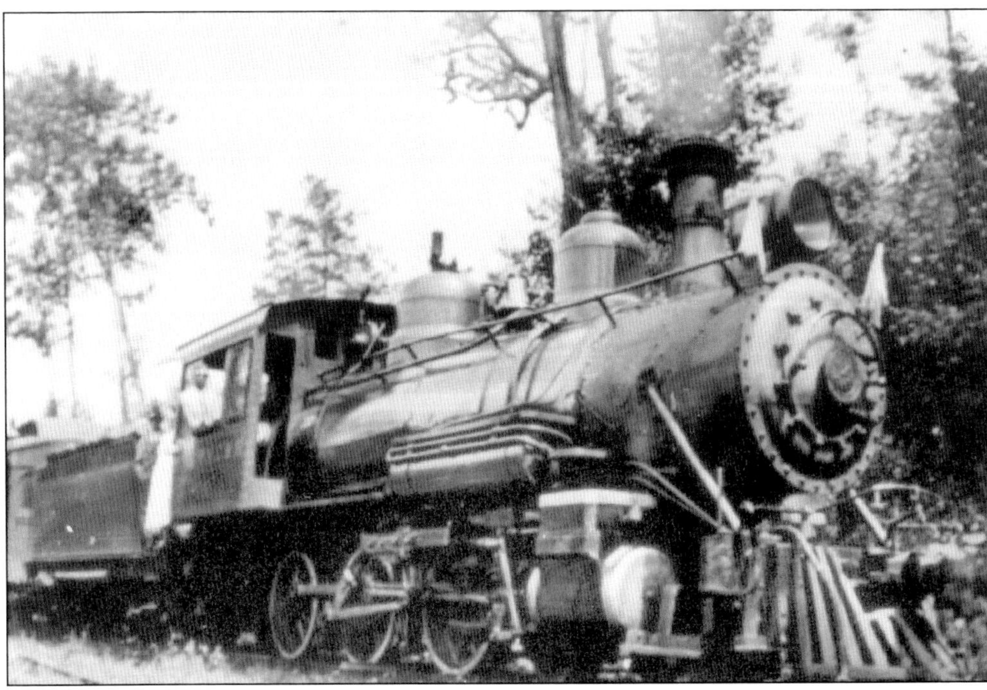

East Tennessee and Western North Carolina Railroad locomotive Number 14 stops in Linville Gap in 1932. (Courtesy of the Cy Crumley Collection/Johnny Graybeal.)

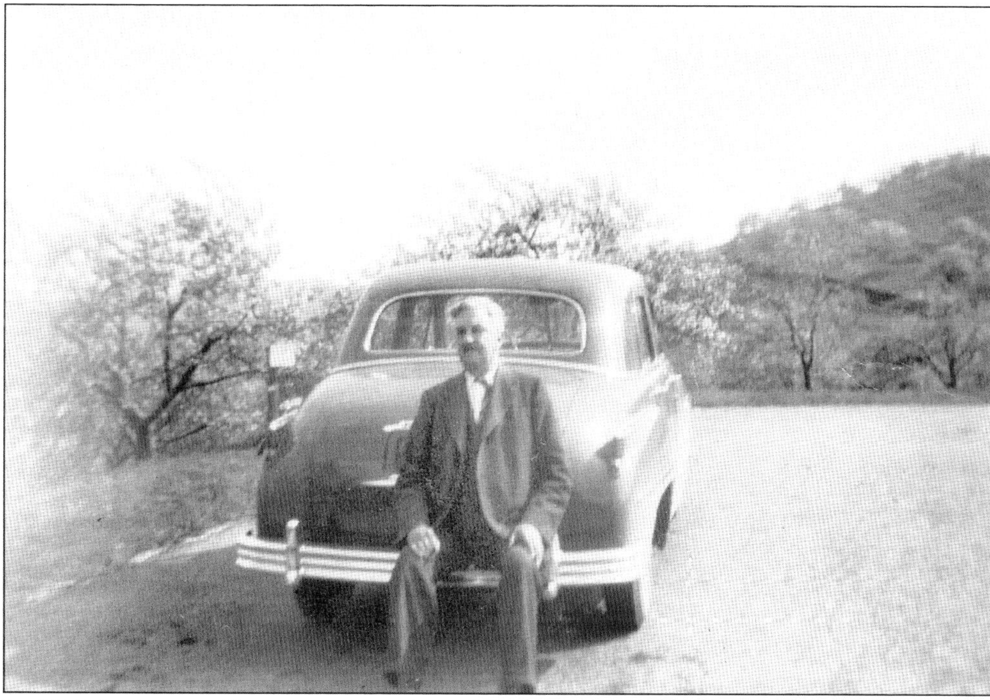

Dr. W. B. Burleson and his car are shown here. As a doctor, he could afford "modern transportation," and it was an essential part of his practice, allowing him to reach patients as quickly as possible. (Courtesy of the Avery County Historical Museum.)

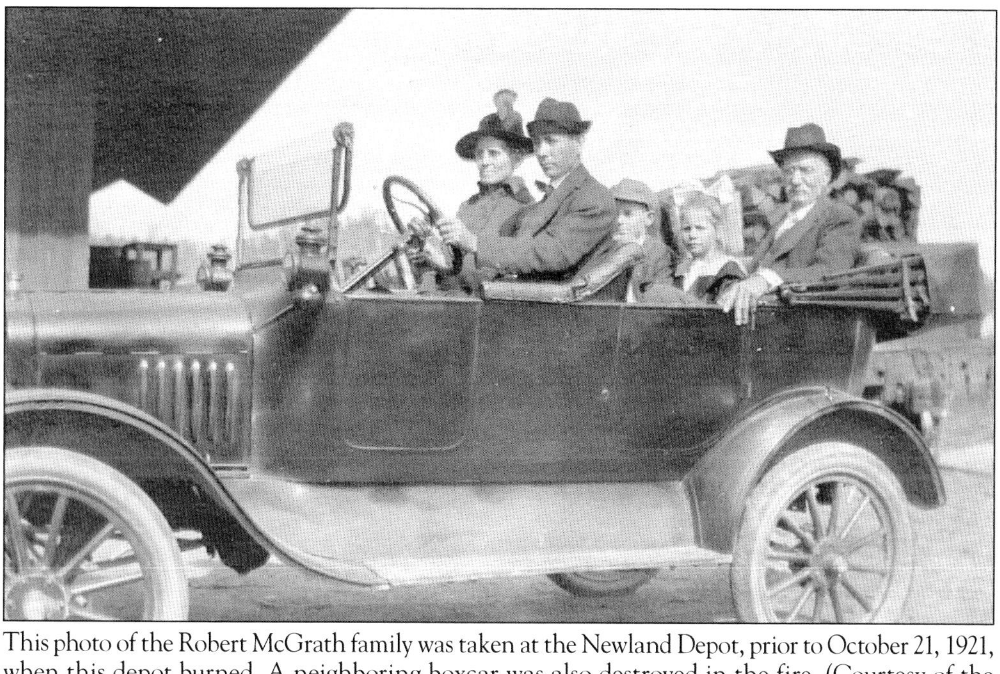

This photo of the Robert McGrath family was taken at the Newland Depot, prior to October 21, 1921, when this depot burned. A neighboring boxcar was also destroyed in the fire. (Courtesy of the Avery County Historical Museum.)

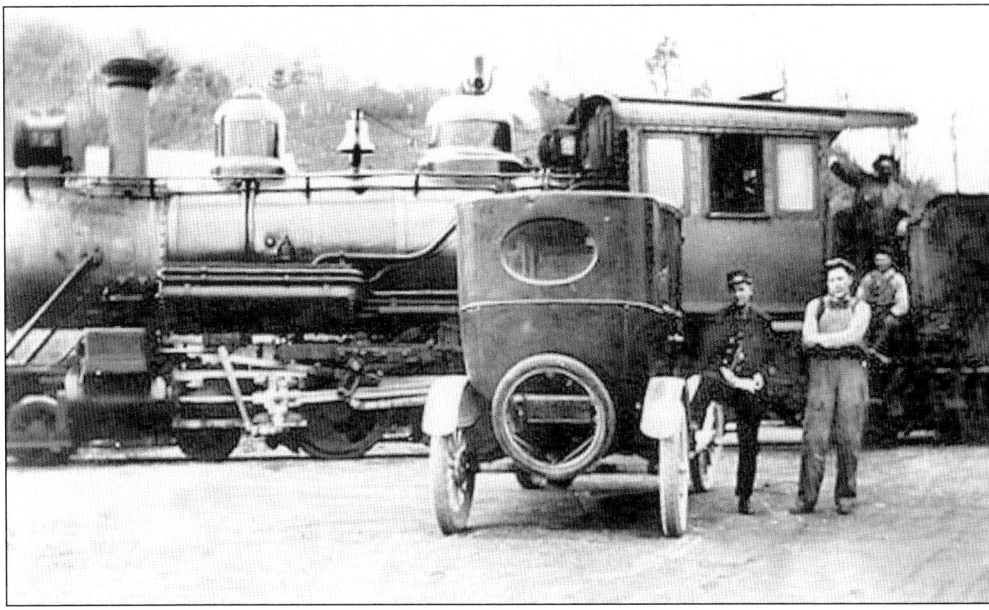

Nat Fletcher's Model T and the East Tennessee and Western North Carolina Railroad's locomotive Number 12 in Newland demonstrate varied transportation methods. Nat Fletcher was railroad agent at the Newland Depot from 1917 until 1937. (Courtesy of the Cy Crumley Collection/Johnny Graybeal.)

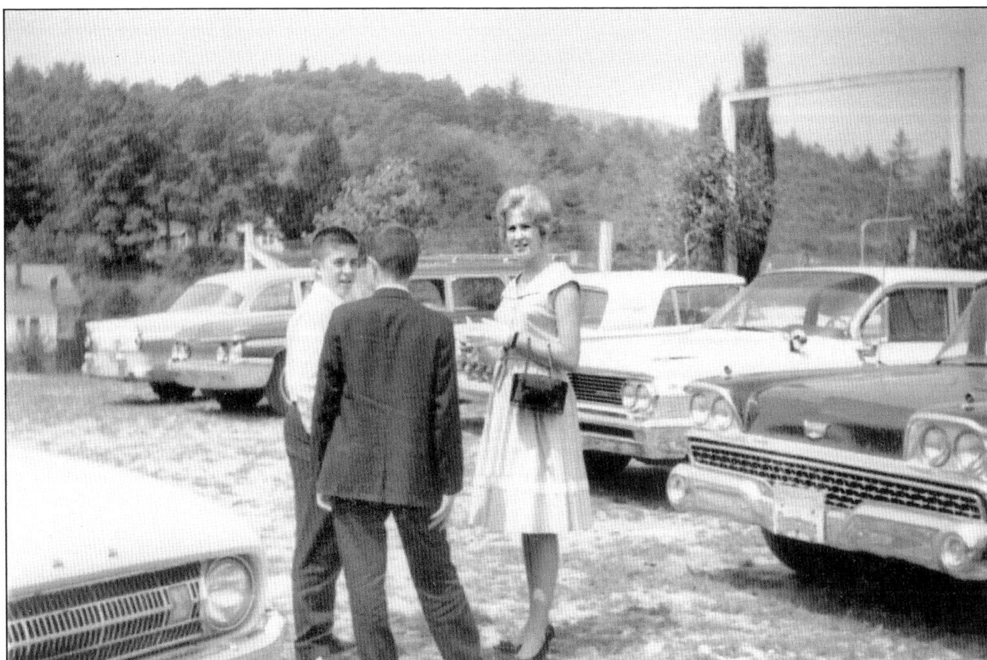

Jimmy Thompson (left), John Thompson (center), and Susie Loven visit in the parking lot of the Pine Grove United Methodist Church, where a variety of cars can be seen. (Courtesy of the Phillips family.)

Six
EVENTS AND MUSIC

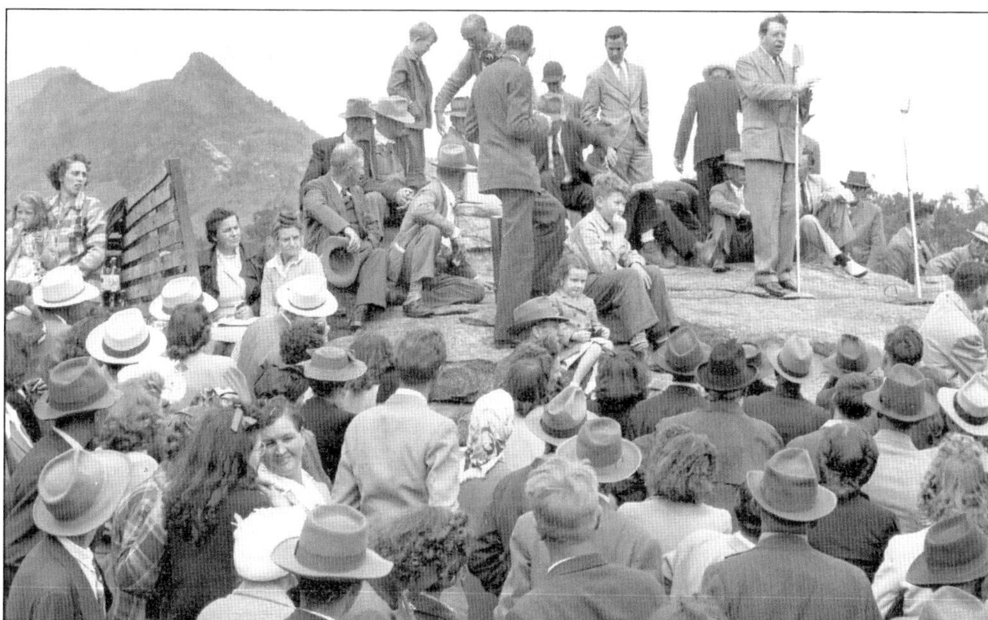

Singing on the Mountain at Grandfather has been a popular event since 1924. The festival features gospel musical groups and draws listeners from all over the country. Here Gov. J. Melville Broughton prepares to deliver some remarks. (Courtesy of Hugh Morton/Grandfather Mountain.)

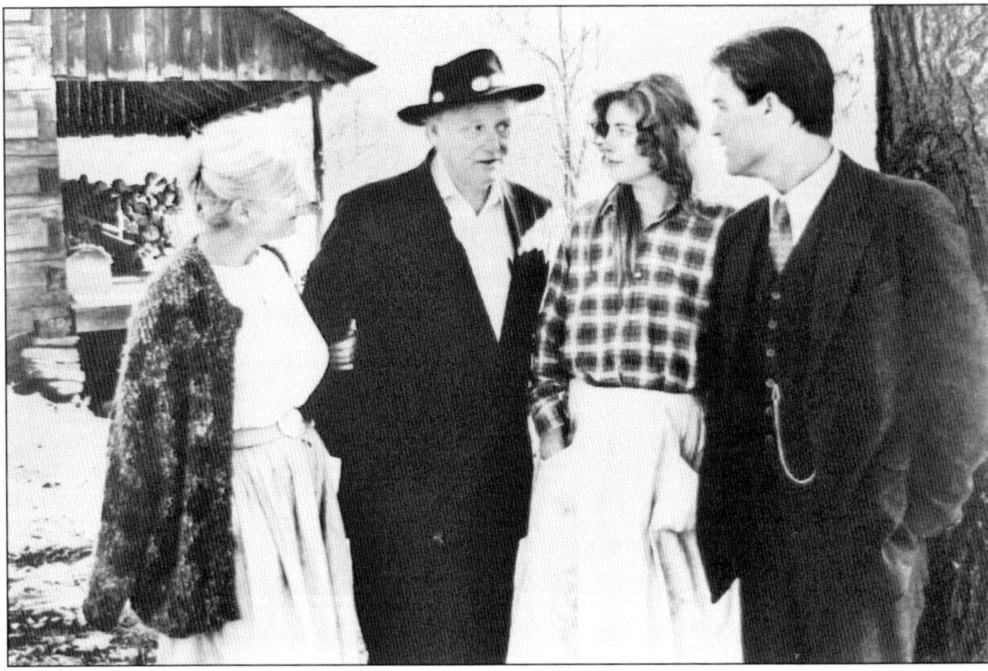

From left to right, Rosemary Harris, John Ehle, Kelly McGillis, and Kurt Russell are seen here on the set of *The Winter People*, based on Ehle's novel and filmed in Plumtree in 1989. Several sets, including a clock tower, were constructed for the film and remained standing for over 10 years. (Courtesy of the Avery County Historical Museum.)

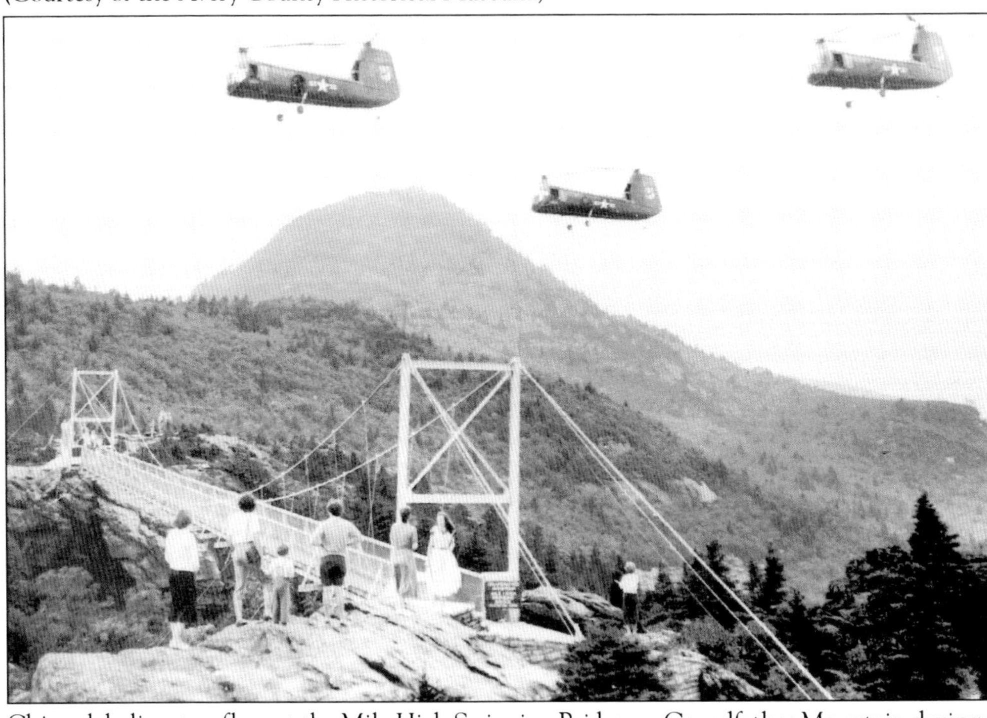

Chinook helicopters fly past the Mile High Swinging Bridge on Grandfather Mountain during a training exercise in the 1950s. (Courtesy of Hugh Morton/Grandfather Mountain.)

Audry Guy Estep (left) and Francis Guy Estep were sisters whose husbands were brothers, hence their double maiden and married names. W. R. Trivett, who took this photograph around 1932, made the banjo that Audry is holding. The instrument had a traditional groundhog-hide head, believed to create the best sound. (Courtesy of the W. R. Trivett Collection.)

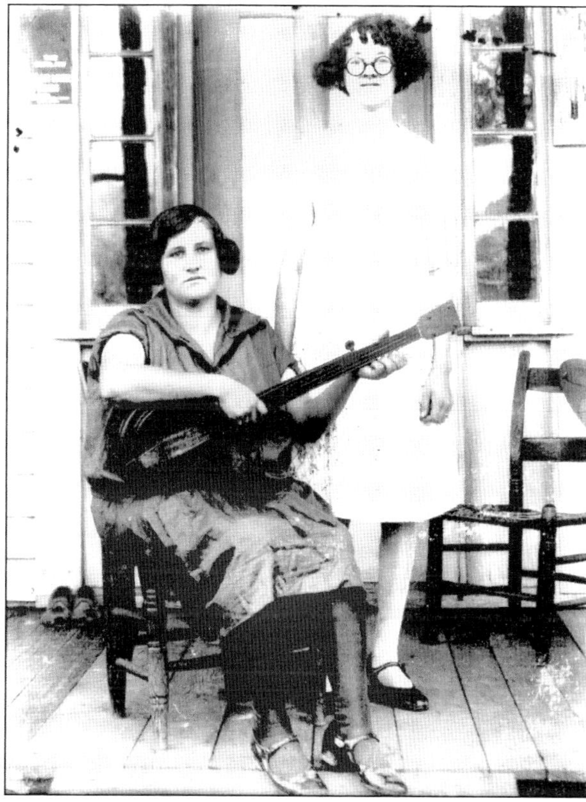

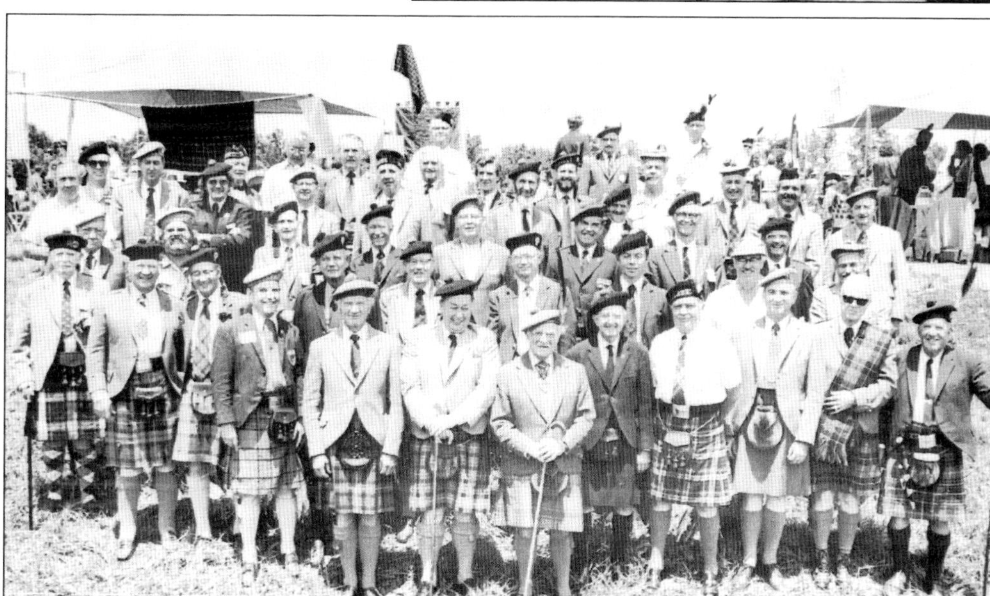

Scottish clan chiefs gather at Grandfather Mountain in 1973. The Highland Games at Grandfather is the largest such event in the country and continues to be a major event that draws tourists from around the world and contributes to the local economy. (Courtesy of Hugh Morton/Grandfather Mountain.)

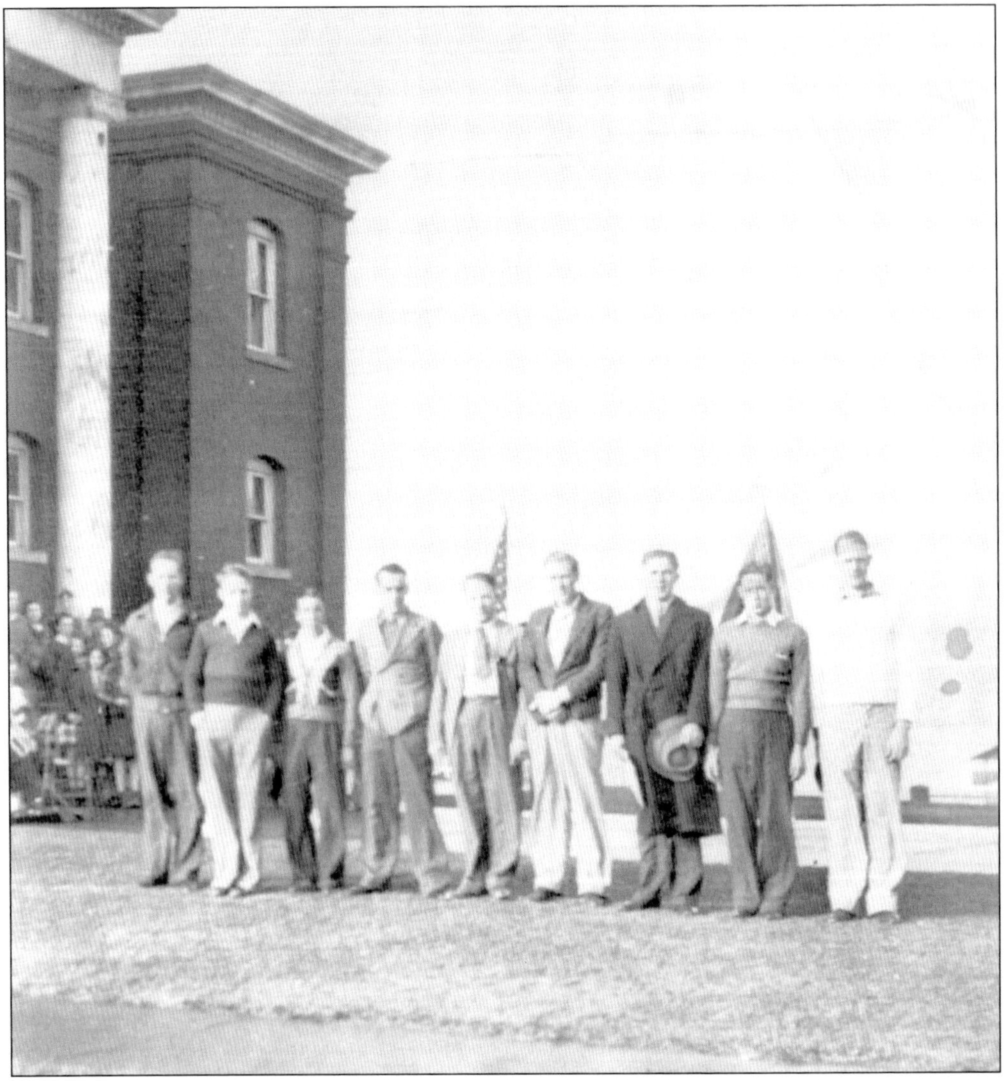

Some of the first men in Avery County drafted during World War II paused to have their photograph made. Pictured here from left to right are four unidentified, Dewey Calloway, Bob Church, Luke Hartley, Nat Johnson, and Frank Mayberry. This image was taken on the grounds of the Avery County Court House with the high school band in the background on the left. (Courtesy of Howell Campbell.)

These patriotic citizens of Avery County were captured by W. R. Trivett. (Courtesy of the W. R. Trivett Collection.)

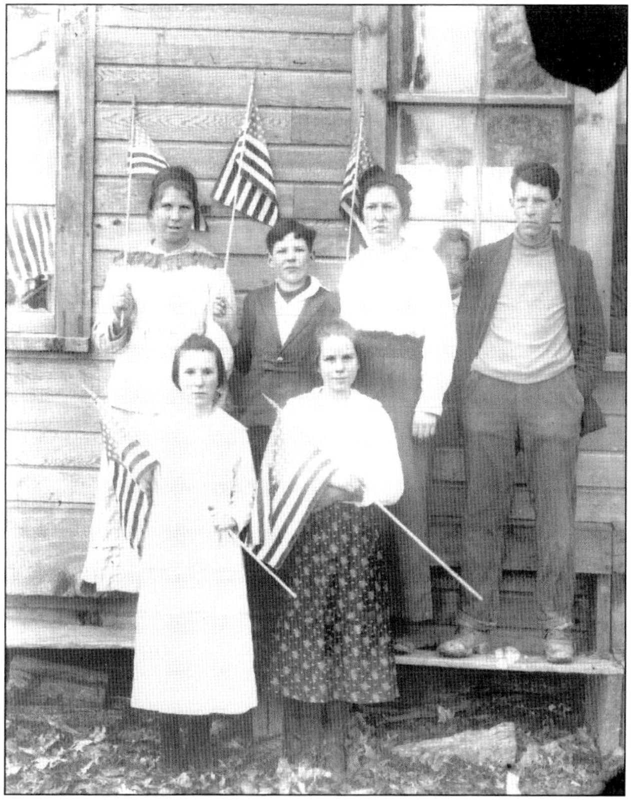

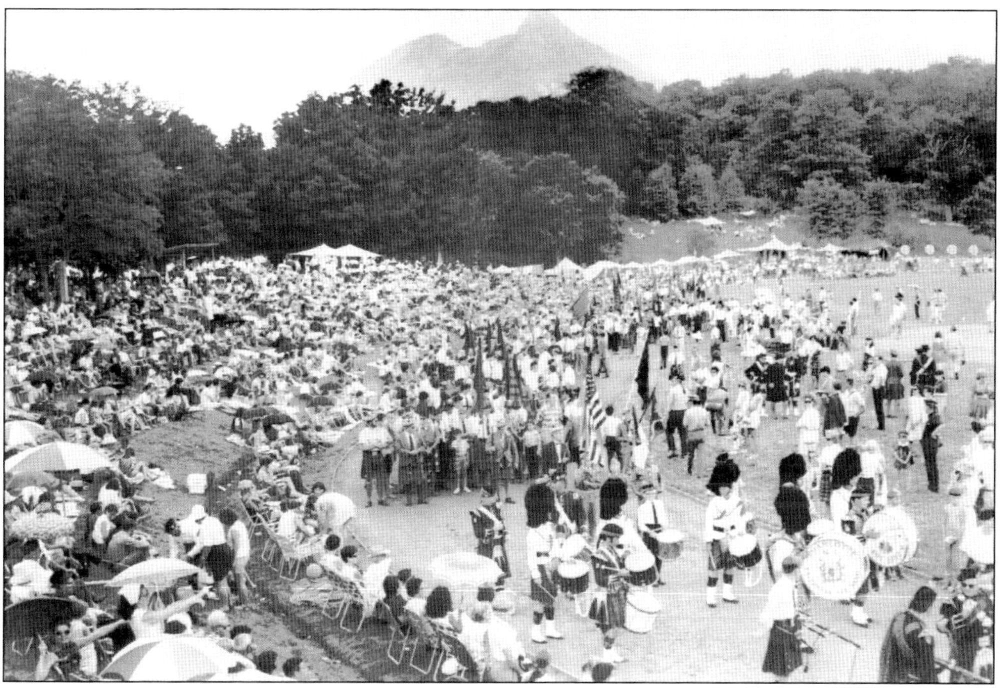

A parade of Highland bands and clan chiefs prepares to kick off the festivities at a Grandfather Mountain Highland Games in the 1950s. (Courtesy of Hugh Morton/Grandfather Mountain.)

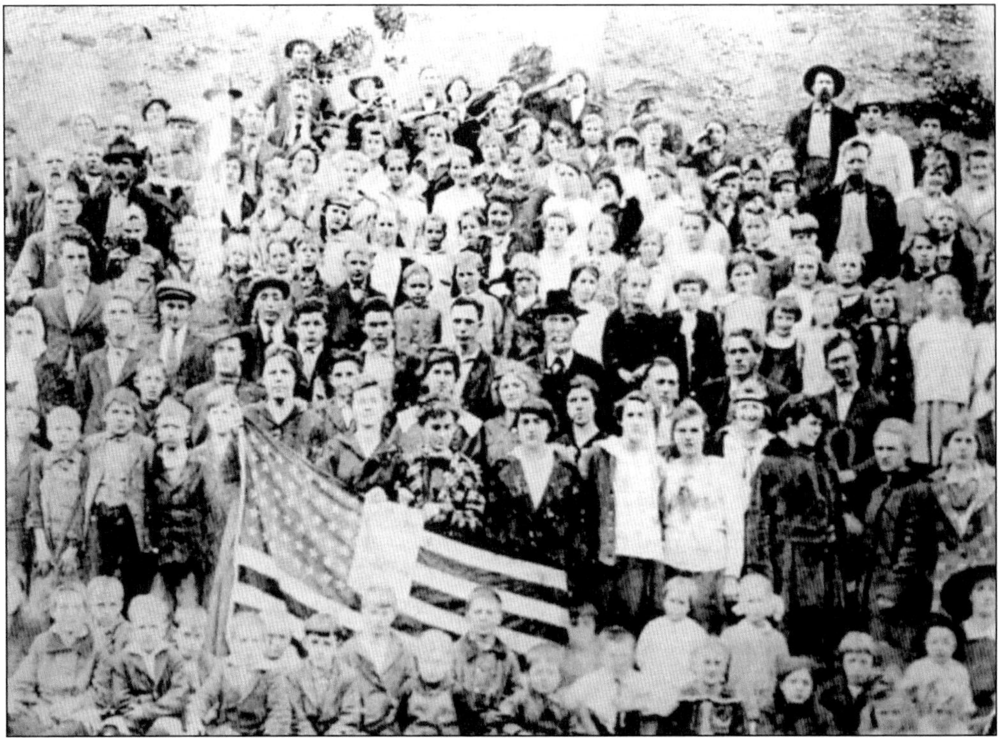

At a Fourth of July celebration in Crossnore, c. 1911, citizens gather around the flag. Crossnore still features a lively Independence Day celebration each year. (Courtesy of the Avery County Historical Museum.)

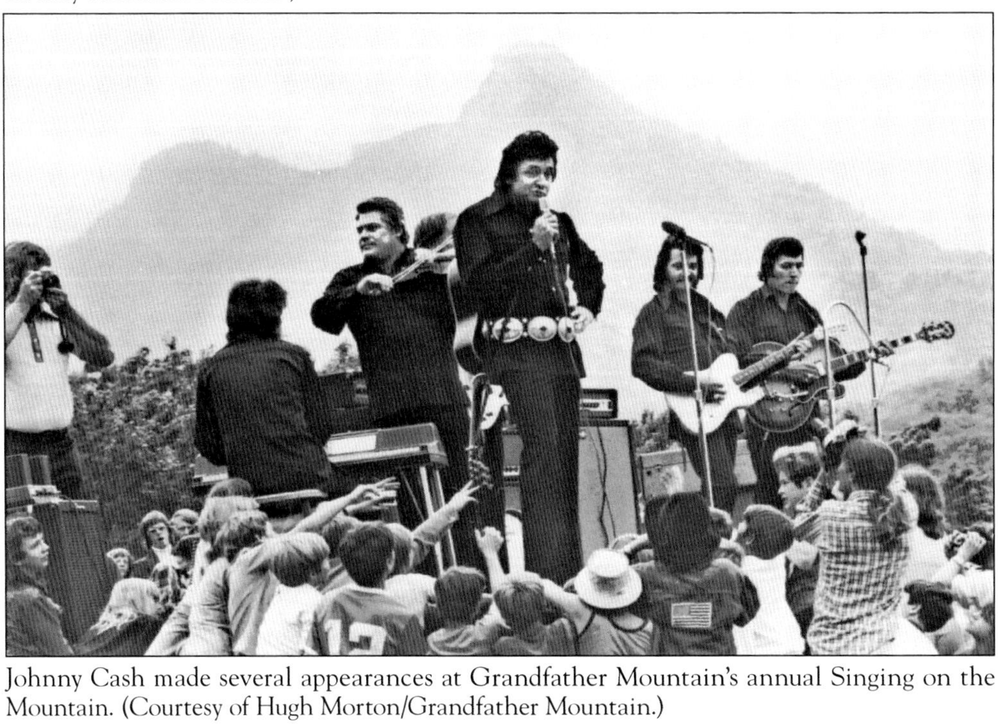

Johnny Cash made several appearances at Grandfather Mountain's annual Singing on the Mountain. (Courtesy of Hugh Morton/Grandfather Mountain.)

Thanks to rail service and mail-order catalogs, Avery County citizens could purchase commercially produced instruments, such as guitars, to add to the county's musical traditions and to entertain family and friends. (Courtesy of the W. R. Trivett Collection.)

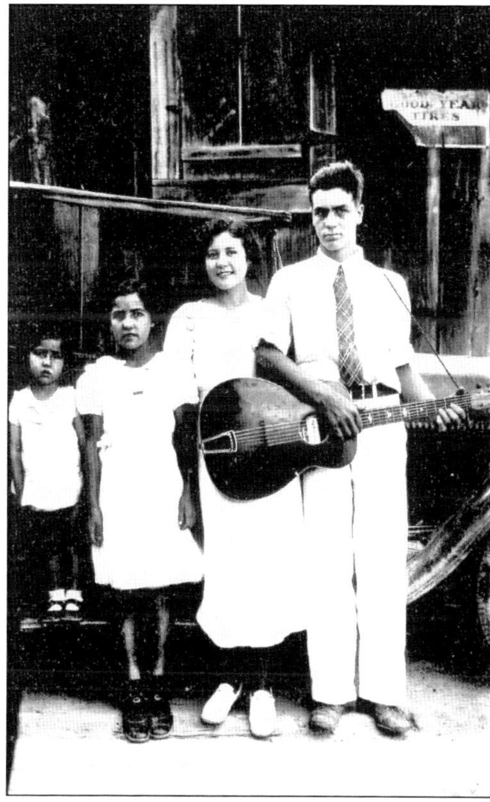

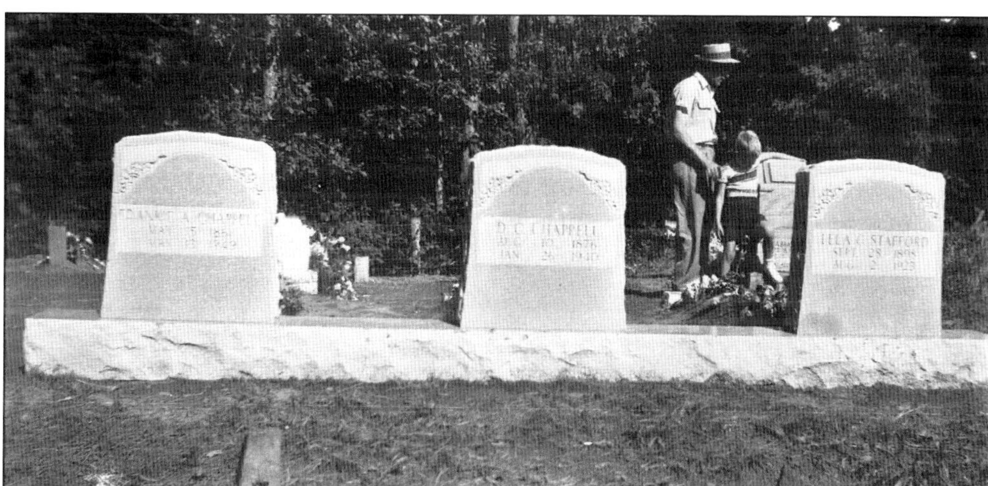

During Decoration Day at the Ashley Chapel Cemetery, family members clean graves and honor the deceased with flowers. (Courtesy of the Avery County Historical Museum.)

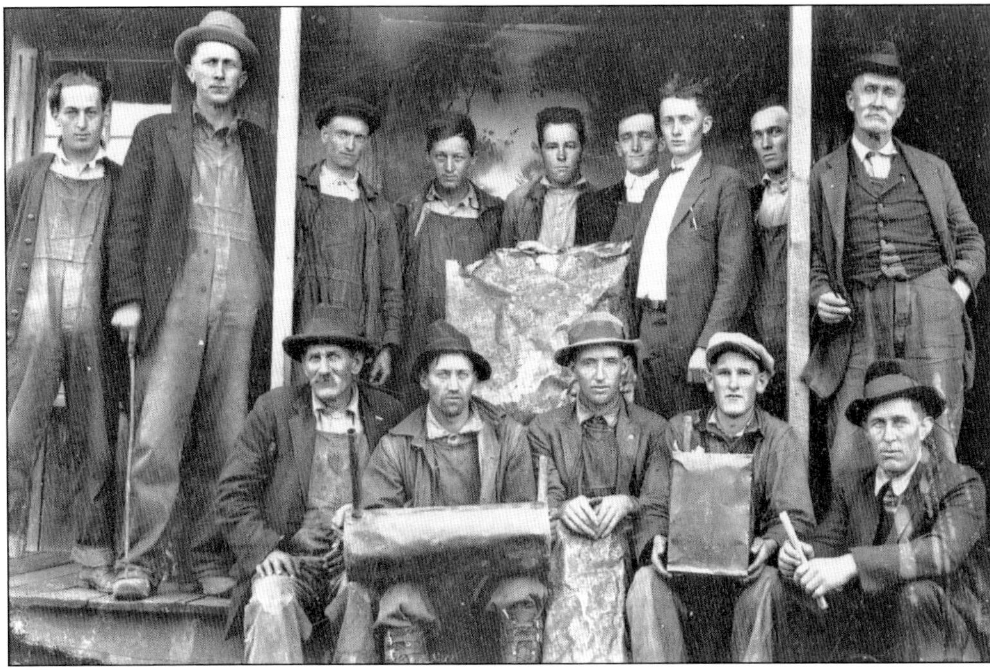

"Revenuers" on Dark Ridge pose with the remains of a moonshine still they discovered and destroyed in 1925. Pictured here from left to right are (seated) Bill McCloud, Fred Moore, George Harmon, Pashley McCloud, and Everett Cook; (standing) Jimmy Norris, Tillet Gryder, John Parlier, Grady Norris, Clyde Gryder, Ivey Storie, Deputy Sheriff Lawrence Storie, Cloyd Parlier, and Marion Storie. (Courtesy of the W. R. Trivett Collection.)

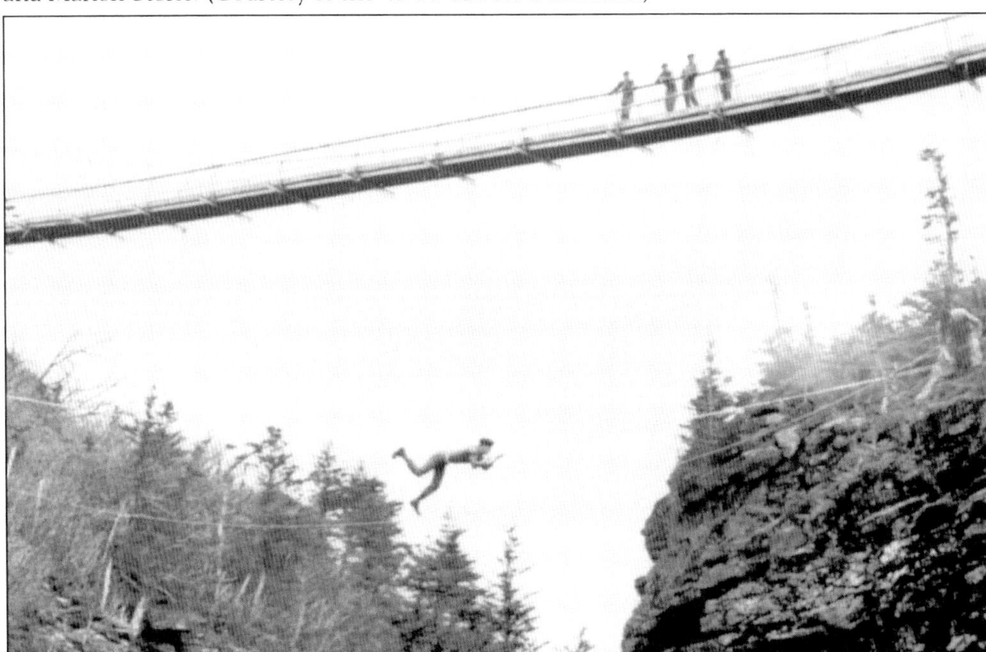

U.S. Army soldiers practice rappelling underneath the Swinging Bridge on Grandfather Mountain. (Courtesy of Hugh Morton/Grandfather Mountain.)

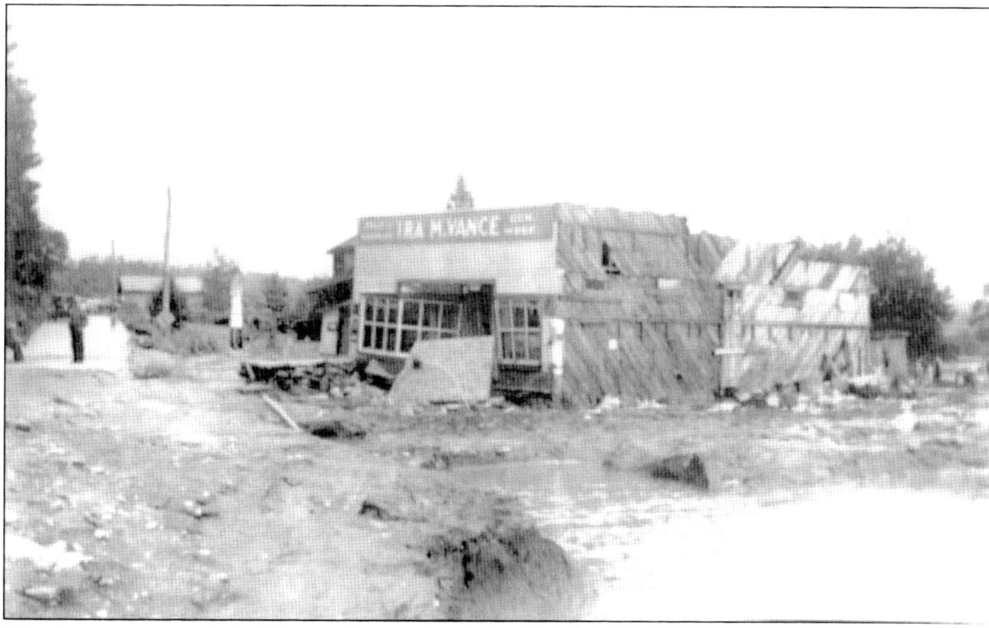

The devastating flood of 1940 wiped out railroads, highways, homes, and businesses such as the Pineola store pictured here. Many never recovered from this tragedy. (Courtesy of the Stewart family.)

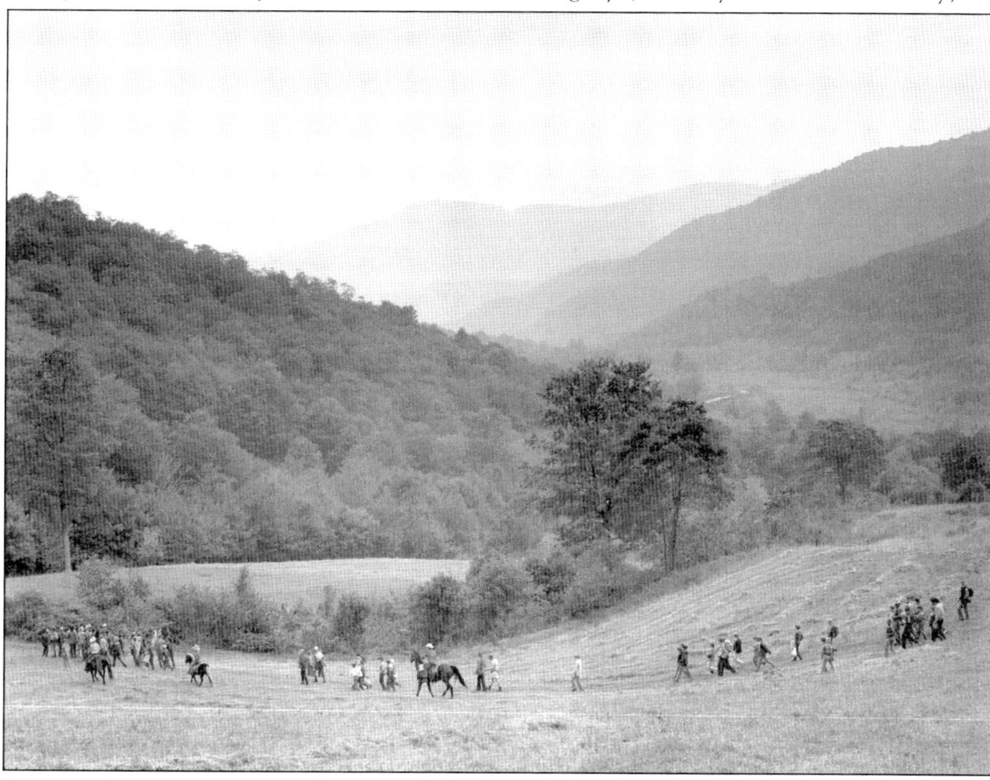

A group of interpreters retrace the steps of the Overmountain Men, patriot soldiers who helped turn the tide of the American Revolution with their defeat of Maj. Patrick Ferguson and his Tory forces at King's Mountain on October 7, 1780. (Courtesy of the Avery County Historical Museum.)

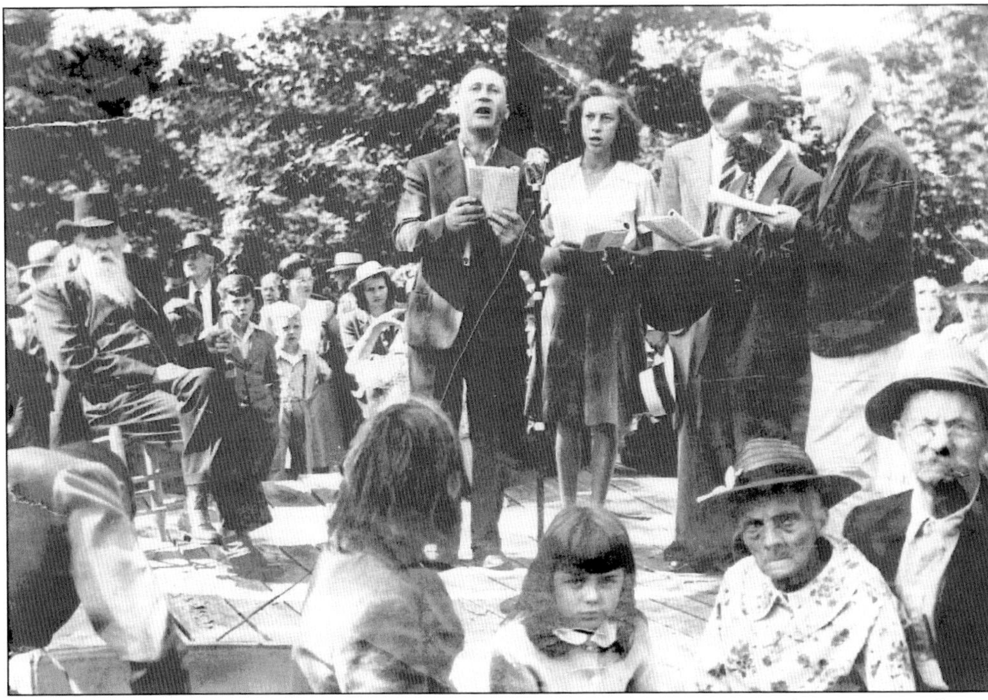

The faithful gather to hear the Word proclaimed through song at Singing on the Mountain during the 1930s. (Courtesy of Hugh Morton/Grandfather Mountain.)

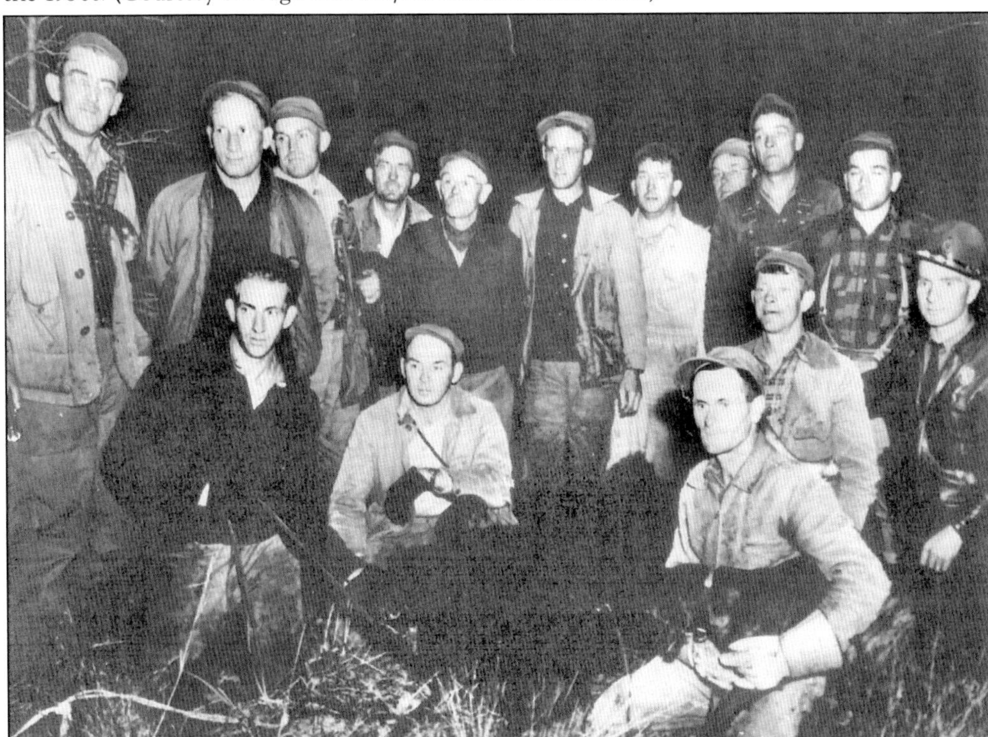

A group of local bear hunters display their prize. (Courtesy of Betty Wright Erhart.)

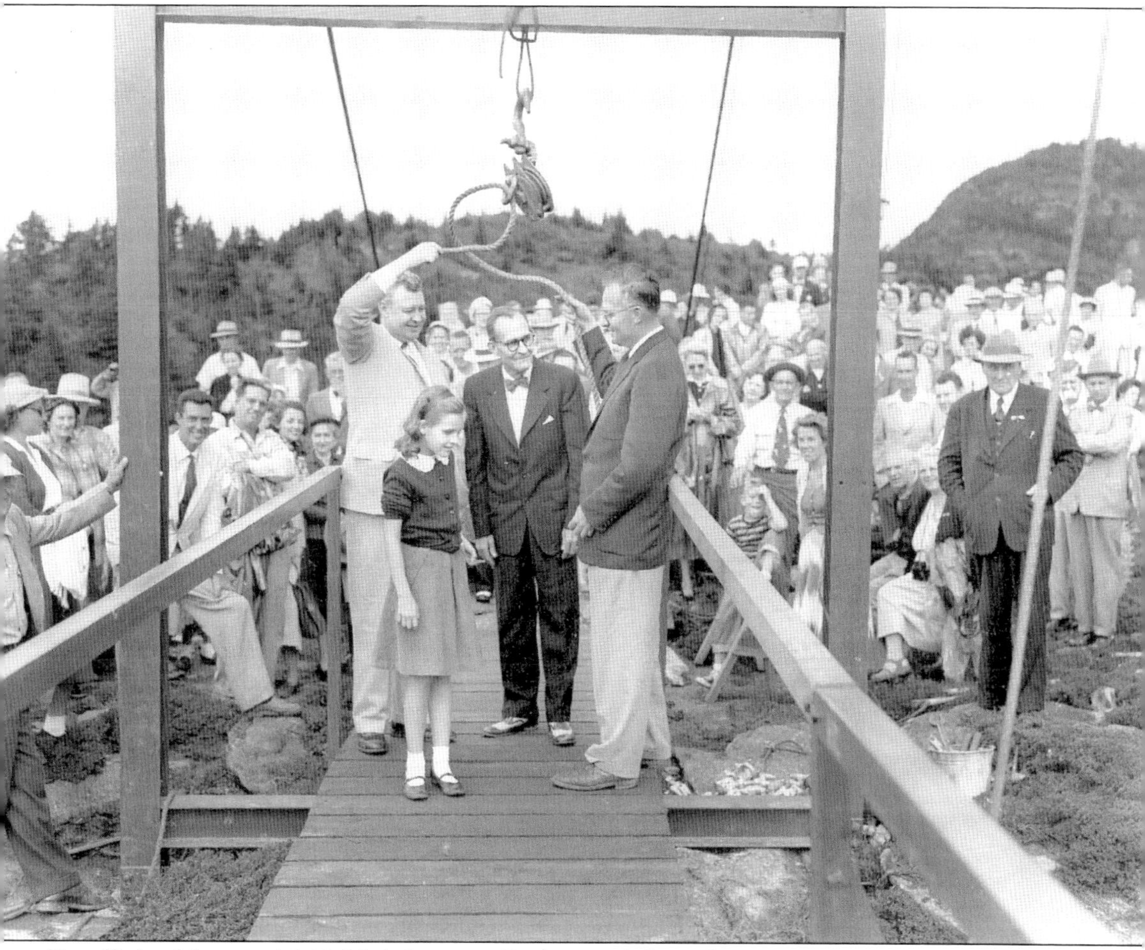

Grandfather Mountain's Mile High Swinging Bridge was dedicated on September 2, 1952, by North Carolina governor William B. Umstead. (Courtesy of Hugh Morton/Grandfather Mountain.)

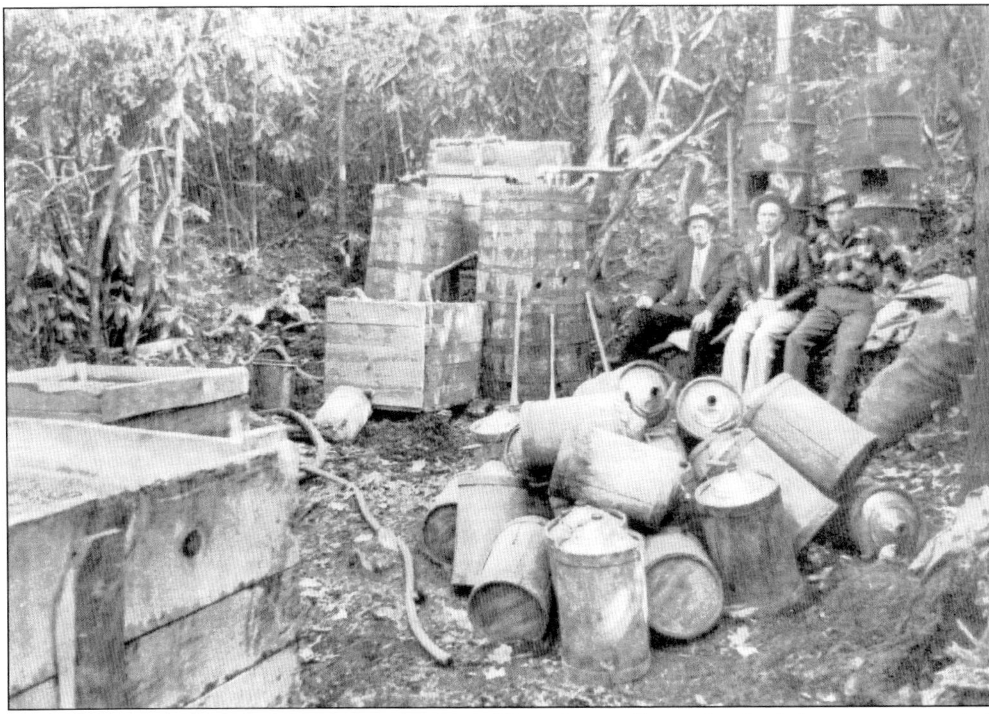

Raids on liquor stills were common in the days of Prohibition. Even after Prohibition was repealed, moonshining remained illegal because the distillers paid the government no taxes on the whiskey. This still was found on Grandfather Mountain in the mid-1950s. Sheriff Wilburn Hughes (on left), Stuart Buchanan (center), and Deputy Julian Greene (on right) are shown here. (Courtesy of the Avery County Historical Museum.)

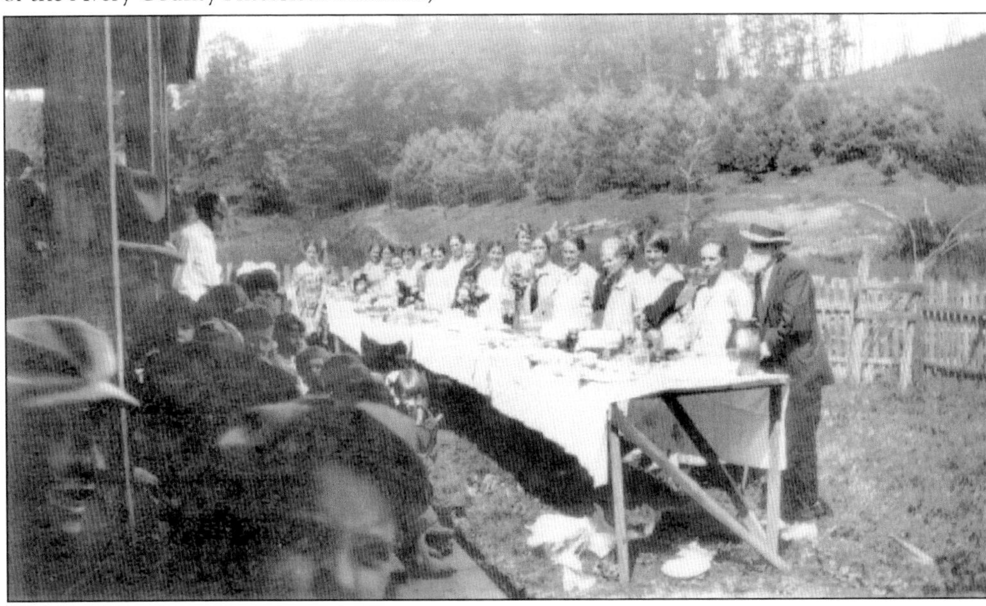

A birthday party for Joe Ollis featured an impressive covered-dish dinner. Even more impressive were his 89 grandchildren and 54 great-grandchildren; many of them were present at the party. (Courtesy of Doyle Ollis.)

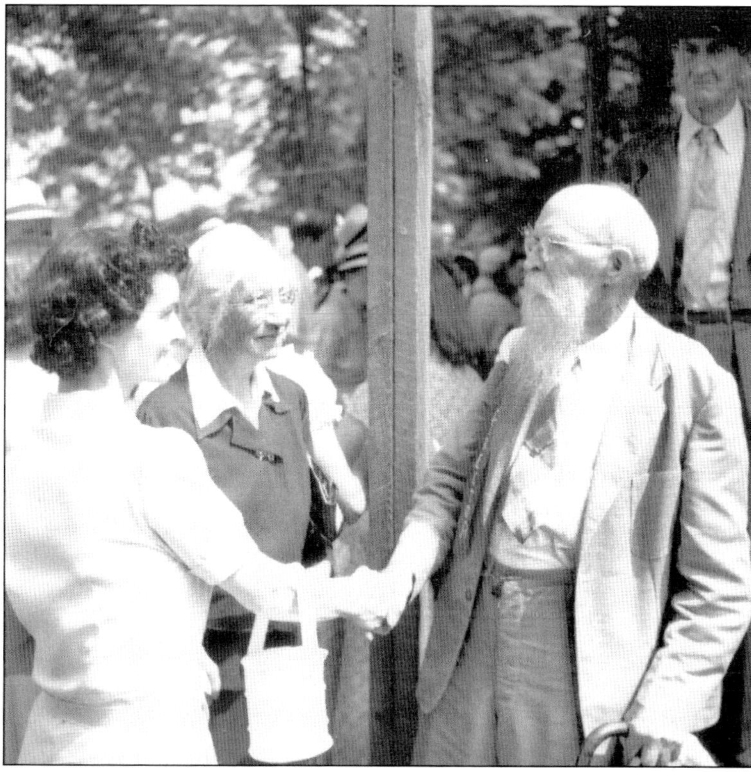

Rev. Shelby E. Gragg, a Watauga County native, was 90 years old when this photograph was taken at Singing on the Mountain in 1951. (Courtesy of the North Carolina Division of Archives and History.)

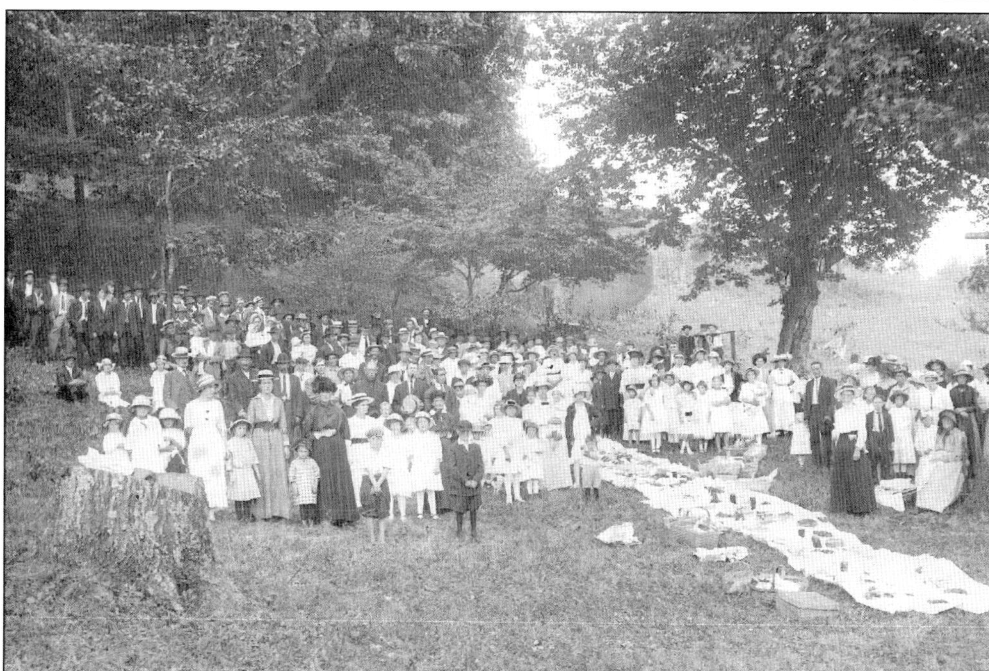

At the Vance-Wiseman family reunion, *c.* 1916, Mary Ann Wiseman is seated at the far right beneath the tree. This photograph was taken at the Yellow Mountain Cemetery. (Courtesy of the Avery County Historical Museum.)

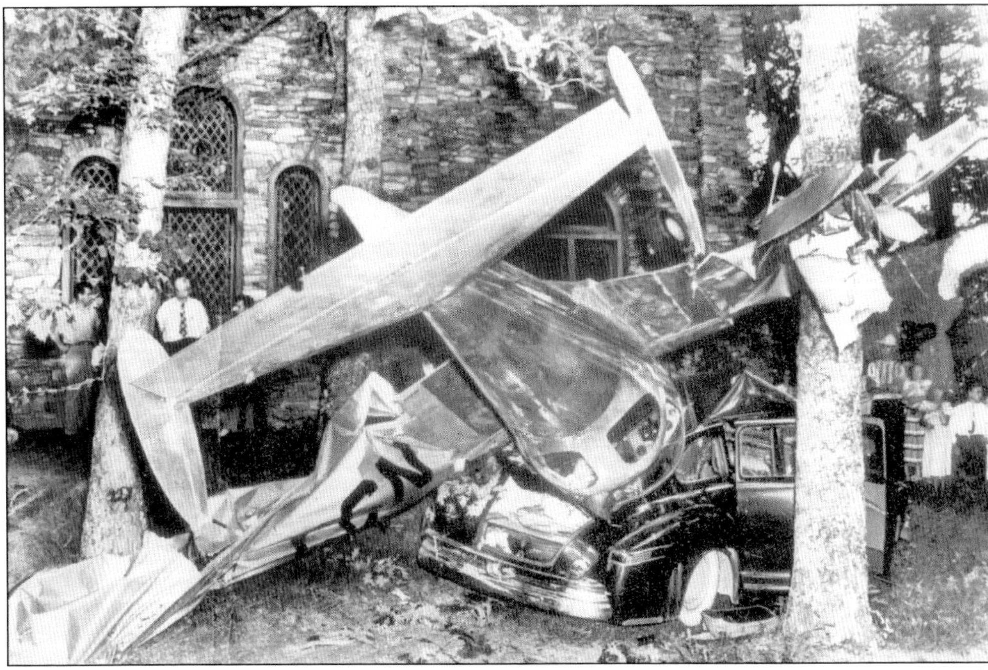

This bizarre plane-car crash took place on June 18, 1949, at the Crossnore Presbyterian Church. The plane belonged to the Nicholson Flying service out of Black Mountain and was piloted by Winifred "Wimpy" Holloway, the foster son of Dr. Eustace and Mary Sloop. Holloway was 22 years old and a student at Warren-Wilson College. He received some slight bruises to his face. The only other person injured was Obie Johnson, one of the attendees of the church, who had his ear clipped by the wing of the plane. "I prayed while coming down," reported Holloway. (Courtesy of the Avery County Historical Museum.)

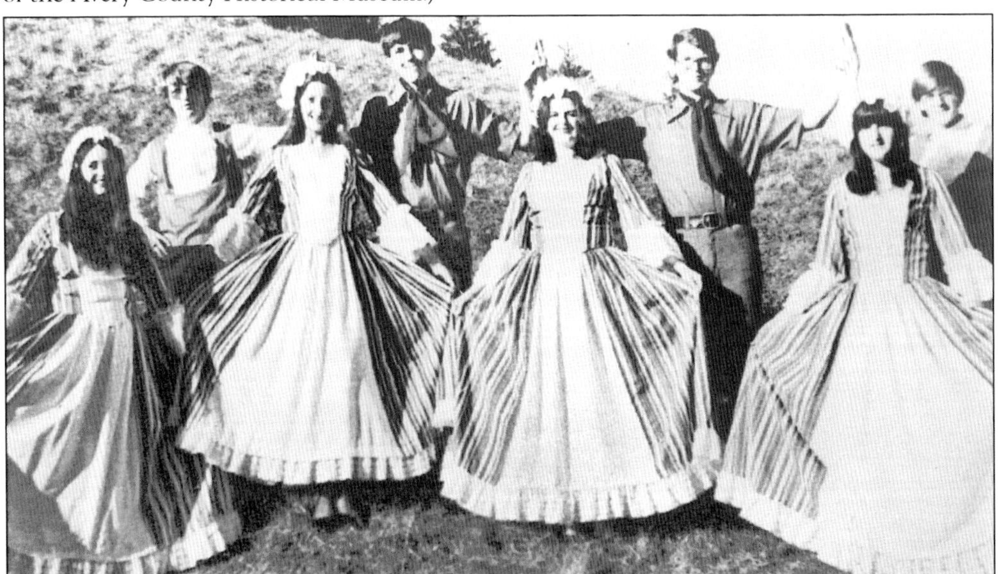

The Avery High School Bicentennial Dancers prepare for special activities in 1976. The popular smooth-dancing team has traveled widely and continues to be an important program at the school. (Courtesy of the Avery County Historical Museum.)

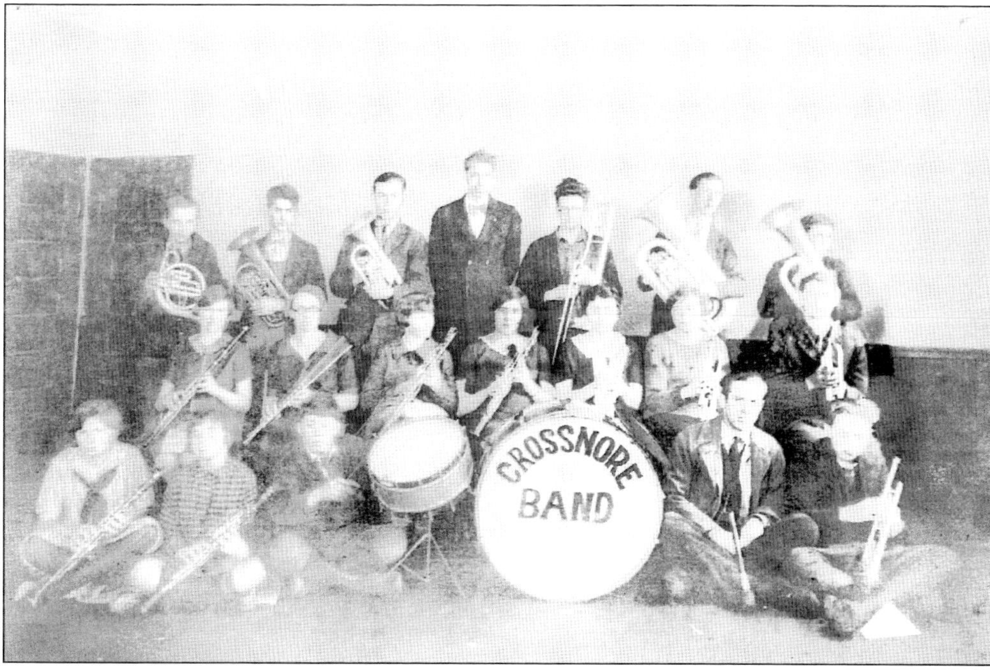

This early image of a community band in Crossnore demonstrates that local citizens could acquire nearly anything, even musical instruments, thanks to the railroad. (Courtesy of the Avery County Museum.)

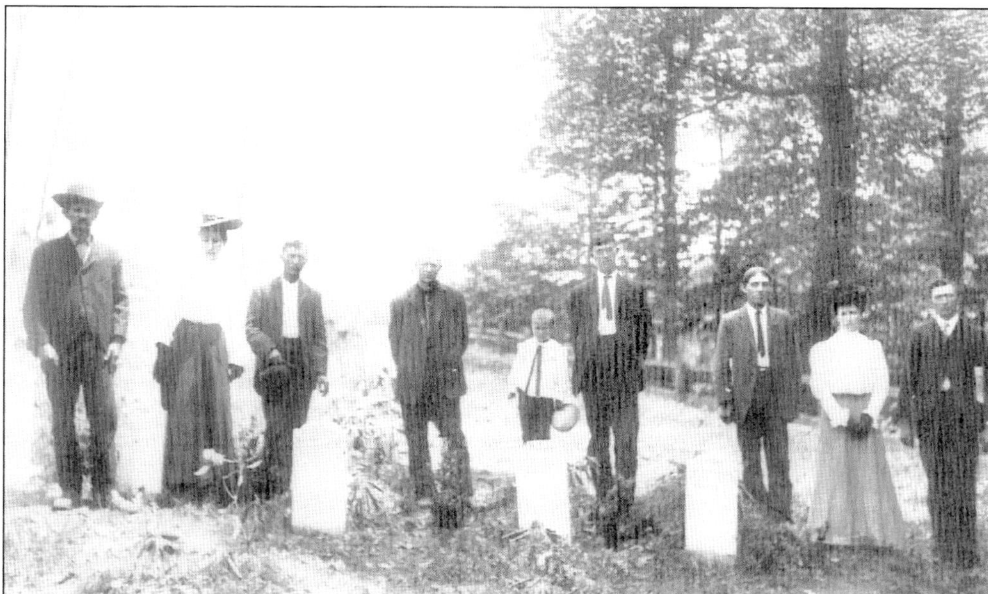

At the Pisgah Methodist Church Cemetery, from left to right, Mitch Burleson, Lottie Wiseman Burleson, John Wesley Wiseman, Hickey Wiseman, an unidentified child, Walter Wiseman, Aden McKinney, Minnie McKinney, and Fred McKinney visit the graves of their siblings who died during the devastating influenza pandemic that occurred after World War I (1918–1919) and killed an estimated 22 million people worldwide, including more than 500,000 in the United States. (Courtesy of the Avery County Historical Museum.)

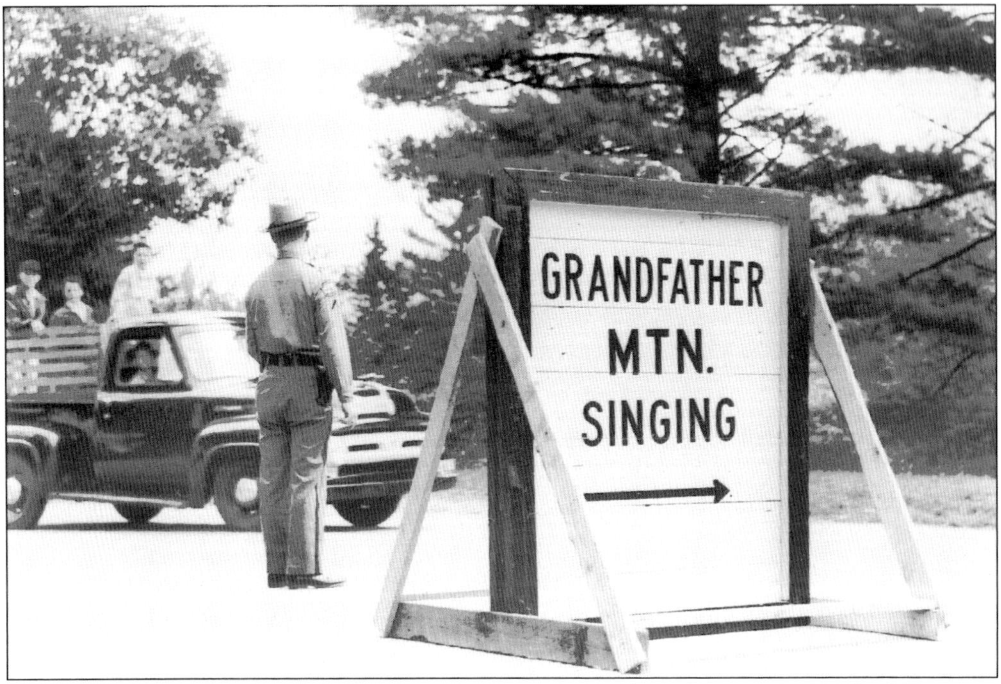

A truck carries a load of folks heading up to MacRae Meadows for Singing on the Mountain. (Courtesy of Hugh Morton/Grandfather Mountain.)

BIBLIOGRAPHY

Avery County Heritage. 7 vols. Newland, NC: Avery County Historical Society, 1976–present.
Blake, Christopher. *River of Cliffs: A Linville Gorge Reader.* Boone, NC: Parkway Publishers, 2005.
Cooper, Horton. *History of Avery County, North Carolina.* Asheville, NC: Biltmore Press, 1964.
Graybeal, Johnny. *Along the ET&WNC*. 5 vols. Hickory, NC: Tar Heels Press, 2001.
Hardy, Michael C. *A Short History of Old Watauga County.* Boone, NC: Parkway Publishers, 2005.
Hawthorne, Ann, ed. *The Picture Man*. Chapel Hill, NC: The University of North Carolina Press, 1993.
Lentz, Ralph E. II. *W. R. Trivett, Appalachian Pictureman: Photographs of a Bygone Time.* Jefferson, NC: McFarland and Co., 2001.